Practical Utopia

T0154168

KAIROS

In ancient Greek philosophy, *kairos* signifies the right time or the "moment of transition." We believe that we live in such a transitional period. The most important task of social science in time of transformation is to transform itself into a force of liberation. Kairos, an editorial imprint of the Anthropology and Social Change department housed in the California Institute of Integral Studies, publishes groundbreaking works in critical social sciences, including anthropology, sociology, geography, theory of education, political ecology, political theory, and history.

Series editor: Andrej Grubačić

Kairos books:

In, Against, and Beyond Capitalism: The San Francisco Lectures by John Holloway

Anthropocene or Capitalocene? Nature, History, and the Crisis of Capitalism edited by Jason W. Moore

Birth Work as Care Work: Stories from Activist Birth Communities by Alana Apfel

We Are the Crisis of Capital: A John Holloway Reader by John Holloway

Practical Utopia: Strategies for a Desirable Society by Michael Albert

Practical Utopia
Strategies for a Desirable Society
Michael Albert

KAIROS

PM

Practical Utopia: Strategies for a Desirable Society
Michael Albert
© 2017 PM Press.

ISBN: 978-1-62963-381-7
Library of Congress Control Number: 2016959606

Cover by John Yates / www.stealworks.com
Interior design by briandesign

10 9 8 7 6 5 4 3 2

PM Press
PO Box 23912
Oakland, CA 94623
www.pmpress.org

Printed in the USA by the Employee Owners of Thomson-Shore in
Dexter, Michigan.
www.thomsonshore.com

Contents

Preface

Noam Chomsky

It is tempting, and plausible, to regard the current historical period as an "interregnum" in Antonio Gramsci's sense, recalling his words on the crisis of his day, which "consists precisely in the fact that the old is dying and the new cannot be born; in this interregnum a great variety of morbid symptoms appear."

The morbidity of many of the symptoms is all too apparent, and the crises are all too real.

The crises of our day come in two forms: some are merely very serious, while others are literally existential. In the latter category there are two crises, each posing challenges that have never arisen before in human history—literally challenges of survival, for humans and innumerable other species.

In their most critical form, both of these crises can be dated to the end of World War II. The first crisis is the nuclear age, which dawned on August 6, 1945, a day when those with eyes open understood that human intelligence had devised the means to destroy the species, and much else along with it. A review of the record of near accidents and reckless actions of leaders reveals that it is a near miracle that we have survived this long, and such miracles are unlikely to persist. One of the most sober, respected, and experienced nuclear strategists, William Perry, never given to exaggeration, says that he cannot understand why everyone is not as "terrified" as he is at the realization that "today, the danger of some sort of a nuclear catastrophe is greater than it was during the Cold War." And as he knows very well, the world has come ominously close to terminal war all too often.

Perry's judgment is not readily dismissed, particularly when one considers what is happening at the Russian border and the policies and rhetoric of the two major nuclear powers.

The permanent crisis of the nuclear age, with its regular near-explosions to terminal catastrophe, is deeply rooted in the structure of the nation-state system that has developed in recent centuries and will not be easy to dismantle in favor of a more humane and civilized social and political order.

The second existential crisis, which is already well underway, is also deeply rooted in core institutional structures of modern society, which will also not be easy to dismantle: the environmental crisis, termed by geologists the Anthropocene, a new geological epoch in which humans are radically altering the environment in ways that portend major catastrophes. These catastrophes are already being endured by species that are rapidly succumbing during the Sixth Extinction, now in progress, and threatening to rival the Fifth Extinction some sixty-five million years ago when 75 percent of plant and animal species were destroyed after a huge asteroid hit the earth.

There has been debate about the dating of the onset of the Anthropocene, but professional opinion is converging on the same time as the onset of the nuclear age, the end of World War II. Whether this crisis can be brought under control in time is not at all clear. And as in the case of the nuclear age, a look at the reactions of systems of power is far from reassuring. Instructive illustrative examples include Denmark, Germany, China, and the United States. Denmark and Germany are aiming to reach full reliance on renewable energy within several decades and are taking serious steps towards that goal. China, already well in the lead in developing and producing renewables, primarily solar and wind, has announced plans to spend more than $360 billion through 2020 on renewable power sources, also creating over thirteen million jobs in these industries.

What about the United States? It had been a participant, even sometimes a prominent participant, in the enterprise of confronting the crisis of global warming, but that changed radically on November 8, 2016, with the victory of a political organization that is, quite literally, dedicated to destroying the hope for the survival of organized human life.

The last comment should strike readers as extreme, if not scandalous, until they look at the simple facts. In the Republican primaries, every candidate either denied that what is happening is happening, or said that maybe it is (who knows?) but we shouldn't do anything about it. The candidate hailed as the adult in the room, Ohio governor John Kasich, declared proudly that "we are going to burn [coal] in Ohio and we are not going to apologize for it." The winning candidate, who dismissed global warming as a hoax, calls for rapid increase in use of coal and other fossil fuels, dismantling of regulations, rejection of help to developing countries seeking to move to sustainable energy, and in general racing to the cliff as fast as possible.

In brief, all three branches of government in the world's most powerful state have been taken over by a political organization dedicated to destroying the hope for the survival of organized life, no exaggeration, and a fact that should elicit regular screaming headlines in a free press.

All of this came to a head on November 8, when some two hundred nations were meeting in Marrakech, Morocco, to try to put some teeth into the 2015 Paris negotiations (COP21) on climate change. It had been hoped that COP21 would lead to a treaty with verifiable commitments. But that hope was dashed by the refusal of the Republican Congress to accept binding commitments. The Marrakech COP22 meetings intended to address that stunning failure. On November 8, as the electoral results came in, the proceedings pretty much came to a halt. The prevailing question was now whether the enterprise could even continue with the most powerful country in history in the hands of an organization that not only refuses to participate but is dead set on undermining possibilities of success. Delegates looked to China as the hope for rescuing the world from the wrecking machine that now controls the leader of the Free World. An astonishing spectacle, which passed with virtually no comment.

The scale of the crisis is hard to exaggerate. And it is also hard to find words to capture appropriately that all of this is passing with scant notice right where the lethal sore is festering.

Even if the U.S. were to rejoin the world, the path forward is by no means clear. On November 8, before the electoral results began to appear, the World Meteorological Association delivered its verdict on the state of the Anthropocene to the nations assembled at Marrakech. Though no surprise to those who have been following the reports in scientific journals, and sometimes the general press, the verdict was grim. The limits set as goals in Paris were already being approached. Major steps have to be taken, and soon, or it may be too late to avert truly dire consequences.

Furthermore, as already mentioned, much as in the case of the terrifying threat of nuclear weapons, the environmental crisis is institutional, deeply rooted in economic institutions geared to accumulation, profit, and often sociopathic forms of growth. These institutional structures are not easily dismantled, but dismantled they must be, at least significantly changed, if life on earth is to persist in anything like the form to which we should aspire.

Attention to the institutional structures that lie at the roots of the two existential crises brings us to the second category of crises, those that are merely extremely severe. And as should be clear, the graver and lesser crises are intimately related. Without significant and perhaps dramatic changes in the institutional structures, the existential crises are likely to determine the fate of the species.

For a generation, under U.S. leadership much of the world has—not for the first time—been subjected to the doctrines of the "religion" that the market knows best, to borrow the phrase of economist Joseph Stiglitz twenty years ago, warning against blind faith in the religion. We should bear in mind, however, that like many others, the neoliberal religion readily accommodates what Pascal called "the utility of interpretations" in his satirical account of how the guardians of the faith devise modes of escape when convenient.

The neoliberal assault on the world's population in the past generation has been regarded very highly by elite opinion. Much has been made of the remarkable decline in global poverty during the neoliberal period, commonly overlooking the not insignificant fact—pointed out by political economist Robert Wade among others—that the achievement relies very largely on China, which paid little heed to the doctrines of the faith, and others who took the same path. In the United States, professional and other opinion was awed by the grand success of the "Great Moderation," managed by the skillful hands of Alan Greenspan—"Saint Alan" as he was sometimes called, until the whole edifice crashed magnificently in 2008 with the bursting of a multi-trillion-dollar housing bubble that somehow escaped notice, apart from a very few perceptive economists like Dean Baker.

Not all were awed by the successes of the Great Moderation. Notably missing from the chorus of approval were American workers, who were not cheering loudly in the streets about the significant decline in real wages for (non-supervisory) workers from 1979, when the experiment was in its earliest stages, to 2007, when euphoria about its successes was at its peak right before the crash. The performance is reminiscent of the days of the Brazilian military dictatorship, when ruling general Emilio Medici commented, "*The economy is doing fine, but the people aren't.*"

The achievements were summarized accurately in the title of an instructive report of the Economic Policy Institute: *Failure by Design*. Contrary to Thatcher's famous TINA slogan, "there is no alternative," alternatives were always quite feasible. And as the study points out, the "failure" is class-based. As commonly the case, there is no failure for the designers—who can count on the public to bail them out when they get into trouble. The public bailouts are the least of the public subsidy to the financial institutions that increasingly dominate the neoliberal economy. An IMF study revealed that much of the profit of the top U.S. banks derives from the implicit insurance policy provided by the government, providing them many advantages.

Others suffered far more severely from the neoliberal onslaught. The imposition of "market reforms" in Russia devastated the economy and led to millions of deaths, setting the stage for much of the ugliness of the subsequent period. Latin America suffered two "lost decades," finally breaking out of the stranglehold, partly at least, in this millennium. One sign is that the IMF, pretty much an agent of the U.S. Treasury Department, has been expelled from the region, as from East Asia after the late '90s crisis there. The savage neoliberal austerity programs of the European Union bureaucracy, heavily under the influence of northern banks, have been so irrational on economic grounds that even the IMF economists have sharply criticized them—while the IMF political figures have joined in imposing harsh and destructive austerity programs on the most vulnerable, with grim effects. The economist Marc Weisbrot, in a careful and well-documented review of the general history in his book *Failed: What the "Experts" Got Wrong about the Global Economy*, makes a persuasive case that one goal of the policies has been to dismantle the social democratic policies that were one of Europe's contributions to civilized life in the post–World War II period but were unwelcome to major centers of traditional power.

One important element of the neoliberal onslaught is the severe decline in functioning democracy, revealing itself in many ways, even more so in Europe than in the United States.

Returning to Gramsci's phrase, the current interregnum has evoked popular reactions, some of them morbid indeed, notably the rise of neofascist movements particularly in Europe, and some much more hopeful: in the U.S., the remarkable success of the Sanders mobilization, which probably would have taken over the Democratic Party if it had not been blocked by the maneuverings of the apparatchiks. Among the young, a large majority favored Sanders, whose campaign departed sharply from the norm of "bought elections" that has long prevailed. There are similar developments in Europe. It is true that "the new cannot be born," yet. But the forms it might assume will depend on actions taken now and the visions of a future society that animate them.

It is to these critical questions that *Practical Utopia* is dedicated. Few have thought as long and hard about these matters as Michael Albert, along with constructive efforts to planting the "seeds of the future in the present." What he presents here is the distillation of a life of searching thought and dedicated activism that merits great respect and close attention.

Acknowledgments

The material in this book comes largely from a prior collection of three short volumes called *Fanfare for the Future*. On that project I had help from a number of people, and their contribution to this book therefore remains notable and central. They are Mandisi Majavu (who helped with Part One), Mark Evans (who helped with Part Two), and David Marty and Jessica Azulay (who helped with Part Three). Various formulations of the ideas throughout this book owe much to Lydia Sargent, Eric Sargent, and in the case of Participatory Economics, particularly to Robin Hahnel. Additional aid at various points in the long process that rests on ideas as well as their formulation came from Noam Chomsky, Stephen Shalom, Cynthia Peters, Peter Bohmer, and the many other writers and activists I have worked with over the years.

Introduction

This is a book about understanding society and history, envisioning a new future, and attaining it.

We are born, nurtured as children, schooled, socialized, and grow up.

We work for incomes. We celebrate particular heritages and beliefs. We romance partners and create families. And then it all happens again, assuming war, poverty, and other disasters don't interfere.

Societies have important aspects that mediate key social functions like being born, nurtured, and socialized; contributing to and consuming society's produce; learning and enjoying a language, heritage, and culture; enjoying or suffering environmental effects; and enjoying or suffering relations with other societies.

Indeed, helping people accomplish these many functions is society's reason for being, so to understand societies we should understand how accomplishing these diverse functions affects our options in life.

A society is a set of relations that enables its citizens to get together to accomplish key kin, community, economic, and political functions. If new social relations exist that would work significantly better than the old social relations for fulfilling the necessary functions, and if the costs of attaining the new relations wouldn't outweigh or subvert the benefits, then it is time for a change.

As we write this introduction, across the Middle East and North Africa, from Spain to Greece and throughout Europe, in unexpected but expanding parts of the U.S., in large sectors of Asia, including India and China, and perhaps most compellingly in South and Latin America, substantial and sometimes majoritarian populations are rejecting existing relations and militantly and publicly pursuing new desires.

Minds are changing. Regimes are falling. New structures are emerging. Tumultuous times, tumultuous changes.

Yet victories are not inevitable. To win sought-after goals people must advance from pain and anger to action, from separated to entwined, and from struggling to victorious. Beyond momentary victories, we need trajectories of gains that accumulate and diversify into new social relations.

Revolutions replace that which conditions events and arrangements. They go to the roots of how people live. They transform nearly everything. And that is the aim.

Everything Is Broken
Billions of people around the world live in abject poverty. Billions are hungry. Even greater numbers lack the free time and healthy space to experience life fully and fruitfully.

Even where more wealth exists and life lasts longer and is less hellish, dignity is scarce. Lying, cheating, aggrandizing, and even killing are the basic touchstones of much of daily life. Economics, politics, community, and family too impose horrendous costs on humanity. Why should survival require vicious venality?

The rich get richer. The poor get poorer. Wall Street counts profits, ignores suffering, and proclaims an upturn.

Bombs burst over daily lives. Politicians salute the rubble. Arms makers celebrate bloated dividends. Soldiers inhabit rotting caskets or face life anatomically and psychologically maimed.

Producers of medicines, houses, food, and virtually everything else pursue profits for a few while curtailing generalized well-being for all. Food chains and megafarms guard their blessings while significant portions of humanity lack food or endure processed food's dietary debits. Palaces of power. Orgies of wealth.

Temperatures and storms accelerate on a doomsday trajectory while the rich and powerful sip margaritas on the deck of Spaceship Earth, glorying in the pretty vistas they see through blind bloodshot eyes.

Society's monarchs have their heads stuck in appetizers. Their eyes face the ground. Their noses sniff in the troughs of other people's pain.

Every person on this planet who dies of preventable disease or starvation—and that is tens of millions of people each year—was socially murdered. Every child who never gets to experience their own full talents and capacities or to enjoy a loving, stable environment is a soul-crushing crime against young humanity. Every person laboring in comprehensively boring, debilitating conditions, enjoying no stature and meager income, is one more soul subordinated to greed and power.

The interpersonal rapes, thefts, and murders that clog streets with victims, the large-scale systematic bending of wills and motives, and the subordination, impoverishment, psychological rape, material denigration, and social and even biological murder of countless souls encompasses a massively unjust misallocation of knowledge and circumstances that doesn't have to happen. And that's only in the empire's homeland. Imagine the periphery.

There is only one coherent or even moderately sane argument against fundamentally reconstituting society on a transformed foundation to eradicate all this deprivation and pain. And even that one argument—which is the assertion that a revolutionary redefinition would only make things worse because there is no viable alternative—is itself, as we will see, no more than another transparent lie.

To create a new society an activist "social change team" needs to know where it will start, its final goal, and how to get

3

from start to finish, which is precisely the subject matter of this book.

The only thing hard about getting ready to be skilled at matters of social change is that it entails arriving at and holding on to thought patterns and insights very different than what we are used to thinking and believing. This is not difficult or "deep," but it can be hard because it's "different." And that's where I hope this book will be helpful.

PART ONE: OUR IDEAS

**"The difficulty lies, not in the new ideas,
but in escaping from the old ones."**
—*John Maynard Keynes*

CHAPTER 1

Many-Sided Lives

"I learned very early the difference between knowing
the name of something and knowing something."
—*Richard Feynman*

What Is Social Theory?

Theory is a mental construction we use to explain, predict, and also guide everything from gravity to language acquisition to baseball. A social theory is a theory about some part of collective human activity and engagement. It could be a theory of markets, law, bureaucracies, or families.

In our case, our theory—or toolbox of thinking aids— addresses societies and history in general and also specific types of society or epochs of history, or actual instances of either.

The components of any theory are called concepts. Concepts can be more general and encompassing or more specific. They name patterns or things that we usefully and frequently highlight to think about the topics we consider.

Theories are typically about specific domains—such as gravity or cosmology, baseball or sports, society or history— and they are better or worse insofar as they accurately address the domain we wish to consider and deliver the type of insights we are seeking for that domain.

For example, baseball theory is supposed to help us understand past and upcoming games and seasons. But suppose we are not just spectators or even historians of the sport, but that we are playing and coaching and we want theory to guide actions we can take.

In this book, our theory is meant to explain past societies and historical events as if we were historians or spectators, to predict likely outcomes of particular situations as if we were betting on outcomes, and to guide us in formulating worthy aims and in making choices to attain them because we are activists.

The Ties That Bind 1: Institutions

What is an institution?

Consider the Pentagon in Washington, DC. Is the Pentagon an institution? Yes, of course.

But is the five-sided building what makes the Pentagon an institution? No, the Pentagon could be in any building and it would still be what it is. And if we put a bicycle factory in the building that now houses the Pentagon, poof, the building would no longer be the Pentagon, even though it would still have five sides.

Are the specific people who walk the Pentagon's corridors what make the Pentagon an institution? No, if we replace the Pentagon's current people with new people, it would still be the same institution, albeit with different people.

So what makes the Pentagon an institution? The answer is a set of social relations, or what we might call roles.

In the Pentagon there are various positions with associated responsibilities and permissions. These roles or slots that people fill include chief of staff, five-star general, lower officials, division heads, technicians, secretaries, custodians, and so on. The roles and the ties, responsibilities, options, and limits the roles convey are the heart of the institution called the Pentagon. The roles that define what people who are part of the Pentagon or who are affected by the Pentagon can and will do or cannot and won't do are the essence of "Pentagon-ness."

All institutions exist to fulfill some functions. The Pentagon primarily prepares and enacts violence and war. A family, church, school, legislature, factory, or the whole market system primarily cares for kids, celebrates a shared set of values and ceremonies, conveys information and skills, establishes rules, produces outputs, or allocates goods, services, and labor.

To partake in social functions we must fill roles that family, school, church, legislature, court, factory, or market offer.

Consider a corporation. Some of its general roles are owner, manager, and worker, which take on special attributes in an auto plant, software publishing house, or hotel chain. If you want to be part of a corporation, to earn a living and thereby survive, you must fulfill the dictates and responsibilities of one or another role to get some benefits, like an income, but you may also suffer some debits, like being subject to a boss.

You might be an owner of the corporation, taking immense profit and having to do nothing much for your great gain. You might be a manager or a CEO, CFO, engineer, or corporate lawyer doing a range of conceptual, empowered tasks with various relations to more rote workers below and to the owners above. In that case, you typically produce results that enhance the owner's profit while also taking a considerable income for yourself and keeping workers from taking too much income and leaving you too little.

Or you might be a rote worker, say on an assembly line or cooking hot dogs on a grill. In that case, you will do largely or even entirely disempowering tasks controlled entirely from above. You will earn a modest, or even horribly low but desperately needed, income.

From churches to police forces, farms to investment houses, and families to hospitals, institutions are society's vehicles of social engagement. We fill roles within institutions to get an income, schooling, entertainment, health care, etc., but the roles require us to interact in particular ways that often dramatically constrain who we can be and what we can enjoy or must endure.

Put differently, institutions are where we operate. We gain some benefits, but we also suffer various limitations. The question at the heart of social change is: Can we have new institutions that provide needed benefits and new benefits without imposing dreaded debits?

The Ties That Bind 2: Beliefs

If institutions matter because of how they impact people, who fills the roles those institutions offer? And what characterizes "we the people" who fill those roles?

Our relative heights and weights, hair color, favorite clothes, TV preferences, reading habits, hobbies, and thousands of personal attributes help characterize us, yet we seek to figure out what is important to understand about people in society in order to effectively and dramatically change society.

Consider a particular friend of yours. What matters most about that person as your friend is likely whatever is unique about them from your perspective. But if you think about a whole society, what matters most about the population is likely to be features that recur in person after person throughout large subsets of the population, because these common features affect many people's behaviors and those many people together in turn have a major effect.

A pursuit, habit, or belief shared by some large constituency might further either the blocking or pursuing of social change. In contrast, some single individual's hair color, or even the total number of people with red hair, isn't likely to matter much for changing a society.

Suppose women in large numbers accept that they are in some way inferior to and deserve to be subordinate to men. That would certainly be a big issue for society, as it has been at various times and places in history. If, instead, women largely became feminist, with the initial impetus being one person's revelation or any other proximate cause, leading in time to women collectively seeking new relations, as has also occurred historically at certain times and places, then that is important.

The same holds for working people, for members of cultural communities, or for citizens facing their governments from below. Each constituency might share pursuits, habits, or beliefs that cement them into subordination and, if so, that will be how their society will maintain itself and the conditions of its population. Alternately, each constituency might share pursuits, habits, or beliefs that propel them into opposition to existing limits. And that too would certainly be critical to efforts at changing society. Likewise, other people may be wedded to sexist, classist, or racist domination and its perpetuation, again, greatly affecting large-scale outcomes.

Any one mother, one Catholic, one owner, one worker, one elected official will have many preferences, habits, and beliefs that are unique to their particular combination of personal experiences. But each will also likely have many preferences, habits, and beliefs in common with other mothers, Catholics, owners, workers, or elected officials, due to sharing the roles those other people also occupy and due to the implications of the shared roles for themselves and for those other people.

Any individual's preferences, habits, and beliefs—what we can call the individual's consciousness—can arise by way of a vast range of local and personal factors. But when we consider society, we need to know if a substantial group of people share overlapping preferences, habits, or beliefs. If they do, we can be pretty sure that what is shared will have similar origins in common role positions in social institutions, because even if the initial precipitating events generating the first instance of the shared views were highly personal or even unique, their later spread will owe a lot to shared circumstances and realities.

Widely shared consciousness typically arises largely due to people sharing similar roles in some institution or set of related institutions, so that even if the views emerge first in only a few individuals, or even in only one, many individuals in time develop the attributes that their similar roles impose or at least facilitate, perhaps due to resistance to those same roles.

What emerges from these simple observations is that institutions are important for social theory aimed at social change for two primary reasons:

1. Institutions facilitate some possibilities and curtail others in different ways for people who occupy different roles.
2. Institutions convey common preferences, habits, and beliefs to people who fill largely the same roles.

What also emerges is that people are important for social theory aimed at social change for two primary reasons:

1. People are the carriers of the implications of institutions, as well as being the creators of institutions.
2. People react, conceive, and create, not only in accord with the roles they occupy but also in opposition to those roles.

Judging Societies

Suppose we value a society that produces the absolute maximum possible output, or one where the largest possible output goes to a small percentage of citizens, or one where the same amount of output goes to everyone, or some other outcome regarding society's product.

Or suppose we value men dominating women materially, socially, psychologically. Or we abhor that result. Or we think some cultural group should benefit greatly at the expense of others. Or we abhor such a prospect. Or we feel the broad public should or should not have decision-making influence in legislative and judicial outcomes, and that the direction of outcomes should benefit all or only a few. Or we like war and domination of other societies, or we prefer peace and mutual aid. Or we think the environment is an endless pool to piss in, or we think it is a limited treasure we must protect.

Of course we could go on listing possible divergent preferences about various aspects of social life. The point is, once we establish our own values, a question emerges: Do society's institutions and people's personalities and inclinations further, impede, or obliterate any possibility of the values we favor being met?

Social evaluation is no different in broad logic than evaluating anything else. Are society's attributes in accord with what we favor? Or do its attributes violate what we favor?

Conclusions

Polity, economy, kinship, and culture are all aspects of a complex society. In a sense each is like a biological organ in a human. No heart, lung, kidney, arm, or eye usefully exists other than in complex entwinement with the rest of a person, yet each of these organs can also be usefully considered a system unto itself.

The words *polity*, *economy*, *kinship*, and *culture* name some "organs" of society, all entwined, but each also viewable as an identifiable conglomeration of institutions for accomplishing a defining flexible function. Viewed as components, some institutions in each of the four spheres of social life are more central and critical than others.

Taken together, the institutions in the four spheres create a kind of boundary of available roles with various accompanying implications that people in society have no choice but to relate to.

Living in a society, we fill its roles or not, sometimes by choice, sometimes without any alternative other than to be entirely excluded from social relations.

And who are we? We are unique breathing, feeling, thinking beings with very complex and diverse preferences, habits, and beliefs, albeit all built on quite similar genetic natures. Yet we each share various roles with many other people. Often that commonality with others causes us to also share associated preferences, habits, and beliefs in broad patterns of group allegiance based on gender, sexual preference, age, race, religion, nationality, ethnicity, class, and being citizens or government officials of various sorts.

So what is a society? In the view we are slowly elaborating, a society is the immensely rich and varied combination of a "human center," which is us with our consciousnesses, capacities, and agendas, plus an "institutional boundary" in the form of the roles that we must fulfill or avoid as a means to gaining various ends in society. Taken this way society is like an incredible mosaic with each multifaceted part affecting and even defining all the other multifaceted parts.

And how do we judge a society? We decide on the broad kinds of outcomes and relations that we desire and appreciate, and we then ask: Does society's human base and institutional boundary, or the base and boundary in each of its social spheres, further those preferred values or violate them?

Given these simple insights, a reasonable next step for becoming better able to understand societies is to refine our means for understanding each of the four social spheres as a basis for saying more about how their aspects interrelate and about change and history.

CHAPTER 2

Redefining Four Views

> "The illusion that we are separate from one another
> is an optical delusion of our consciousness."
> —*Albert Einstein*

General Character of Social Spheres

One way to rapidly progress in understanding society and history is to make some generalizations that apply to all four spheres of social life—kinship, culture/community, polity, and economy—even while we remember that these four spheres always overlap.

In the various acts of kinship family life, community cultural identification, political legislation, implementation, and adjudication, and economic production, consumption, and allocation—especially as a result of the requirements of the roles for carrying out those acts—people are typically divided into groups which contend for influence, status, material well-being, and overall quality of life.

Further, while particular features differ for race, gender, sexual, and economic hierarchies, much is also similar. Members of groups on top in each sphere of life do not typically get up each morning and smugly tell themselves, "We are on top because the system is rigged to our advantage, and we act to keep those who are beneath us below by whatever means we can muster." Rather, those above typically tell themselves, "We are superior and deserve our advantages, while those below are inferior and, in any case, don't deserve as much." Those above also typically tell themselves, "Our being rewarded more than others benefits everyone, because we are smarter, more creative, harder working, and more responsible." They may even tell themselves that those below "wouldn't even enjoy the benefits we receive were they to have them—at least as much as we enjoy them—because they just don't have the refined taste and creativity to make good use of such riches. In fact, our underlings would likely be burdened if they had all the wealth we have. What would they do with it—other than waste it?"

Those above therefore conclude that for the most part "society is just." This set of self-elevating attitudes appears in racism, sexism, authoritarianism, and classism, which in turn elevate dominant cultural community, kinship, political, or economic groups above those subordinated below.

Reciprocally, those on the bottom won't always furiously tell themselves, "We are on the bottom unjustly. We suffer because the system is rigged to keep us down and because those arrayed above work hard to keep things as they are, and we damn well ought to change it." Rather, those on the bottom may instead tell themselves, or at least at some level harbor the suspicion that "We belong down here. We didn't try hard enough. Or we weren't able enough. Or we were unlucky. Or our kind just doesn't have what it takes."

Those below may even sometimes feel that they "do better with those above staying above, because the men/owners/whites/politicians are better at what they do and we get trickle-down benefits." Or they may tell themselves, "We like it down here. We have less responsibility and less hassle."

But while those self-deprecating formulations were the primary rationalizations and justifications for many decades, and while they still hang on naggingly for quite a few people living on the downside of society's hierarchies, impressions suggest that they may no longer be the predominant view of those on the bottom. Rather, in the past few decades, and increasingly as time passes, a new motif contends in oppressed people's rationales for accepting their plight.

Those below have come to realize they are below because the system is rigged. They have come to realize, even if they don't dwell on it, that their plight is not inevitable but imposed. But at the same time they have also come to believe that "there is no alternative, no better arrangement, or at least no way out. To fight the system is like rolling big rocks up steep inclines, only to be crushed when they finally roll back down. Futile."

More positively, being on the bottom sometimes leads people to examine their situation, define alternative arrangements, seek levers to win changes, and pursue further insights to fuel each investigation and practice. And, indeed, this has happened repeatedly throughout history and has led to various oppositional, radical, and revolutionary perspectives that have dramatically advanced the interests of those below.

So we might expect these past rebellious perspectives to provide tools we can use ourselves in our own future. And indeed, we can do just that, quite successfully and largely without need for fundamental alterations for at least three of the four spheres.

Three Spheres: Theory the Easy Way

Suppose we start with gender and sexuality. Women and homosexuals live at the bottom of sex/gender hierarchies and have, over time, elaborated concepts and ideas for understanding sexist hierarchies and alternative institutions that might fruitfully replace existing kinship institutions.

Taken together, we can reasonably call frameworks that elaborate the interests of women and gays feminism. They combine concepts, insights, aims and methods people use to alter gender relations, focusing on what needs highlighting, leaving out nothing critically important, pointing in useful directions.

The functions defining the kinship sphere are those of family life, including bringing into the world and raising the new generation. They are about living units and sexual and daily life interactions more broadly. Some central associated roles are man and woman, mother and father, and, for that matter, sister and brother, uncle and aunt, as well as gay, straight, transsexual, and bisexual.

Feminist analysis has explained the features of sex/gender hierarchies and the tremendous toll they take. It has uncovered the differences in circumstance and material well-being, the psychological and physical abuse, the different allotments of time and energy that accompany being in different sex/gender roles, including tracing implications into all features of social life, religion, work, government, education, culture, and home life. And, to an extent, feminists have also explained the origins of the sex/gender hierarchies and have elaborated ideas about alternative roles and structures that would eliminate those hierarchies and establish just relations in sexual and familial interactions.

But why are man and woman social roles?

Samantha may biologically be a woman and Samuel biologically a man, but the behaviors and responsibilities that Samantha and Samuel carry—and the habits and preferences they arrive at—go way beyond their innate biological differences.

Being a man or woman amidst sexist hierarchy is very different than being a man or woman when men and women are different only by virtue of actual biological imperatives. Biology imposes some differences vis-à-vis birthing, nursing, and more. But social structures by their roles impose much broader and more stringent differences regarding how we must act, who we can be, our jobs, behaviors, feelings, status, income, and position.

Similarly, you might think being a mother or father is defined by biological dictates in our natures. And yes, biology is certainly part of being a mother or father. But being a mother in our society typically means having an array of very specific nurturing, caring, cleaning, and organizing responsibilities which are on average quite different from what fathers do, with the differences having literally nothing to do with biology. And, similarly, being a father in our society carries a very different set of responsibilities and expectations than being a mother, often financial and disciplinary, that are more authoritative as well as less time-consuming, and that again have zero to do with biology.

Of course, the nonbiological attributes of being a mother or father, and even how the actual biological aspects are practically manifested, can change due to institutions changing, while the actual biological imperatives are far more fixed.

For now, let's just assume that much of what feminism has asserted and still asserts can be carried over pretty much as it currently stands to become part of our development of a multi-focused perspective. We'll test that assumption as we proceed.

Next, consider cultural community. The situation is similar to sex/gender relations. Historically, communities that have suffered the indignities and gross violations of racism, nationalism, and ethnic and religious bigotry have sometimes given in to despair and even become resigned to their situations while trying to carve out the best possible circumstances within the dictates of the oppressive limits they have confronted. At other times, however, subordinated communities have developed ways of thinking about their plight—including developing related concepts and commitments about racism and other cultural oppressions—that we can pretty much adopt in full.

The heart of this has been understanding that racial, religious, and other cultural hierarchies typically involve one community dominating and seeing itself as innately or at least historically superior to one or more other communities, with institutions throughout society elevating members of the dominant community while suppressing members of the subordinate communities.

An additional key insight of those rebelling against community hierarchy and seeking community/cultural liberation has been that these racial, ethnic, national, and religious hierarchies are actually social. The power and material advantages of one community over another arise from social relations and history not biology. Indeed, no real biological boundary exists between communities and there is no significant biological basis for cultural community distinctions. On average the genetic difference between two randomly selected individuals in any single cultural community are typically greater than the genetic differences between average representatives of two different communities. Role differences not biological destiny deliver unequal circumstances and benefits whose rationalization then fuels derogatory misconceptions of self and others, often including domination and resignation, all backed by power differences which create and sustain cultural hierarchies.

Next we have issues of polity. Again, critics of existing political relations—the best practitioners of what is often called anarchism—have developed highly useful insights that we can largely adopt and work with in our own developing perspective. They focus on political institutions that serve narrow interests and exist separate from and above the population, including ruling over it. The polity that anarchists reject is not one that is limited by and manifests the will of the population as an extension of it. The rejected polity, whether dictatorial or parliamentary, is instead an encumbrance on the population, weighing it down and manifesting the will of a minority.

One anarchist insight, for example, is the observation—long asserted but rarely seriously considered—that power corrupts and absolute power corrupts absolutely. This means, basically, that if some people have excessive power they will rationalize it in ways that extol holding power as a virtue, in turn leading to their trying to accrue even more power, and they will then most typically use that new power in pursuit of more power. The results become steadily worse the more power is centralized into ever fewer hands.

As was true for our view of feminist and intercommunalist approaches—there are no grave and fundamental problems in the basic ideas of antiauthoritarian projects such that we would need to reject or dramatically amend the perspective to make it a part of our intellectual framework for understanding society and history. Rather, in building our own framework, we can mostly incorporate the insights of effective anarchist practitioners, meshing them with the best insights of feminist and intercommunalist schools, making modifications mainly—as we will see next chapter—so that each approach respects and incorporates the wisdom of the other two.

One Sphere Takes More Work

The fourth sphere, economics, presents a different problem than the other three. Economics, it turns out, needs significantly more alteration of past views to make useful progress.

Typical dissident understanding of the economy addresses material inputs and outputs and produced services, as well as the condition of workers and consumers involved in these acts. These perspectives address production, consumption, and allocation and unearth key roles regarding all these, including seeking to understand the implications of those roles for contending groups. The path taken is much like that for the three other spheres: identify functions, identify institutions, and examine the implications for contending groups.

But for economics, something went awry. Almost all dissidents examining economics agree that the key to understanding economic prospects and possibilities is understanding contending groups, called classes, and the attitudes, behaviors, and interests largely imposed on classes by their economic roles. But then almost all dissident approaches to economics rightly identify one critically important aspect of economics that affects its creation of contending groups but overlook—and even obscure—another comparably important but quite different aspect that also affects the creation of contending groups.

The usual approach goes like this. Economies must produce and distribute so that people can then consume. We produce potatoes to consume potatoes. In our capitalist economy, particular ownership relations and the roles they impose generate the working class and the owning class as contending actors with different motives, agendas, and views of each other.

The anticapitalist analysis of this contentious relationship next uncovers how private ownership of workplaces and production assets leads to the pursuit of profit by owners and of better salaries by workers—including owners trying to diminish wages, lengthen the workday, and speed up and intensify work, while workers seek to raise wages, shorten the workday, and enjoy less frantic and dangerous conditions.

Here is the problem. People are divided into contending classes due to their different roles in the economy, giving them opposing interests. One factor causing such differences is different ownership positions—as in some people owning means of production and others just owning their own ability to do work. So far, so good. But another factor causing people to occupy different classes is the type of work we do in the economic roles we play. Economic class is not solely about who owns what but also who does what.

Work, like all activity, affects those who do it. In modern capitalist economies—except for the top owners who constitute only 1 or 2 percent of the population—we all work. Indeed, we all sell our ability to work to owners, and we all get wages for the work we do. This commonality has caused anticapitalists over the decades to lump all these people who sell their ability to do work for a wage into a single working class.

A different view agrees that at the top there are owners, or capitalists, and at the bottom workers. But in between the lowly laborers and lordly capitalists, this contending view says there is a third class, the coordinator class, which includes those who do mainly empowering work, unlike workers at the bottom who do overwhelmingly disempowering, rote, and tedious work.

This third class—between labor and capital—overwhelmingly does tasks that give its members self-confidence, social skills, workplace knowledge, habits, and experiences of daily workplace decision-making. This empowers them. In contrast, the more typical workers toiling below overwhelmingly do rote, tedious, repetitive, and often dangerous tasks that convey only exhaustion, reduced health, personal isolation, habits of obedience, and disempowerment.

Economic approaches that have in the past informed dissent have focused on two key classes, while we claim they should have focused on three. They have highlighted economic oppression related to profit seeking but have largely ignored—or at times even denied—economic oppression related to maintaining the division between coordinators above (usually around 20 percent of all waged employees) and workers below (typically constituting the other 80 percent of all waged employees).

A rightful rejection of economic oppression got sidetracked, one might say, into aggressively examining property relations without equally examining the division of labor relations having to do with empowerment.

This isn't just that the 20 percent in the coordinator class do much better than the workers below them, while contending with the owners above. It is also that focusing on only two classes often causes anticapitalists to arrive at a vision they think elevates workers but which in fact elevates coordinators. To get beyond this failing, we must add to past views an understanding of the coordinators that exist between owners and workers. And coordinator-class members—doctors, lawyers, managers, accountants, engineers, scientists, and so on—are not just another kind of capitalist, smaller or smarter, or whatever. Nor are they just another kind of worker, better off but still in the same class. They are not a somewhat deprived part of the class above nor a somewhat advantaged part of the class below, nor are they some kind of a mix of the two. Coordinators occupy a class unto themselves, with very different circumstances from workers below and owners above that can cause them to contend with both.

Regarding the four spheres of society, our aim as we proceed is going to be to understand how to accomplish their relevant functions without generating old or new hierarchies of wealth, power, dignity, status, and comfort. For the economy, this will mean we want classlessness. But you can't get from class divided to classless if you fail to notice a key class whose basis must be removed. This isn't just a plausible hypothesis, it is verified in experience repeatedly in history. What has been called socialism in the past, claiming to be an economy guided by the interests of and ruled by the collective desires of workers, has in fact typically been an economy that has eliminated the owning class by eliminating the role of owning workplaces but that has retained the corporate division of labor and the coordinator class, with the coordinator class ruling workplaces and the overall economy.

Wanting classlessness means we don't want this new boss in place of the old boss. We must attend to the coordinator class when considering what exists, what we want, and how we get to our goals. Our changed theory will affect our new vision and strategy.

Conclusion
Changing society requires an accessible, sufficiently complete, but not excessively detailed set of accurate views about what exists, what we want, and what methods can take us from the former to the latter.

We have identified four spheres and two contexts and the centrality of certain social constituencies and institutions. We have seen that we can borrow from past insights to enhance our understanding of three of the four spheres, and that we can borrow some insights but also must generate some new ones for understanding the fourth sphere.

To move toward more detailed analyses and on to vision—we must now look at how the four spheres intersect and change over time, each affecting and being affected by the others, changing and being changed.

CHAPTER 3

Society and History

"All the world's a stage,
And all the men and women merely players."
—*Shakespeare*

Society Snapshot

In the nearly endless array of people, institutions, and objects composing any society, we need to highlight what is important to pay attention to if we are to avoid errors of omission. We also need to at least initially ignore what is relatively unimportant to avoid being sidetracked by endless peripheral details.

We should pay attention to hierarchies of gender, race and religion, political power, and class, including examining each associated hierarchy's attributes, tenacity, and implications.

Obviously such a varied exploration could proceed for a long time—but suppose we have done all that. Then what?

Well, these spheres of social life are not self-contained and separate from one another. Rather, the four functions all transpire in virtually every nook and cranny of society.

Thus, if we say the kinship sphere is all those places where kinship (sex/gender) dynamics occur, it turns out that while the center of the kinship sphere is families and other locales of intense gender interactions, its outer reaches extend to kin-dominated and kin-affecting relations in workplaces, churches, and legislatures, not just families.

Similarly, community, political, and economic dynamics also extend to the whole of society, well beyond the institutions that define each.

For example, the core of the economic sphere is work-places, markets, and consumption units, while the extremities certainly include families, schools, churches, government agencies, and the like, since in all these institutions at least some production, consumption, and allocation can occur alongside more central kin, community, and political aspects.

If we look at a society in a stable condition, people will largely fill roles within the society's various institutions. The structures of gender, race, power, and class will be continually created by those roles and will continually need people with certain expectations and inclinations to fit the roles. Society in a stable condition requires that some people fit here, some fit there, but nearly everyone fits somewhere.

Suppose that a society is strongly sexist, relegating women to bearing greatly excessive burdens and denying them access to significant benefits that men readily enjoy. This means the kinship sphere's roles, by the practices they impose on people, produce men who feel superior to women and women who largely accept subordination to men. Suppose these men and women are fitting their sexist kinship roles nicely, and by their actions and behaviors in their household and other core kin relations wind up with the expectations, habits, and beliefs of sexism continually reinforced.

Now imagine that in the economy of the same society, at the same time, men and women fare similarly to one another, with little or no gender differentiation, so that men who, by virtue of their experience in households and their upbringing, expect to be above women, instead typically find themselves as often as not economically equal to or even below women in income and influence. And similarly, women, who by virtue of their experience in households and their upbringing expect to be subordinate to men, typically find themselves economically equal to or even dominant.

This disjuncture between the requirements and implications of kinship and the requirements and implications of the economy would pose a problem. The economy and the kinship sphere would be out of alignment—or, to use a term I prefer, "out of whack"—creating tension, dislocation, and possibly also resistance.

We do not expect to see this type of disjuncture between these two spheres of social life—at least not without there being conflict and then changes due to realigning violated expectations or unusual beliefs systems that allow it all to work smoothly—and, indeed, we will talk more about how two or more spheres being out of whack might be resolved. But for now, what we can anticipate when society is quite stable and without conflict seeking fundamental change is that any substantial hierarchy born of one sphere will tend to invade other spheres, creating a degree of consistency for actors in all of them.

The general idea is simple enough. Just as inside a single institution you would not anticipate seeing one important part of it having roles causing people to be X-like and another important part of it having roles causing them to be Y-like— where being X-ish contradicts being Y-ish and vice versa— unless the institution was in turmoil, and we expect something very similar for a society.

We expect, that is, that each sphere of social life—meaning the ways that its main social institutions address and accomplish the four key functions of society—will typically tend to welcome and induce particular habits, beliefs, expectations, and desires in people filling that sphere's roles. Corporations mold us. Families mold us. Citizenship molds us. Communities mold us. Each sphere will have requirements for us, depending on the roles we fill in the associated institutions.

When conditions are largely stable, as is most often the case in typical societies, this might mean that there are habits, beliefs, expectations, and desires consistent with sexism, racism, political authoritarianism, and classism within the institutions of the four spheres. But the four spheres overlap so much and so intimately that each sphere's implications radiate a field of social influence beyond their own structures and into the other structures in society, and we expect this to cause the sexism, racism, authoritarianism, and classism to expand from each originating institution and sphere into the rest, so that there is at least compatibility.

Past and Future History
Elaborating the above observations leads to a view not only of society at a moment but of society changing from moment to moment—which is history.

Social Accommodation
If we look at the history of any society, one of the ways the four spheres entwine with one another we can call "social accommodation."

A social sphere, let's say kinship or economy, creates a particular set of social expectations, habits, and beliefs, let's say sexism or classism, by the behavioral requirements of its roles. This typically means that these social spheres each impose a hierarchy on the actors filling their roles.

Accommodation occurs when the hierarchy created by one sphere is respected by others. Thus, if kinship creates a gender hierarchy and the economy accommodates kinship's sexism, it will, overall, not pay women more than men or give women power or status above men. It will obey and specifically not violate the expectations and patterns of behavior emanating from kinship.

Similarly, if the economy creates a class hierarchy and kinship accommodates the economy's classism, it will, overall, "produce" young men and women who are ready to fill the class-divided role slots of the economy rather than producing folks not suited to their likely positions.

Think of each sphere as a kind of school that—along with accomplishing its own functions—conveys to people filling its roles various beliefs, habits, knowledge, skills, and expectations. If what one sphere creates and requires of people is contradicted or even undone by what another sphere creates and requires, then the two spheres are at cross-purposes, disrupting one another's operations. Each sphere would prepare people who would not fit the other but would instead clash with the other. This would not likely persist without changes occurring. So in stable situations, after such corrections occur, we tend to see what we are calling accommodation in the alignment of any two of the four social spheres.

Accommodation means one sphere creates and re-creates a set of powerful patterns the other three do not seriously violate or contradict in their own different contexts. The basic attributes of kinship, racial, political, and economic hierarchies are at least not seriously violated and are in fact typically abided by other spheres. To the extent that there are features that are "out of whack," there will be tension, resistance and disruption, and forces pushing for recalibration. In stable contexts, social spheres cannot long cause people filling their roles to fail to fit the roles of other social spheres in the same society without turmoil occurring.

Social Co-reproduction

Beyond accommodation, co-reproduction exists when the field of influence emanating from the kinship sphere, to continue with that example, is so powerful that it actually redefines the roles in other spheres of social life to the point where instead of simply not violating sexist hierarchy, the roles in those other spheres actually produce and reproduce sexist hierarchy.

For example, with co-reproduction it isn't only that women earn less than men. Rather, the actual role requirements of work (and of allocation and consumption) are transformed by the influence of sexism to themselves generate sexist behavior and expectations. Economic roles become imbued with sexist assumptions and patterns to the extent that they literally impose those attitudes and behaviors on the actors. The field of influence of the patriarchal kinship sphere insinuates itself in the very manner of carrying out economic functions—not just in who does what but in what is done—thereby altering the makeup of economic roles.

What it is to be a male businessperson and his female secretary or a male doctor and his female nurse or a male X and a female Y changes from what economics alone would dictate of those roles. Instead of gender-neutral definitions of how to carry out tasks, tasks incorporate gender attributes that assume and continually re-create sexist outcomes. The economy becomes a seat of the creation and re-creation of sexism. What people do in their economic roles generates sexist assumptions, beliefs, habits, and expectations. Even if the kinship sphere were to be somehow changed so that its sexism generating attributes were eliminated, an unchanged economy that had become co-reproducing with kinship in its old form would still produce sexism.

The scholar Batya Weinbaum was the first person I ever encountered to make this sort of observation. She looked at workplaces in the U.S. through feminist eyes and she didn't just see in men earning more than women or having jobs that were better and more often on top the result of accommodating kinship in who gets what positions. She instead saw that the actual composition of work—the role structures, the positions themselves—changed so that some work was not just done by a woman or a man but was altered in how it was undertaken and in its tasks, and thereby in the expectations and requirements associated with it, until it was literally man's work or woman's work—meaning work that imposed on those doing it male and female assumptions and habits.

Indeed, Weinbaum looked at workplaces—and as highly attuned as she was to the dynamics of gender roles, she could literally see mothers and fathers, even sisters and brothers, inside the workplace—and she saw people doing things in the manner and with the implications that were typical of sexist families. This is co-reproduction is a condition that is powerfully important, particularly when we later consider what is required to make fundamental and lasting changes in even one of the social spheres, much less in all four.

To pin it down, in a co-reproducing situation, the dynamics of the origin sphere are incorporated elsewhere, substantially redefining other spheres' qualitative ways of accomplishing their functions such that the other spheres start to also produce and reproduce the features emanating from the original source sphere. The economy not only doesn't violate the sexism of kinship, it alters so much that it reproduces sexism—and likewise the kinship sphere reproduces classism rather than merely accommodating to it. Similarly for the polity and culture regarding all others and vice versa. When a sphere is strong enough in its field of force, other spheres alter so as to incorporate its logic, reproducing its features and not merely abiding them.

History's Engine

With all these pressures causing accommodation of different parts of society, and even their mutual reproduction, it is reasonable to wonder why there is any change at all. Why do societies change as time passes?

With history the situation is different. Yes, time passes, but changes are not inevitable. More, there is no limited group of causes.

If we look way back to the great Egyptian societies around Cairo six millennia ago, we can see that there is a real question lurking there. It is 4000 BC. We stroll around in ancient Egypt and take an inventory of the society we find. We know enough to look first at the four spheres of social life, specifically at the roles people fill in the economy, polity, kinship, and culture. We easily examine visible indicators of the character of those roles evidenced in the look, feel, and features of their outputs—for example, the details of technologies, buildings, clothes, rituals, government, daily work, and so on.

We take our leave for a bit, indeed for many years, and then we return. We look again. We find that there are new people, as old ones have died and their offspring come of age. That's change. There are also new buildings and houses, some from the past having collapsed. That's change. There are new clothes. There are a few modest new rituals, and so on. But we also notice that in a very profound sense almost everything is unchanged. And this isn't surprising, because when we then also look at the religious, decision-making, productive, and cultural roles, those are all as they were too.

Time has certainly passed. Some modest changes have happened, but history, writ large, has stood still. Strolling around after the time warp delay, we could easily be in the same society and the same place as we were before the time warp delay. It would take a discerning eye to even know time had passed.

Now this little thought experiment didn't occur regarding a passage of ten years, fifty years, or even a hundred years, but regarding a passage of three thousand years. Yet, despite the passage of such eons, the basics and even most of the details remained as they were on the earlier visit. After three thousand years, less change was visible than between 1900 and 2000. Hell, it is possible there was less change visible than between 2000 and 2010.

There was, in ancient Egypt, very modest, snail's pace social evolution. That is, there were very modest changes consistent with the continuation of the defining features of the four spheres of Pharaonic (Egyptian) society—though actually, in fact, there was not even much of that.

The same descriptive label was accurately applicable to the society before and after the three-thousand-year passage. The same social roles pertained, and not much that was second, third, or even fifth order had changed either. Social evolution happened, pretty much by definition, with the ticking of the clock. The calendar's pages turned. People were born and died. New leaders replaced old leaders. New priests replaced old priests. New clothes were worn instead of old worn-out clothes. But if you look at the hieroglyphics—the pictures revealing style and substance—it is hard to distinguish before and after. And if you dig around archeologically, there was virtually no change in the substance of the defining roles in society. History, one could say—if by history we mean substantial changes in structures—apparently doesn't necessarily always happen but instead occurs only sometimes.

Why does history in the form of social evolution happen at all? Why do more or fewer changes happen consistent with the existing defining order—the four existing social spheres and their defining roles, and thus the existing human center of attitudes, consciousness, and expectations common to various constituencies in society, and the existing institutional boundary or totality of critically influential social roles?

There are lots of reasons. New ideas may be hatched. New technologies can flow from those ideas. Changes in weather or geography can occur and impact housing and clothing and some habits, as can somewhat altered tastes or talents. There could also be migrations. Births could accumulate. This type of change happens, sometimes less, sometimes more, but always at least somewhat. So this type of history—called social evolution—always happens.

When some infamous commentators have said about modern times that "History Is Over" or that "Capitalism Is Forever" or that "There Is No Alternative," they must be talking about something other than social evolution, because they know there will always be changes of that sort. There will be new styles, new designs, and new knowledge. There will be new applications of it all, yielding not only new trends and fashions but new options, behaviors, and outcomes.

Folks who proclaim an end to history know all that. What they really mean is there will not be new defining roles leading to and deriving from new defining institutions. There will be more social evolution, yes, but there will be no more fundamental transformations of how we accomplish social functions.

Sometimes, "history" just refers to time passing. That's true when we call social evolution, which more or less always happens, history. Other times, however, by "history" we mean the social revolutions in defining role structures that are more rare. An end to history in the former sense would mean there is no further change at all. An end to history in the latter sense would mean new things keep happening but the basics remain in place.

Okay, to be in accord with the most familiar and frequent practice, let's use the word *history* to refer to all of it. Time passes, changes happen—or not—and that is history. You can reasonably reference it mainly by noting years passing. Social evolution, no matter how modest or grand, is change occurring over time that reproduces the defining features of the old order. Social revolution, however, which is also part of history, also occurs over time but only when there are changes that overthrow the defining features of the old order and introduce, in their place, new defining features that bring new roles that dramatically change life's options and prospects. As to social evolution's engine, we know that many things can play a role— ideas and their applications, natural changes in weather or geography, new tastes, and many other variables.

As to social revolution, what causes that is not so obvious. We know that by definition social revolution means change in the defining institutions and, thus, in the roles that are available for people to fill in one or more of the four social spheres.

Social revolution doesn't mean violence. It doesn't mean chaos. It doesn't mean progress or reaction. It could involve any or all or none of those, but it means change of a certain type and degree, which may come about in any of a large variety of ways. So in asking for potential causes of social revolution we are seeking to identify phenomena that could cause such changes.

Karl Marx confronted this question of why history in the large sense of social revolutions happens at all. He made great progress but also went significantly wrong. Looking at some specific periods in history and noticing that social evolution was common but that social revolution only happened rarely, Marx suggested—or at least the school of thought named after Marx says that he suggested—that history moves by virtue of a very particular kind of tension embodied within societies.

Marx rightly showed, for example, that in capitalism there is a built-in drive to keep on accumulating—that was his word for it. He famously wrote that for the capitalist the guiding mantra is "Accumulate, accumulate, that is Moses and the prophets." Due to the pressures of competition for profits and market share, Marx taught, a pressure to keep on transforming natural resources and human capacities into more and more outputs, including constantly innovating, was built into the actual logic of the system. This wasn't just an option that might be pursued. It was an inevitable part of the fabric of these societies. It was built into the defining relations and role structures. This pressure would persist regardless of whether people liked the results or not. And the ensuing perpetual drive to accumulate clearly meant there would at least be significant social evolution—indeed, he contrasted this positively with prior systems like the Pharaonic that had no such built-in pressures and were, as a result, far less innovative. But one might note that accumulation could happen and augur social evolution and only social evolution, with the surrounding capitalist system constantly reproduced. Whether it was subjectively because Marx didn't like that surrounding system or objectively because his investigations led him to the following observation with no influence from his hopes and desires, Marx came to the conclusion that the inevitable accumulation drive of capitalism did more than just pile up new products. It also created a tension or a contradiction in society between ever-growing and innovating technical and social capacities, on the one hand, and old forms of organization and exchange that operate incompatibly with the new potentials, on the other hand. Marx argued that in society after society this tension would eventually cause the old social relations to be overcome by the new productive possibilities, leading to new social relations and in that way leading to a new economic sphere with new roles and, therefore, a social revolution.

This is not the place to get too deeply into these claims which seem to us to identify one possibility, which is that technical and even organizational innovations can drive new productive possibilities which, in turn, can fuel social changes by affecting a populations' actions. As with the old Marxist way of seeing class, this is a possibility that is still, at most, only one possibility, while there are actually many other possibilities as well. More, the possibility that social relations will be burst by growing productive forces isn't likely to transpire or to yield comprehensive results if it occurs alone. But whatever one thinks about what Marx called a contradiction between "forces and relations of production" as a possible locus of revolution, as with our broadening from a narrow two class conception that is often typical of many anticapitalists, we will now also expand our approach to understanding history's engines from that which is often typical of many anticapitalists.

Consider some possibilities. Along comes some kind of technical innovation—like birth control. This innovation, in turn, leads to changes in social relations and outcomes, fueling new attitudes that cause gender struggle and finally push all manner of evolutionary changes, some highly consequential for life situations. But we can also imagine that this innovation sparks, say, women to see outcomes differently, to resist their subordination, to discover sexism's roots, and to transform defining kin relations. Does this have to happen? No, it doesn't. But could it happen? Yes, a fundamental transformation could be propelled by a technical innovation impacting attitudes and actions in the kinship sphere.

Consider another possibility, the economy and polity—and probably also kinship and culture in some societies—generate a big imperial war. In fighting that imperial war it happens that various historic roles are violated. For example, perhaps there is a severe labor shortage and women who were previously excluded from an economy that was accommodating a sexist kinship sphere now must be incorporated, and even treated equally, so as to take advantage of their talents and capacities, winning the war being paramount. Women begin to discover their own potential, previously deemed to be nonexistent. Likewise, the same could happen if some oppressed cultural community, say that of blacks, is welcomed into the military and, given fair conditions to generate both trust and military efficiency, is treated equally with others rather than in a racist manner. Again, previously subordinated people could discover potential that they had long forgotten they had.

We can imagine, then, that this jolt in circumstances unleashed by the dictates of trying to win a war could unleash new expectations and hopes that would go unmet, or even be dashed, when the war ends and women and blacks return to far more sexist and racist circumstances than existed for them during the war, this in turn fueling resistance, leading to insights into the true causes of gender and/or racial injustices, and then leading to transformations. This would involve at least social evolution, but it could also involve social revolution, affecting certain spheres of social life, or perhaps all spheres of social life.

The general ideas in these examples emerge easily enough. When events and occurrences within one sphere or between two or more spheres directly cause either consciousness to get out of accord with old role requirements in a sphere or cause two spheres to get out of accord with one another, causing consciousnesses to alter as well, it can lead to lasting changes. The turmoil might reestablish or merely innovate old social relations a bit, yielding only social evolution, or the turmoil might cause dramatic changes in defining features, yielding social revolution.

Here is another possibility. Some people create new institutions for immediately addressing some social functions but also to guide fighting to win changes in old institutions. The new approaches, such as new household or neighborhood arrangements or new workplaces, develop wider support and participation by the inspiring way they treat classes, genders, and communities in comparison to the past ways of handling the same functions. The organizations steadily gain more participants by the manner in which their activities reveal new possibilities. Their actions arouse new desires and provide means for collective expression and fulfillment. Both the exemplary functional and fighting institutions—whether we are discussing new families, workplaces, modes of allocation, means of governing, cultural communities, or movements for changes in various spheres of life—may themselves, in turn, have roles that breed new habits, expectations, and desires, popularizing them and militating for the wider acceptance of the innovations. This path too, based on acts of will by the people affected, can lead to social evolution or even to social revolution.

History is not preordained. It is not an inexorable process. It is not an outcome of one simple dynamic. It is not based solely on classes or genders or communities or political constituencies. History can unfold due to many diverse causes, propelled by many diverse motives, engineered by many diverse groups, and inspired and advanced by many diverse acts and insights, including many diverse dynamics within and among society's social spheres and its relations to ecology and other societies—all either due to intentional choices or unintended occurrences. Life is like that. History is like that. But narrow theories are not like that.

Further Refinements

Suppose you have a set of concepts composing your viewpoint that gives you guidance in looking at events and relations, in posing alternatives, and in evaluating and implementing possible paths forward. Think of concepts and viewpoints as being a set of instructions—look here, look there, emphasize this, check for this predicted relationship when you see that, look for that when you see this, and so on. The problem is, one might start to see the world as if through a filter that cleaves very closely to one's viewpoint, sometimes seeing what isn't there or is minor and missing what is there and is perhaps even major.

We know that if we look at the world with a red filter, we will see the red part highlighted but tend to mute out or even miss that which is yellow, blue, or green. The same holds if we look through a yellow filter, seeing only that which is yellow, and not the other colors. Of course the analogy between looking at the world with colored filters and looking at the world with concepts is a bit tortured, yet there is considerable truth lurking in it.

Suppose I adopt a feminist perspective. It highlights for me some important types of consciousness—relations among men and women and institutions, like families, and their roles—and it also orients me away from wasting time on what it deems unimportant secondary or tertiary relations.

But what if some of that other muted stuff is, in fact, key? Indeed, what if some of that muted stuff exposes differences from my expectations that bear upon what I care about accomplishing? I may manage to get beyond my initial views to perceive the unexpected key relations or I may not. I may cleave so tightly to what my framework predicts that I simply can't see beyond its limits.

We have said that in any society, by virtue of inevitably present human needs and social realities, there are four social spheres. We have also said that each of these four social spheres will likely emanate a field of influence that propels its logic outward to produce at least accommodation in other social spheres, and sometimes co-reproduction.

For these reasons, our approach says to the feminist, intercommunalist, anarchist, or anticapitalist that to avoid missing key elements of reality you must become an adherent of the other three perspectives as well as of the perspective you already favor.

Second, our approach notes that a person identifying primarily as being a black person, for example, or a woman or a subordinate citizen or a worker will, in adopting the framework most relevant to their own centrally felt condition, not gain all that much missing insight. That is, regarding their own intensely felt condition, even without taking aboard new and carefully formulated concepts, the person is already quite alert and sensitized. They already almost reflexively highlight the key factors, and even many secondary factors, operating in their priority sphere of focus. Yet their capacity to see that which is central in the other spheres of life is limited, perhaps very heavily limited, by their lack of related experience, and so in a very profound sense those other spheres are where they need the most conceptual help and guidance.

The point is this. If I am a white male worker, I need more conceptual help understanding the roots and implications of sexism and racism than I do understanding the roots and implications of the classism that I am already—by my own situation— attuned to and focused on. Similarly, if I identify as a feminist, it is with the other spheres—not the one I myself most directly and automatically relate to—that I need the most conceptual help. And so the second point is that we not only need to have a fourfold rather than single sphere approach, but individually we need to put more effort into having concepts for the spheres we are weakest at, and even prone to misunderstand, than into the sphere (or spheres) we are strongest at and already largely understand. This is, of course, almost exactly opposite to most people's reflex agenda of pursuing more reading and thinking about their own circumstances. So for precisely this reason it is quite important.

As an example, if I analyze a capitalist market economy in economic terms alone, I will come to the conclusion that in choosing a new working-class employee or a person to become a coordinator-class manager, the key thing the owner will care about is the person's inclination to abide by the dictates of class and economy—which means to work hard without attention to personal dignity and without seeking additional bargaining power, while willingly enduring boredom, taking orders, and putting out in the case of the working-class hire. And for the coordinator-class hire, it means paternalistically administering and keeping subordinate the workers below and enjoying ample income but not working to unduly enlarge it and, in any case, accepting ultimate authority from above without challenge, as well as producing at a frantic rate.

But what if there is a sharply racist or sharply sexist culture at play in the society that contains the workplace. Then things become more complex in choosing among working-class or coordinator-class applicants. There are new variables, such as not violating and indeed perhaps even reproducing the requisites of those two hierarchy-creating spheres. Instead of the woman and/or black I might hire for one position or another—if I ignored race and gender implications and derivative implications for class that I would not see if I was ignoring race and gender—I might instead favor a white and/or male hire. Or, in fact, especially for the working-class position, this could operate in reverse, since I might be able to better control and extract labor from a doubly downtrodden individual. If there is a pecking order of status, security, and influence established elsewhere in society, then in the economy I don't buck it but instead use it.

Another variant of this same type of refining of views was revealed earlier. The Marxist tends to see—or at least some Marxists tend to see society as economy-based, with everything else in a "superstructure." They argue that the economy, their prioritized sphere, is essential—since without it we die. They note that the economy yields opposed constituencies, or classes, and that the one at the bottom, the working class, is key to arriving at new social relations. The economy has its own internal dynamics and those dynamics can (and some Marxists would say must) yield disjunctures which arouse dissent leading to opposition, and finally to fundamental change. And, in this view, this change then imposes a kind of outward field of influence that also changes the rest of society, called society's superstructure.

Can this more or less happen? Yes. But contrary to some formulations, it is certainly not inevitable, nor is it inexorable once elements of it have begun. Even more to the point, it is not the only thing that can happen.

First, the feminist or the intercommunalist or the anarchist (now focused on polity) can argue, quite like the Marxist, that their function is essential. Their sphere also produces opposed constituencies. Their sphere can also affect consciousness and arouse resistance. When the feminist does this, she may see kinship as the base and all else (including economy) as superstructure. Roughly four decades ago a very insightful feminist, Shulamith Firestone, made exactly this case as an argument *ad absurdum* against class relations being solely critical. She literally took Marxism's arguments and words and simply rewrote them with new references to kinship instead of economy.

And so too for the intercommunalists or anarchists, who can just as reasonably emphasize culture or polity as the base and the rest as superstructure, as some have done. So actually it is not the case that only one claim is right and the rest wrong—which is what an adherent of each perspective might, and often will, argue, and what each will often act on as a guiding assumption. Nor are all the claims to importance wrong. Instead, all these claims are possible but none are inevitable. And more, it is also possible for what happens in one sphere to be reversed by pressures from other spheres, rather than to propel other spheres to change in accord.

In essence, we must say goodbye to prioritizing one sphere before analyzing all spheres. We must say goodbye to taking one aspect of society as a priori preponderant in importance. We must say hello to a more balanced and comprehensive stance that sees the mutual interconnectivity and entwined influence of all four spheres.

Conclusion

Think of our effort as slowly filling a conceptual toolbox. We dig into this toolbox when we need to understand existing relations and history and when we need to propose new vision or strategy. In our toolbox, so far, we have the idea of four societal functions essential to a society existing and persisting—economic, political, kin, and cultural. We also have the idea that societies exist in context of the natural environment, influencing it and being influenced by it, as well as by the many other societies that together establish international relations.

We next have the idea of four social spheres corresponding to the four inevitably present and important social functions. And we have the idea that each sphere has defining institutions, which in turn have defining social roles. More, we focus on institutions and their roles, both in each sphere and also taken all together to constitute a kind of institutional boundary of society, and we focus too on people's consciousnesses, values, skills, and expectations, particularly as shared by large groups defined by institutional roles, all together constituting a kind of social center of society.

We have in mind too that each social sphere affects the lives of people via that sphere's roles, often generating hierarchies—for example, of class, gender, sexual preference, race, religion, ethnic and national group, and political power or influence. Each sphere also, again by way of its roles, produces in those who function in it particular shared attitudes, interests, beliefs, habits, and expectations—typically arrayed in ways that line up from one sphere to another so that what each sphere requires and upholds does not seriously violate the requirements that other spheres require and uphold, and, sometimes even tends to reproduce and enforce the requirements born of the logic of the other spheres.

Indeed, we also adopt the insights that have emerged to serve the interests of subordinate populations in each of the four spheres. We adopt three approaches (feminism, intercommunalism, and anarchism) largely whole, just as they have been often used before, with only modest refinements to take account of mutual interconnections and influences. One approach (anticapitalism), however, we substantially modify by seeing three key classes rather than two, adding the new concept of the coordinator class between labor and capital, with its own attitudes and interests.

We also highlight the fact that sometimes the requirements and implications of social spheres can get out of whack, either internally within one sphere or between two or more spheres or, for that matter, with innovations in any one sphere that have been proposed or enacted, sometimes even with the explicit purpose of propelling change. In these ways there ensues social evolution that occurs within the limits of reproducing old defining relations but also sometimes a less frequent and more profound social revolution, replacing old roles with new and fundamentally different ones.

In light of all this, our next task is to broadly apply these ways of thinking to vision and strategy. As we do this, our conceptual toolbox and our broad perspective about social change will get some new resident concepts, while some of the concepts already in it will become sharper and better understood.

PART TWO: OUR GOALS

**"If we don't stand for something,
we may fall for anything."**
—*variously attributed*

CHAPTER 4

Visionary Patterns

"One can never consent to creep when
one feels an impulse to soar."
—*Helen Keller*

This chapter seeks a short list of values to guide our efforts to envision core institutions for a future desirable society. I list seven values—a short list just sufficient to inform our efforts. The values each correspond to an aspect of life and, perhaps unsurprisingly, most of the values are commonplace and uncontroversial.

Relations among People: Solidarity

Societies and each of their four spheres affect how people interrelate. Do institutions cause us to treat each other instrumentally as means to ends? Do we scramble over each other, some winning only when others lose? Do our roles cause us to become isolated and individualistic—even antisocial?

Yes, those debits are normal to contemporary life. But what value would we rather have to organize relations among people? Our answer is, other things being equal, we want our institutions to cause us to have shared rather than contending interests. We want our daily activities to make us more not less concerned with the well-being of others. We prefer empathy to antipathy.

We want institutions that cause looking out for ourselves and looking out for others to be almost always the same thing and to be, at least, nonconflicting.

I benefit, others benefit too. Others benefit, then so do I. None of us should benefit at the expense of others. All of us should benefit to the advantage of others. Institutions in each sphere should cause people to have compatible rather than opposed interests so that each benefits from another's gains, rather than some gaining as others lose. So solidarity is our first value.

Options for People: Diversity

Society and its defining institutions dramatically impact the range of available options people can choose from. None of us live forever. We can't enjoy doing every conceivable thing. None of us are omniscient. We can't always know for sure the best way to proceed.

If everyone does the same things you do—if we all act alike, all follow one path, all explore one solution, all implement one approach—then all other possibilities are gone for each of us. There are two very serious problems with trends toward homogeneity.

With homogeneity, we lose the benefit of vicariously enjoying what we ourselves can't or don't have time or don't wish to do. We can only vicariously enjoy acts that we don't undertake. We can only learn their lessons, enjoy their beauty, be edified by their wisdom, if others undertake them. And that requires diversity.

With homogeneity we also suffer more when there are mistakes because we don't have a fallback position to adopt when a preferred approach proves faulty. We don't have other options we can switch to, because if society is largely homogeneous and we choose a wrong path, everyone else is on that wrong path too.

Our value for options is diversity. It doesn't mean we should multiply available paths without limit just for the sake of a higher tally. But it does mean we should studiously avoid narrowing options at the expense of enjoying vicariously what others can do, as well as being prepared to correct faults. And it means this for each of our four spheres.

We enjoy other people's contrasting and sometimes clashing choices. We don't put all our eggs in one basket. We have options. This is the meaning of diversity, our second value.

Distribution of Benefits: Justice

Society and its defining institutions dramatically impact the distribution of material and situational responsibilities and benefits that people enjoy or suffer in their daily lives.

How much stuff do you get? What is the norm guiding what you get? What circumstances do you find yourself in? What is the rationale for your being in those circumstances? Do you get more or less than others? Why? In disputes, how is the redress of grievances assessed? What level of punishment is warranted and when is it imposed? What level of redress or reward is warranted and when?

Our distributional value is about allocation of responsibility and benefits in all aspects of life. We call distributional outcomes that are fair—when you get that and I get this and we both respect the outcome—just. We call distributional outcomes that we do not like unjust. In other words, we all agree to call our distributional value justice.

We also agree that what makes a particular distribution of benefits and burdens just is that it is fair. This is circular, yet also true, and it will enrich or clarify the definition for some people. We want the amount that each person receives—whether in the form of material reward or desirable circumstances—to be commensurate to that person's efforts to fulfill their responsibilities.

In a very real sense, justice is about each person getting a fair and essentially equal overall mix of benefits minus burdens. If we outlay more from our lives in taking on burdens, we should get back additional benefits to bring us back to an average or fair weight of both combined.

To get more benefits, we endure more burdens. To endure fewer burdens, we receive fewer benefits. Gain and loss should not be by luck, by taking or being taken, by demanding or being demanded.

Society has much that is burdensome to endure and much that is rewarding to enjoy. If we endure some of what's burdensome, we get to enjoy some of the benefits. The gain weighs against the cost. If we do more that needs doing, we get more benefit. If we do less, we get less benefit. If, worse still, we violate our responsibilities and not only don't add to but actually reduce society's bounty by irresponsible behaviors, then we suffer penalties. This is what we typically mean by justice. Justice is fair apportionment of burdens and benefits, and it is the basic norm we shall have in mind and apply, yielding slightly different insights and aims in each of the four spheres due to their specific attributes.

Consider economics. The issue of justice in the economy is about what income and circumstances we enjoy by virtue of fulfilling our economic responsibilities. The economy produces lots of stuff. Think of the output as a giant pie. What size piece do we each receive? That's income distribution.

There are five norms of remuneration advocated by various economists to determine the income (or share of the pie) people should receive:

- the amount our property produces;
- the amount we are strong enough to take;
- the amount we ourselves produce by our efforts and sacrifices;
- the level of our efforts and sacrifices, as long as we are producing desired results;

- and/or our need.

There are two primary considerations in judging these norms:

- the morality of a norm for the person receiving the share of the pie it implies and for all those who then get their share of the pie from what is left;
- the incentive effects of a norm for the size of the whole pie and thus for what anyone can receive.

Which option or combination of options is equitable for determining income distribution? In our view, it is remuneration for need when one cannot work and remuneration for duration, intensity, and onerousness of socially valued labor when one can work that is equitable. Thus, from our list above, remuneration for effort and sacrifice doing socially useful labor. We reject remuneration for property, power, and/or output as not yielding fair benefits minus burdens for each person. All this will be investigated in the next chapter, which will also address additional details regarding equity of circumstance and the incentive aspect of the various norms. But the idea should be clear—we develop values, we explore them, and we use them as a guide in defining institutions.

For kinship and culture, the key justice focus is the apportionment of benefits and responsibilities to people in their kinship and cultural practices. For kinship, do men and women, children and elderly people, gays and straights—both in the home and in kinship institutions more broadly, as well as in the rest of society—have a mix of responsibilities and benefits that distribute fairly from person to person? Within cultural communities, the same calculus needs to apply, but it also needs to apply between communities, so that different communities have the same security and potential to pursue their cultural practices vis-à-vis needed resources, space, safety, and more.

Regarding polity—assuming all the above are dealt with, and thus assuming that legislation abides just norms—the remaining issue is largely one of justice in the oft-used sense of determining just results of conflicts. This is partly about dealing with violations of social laws and norms and partly about resolving disputes with benefits and responsibilities. Legal justice means arriving at results that apportion benefits and punishments appropriately given past actions and future situations, as well as agreed upon norms and laws. Is that vague? Yes, but that is the nature of judicial applications—the range of issues is so broad that what justice means judicially is largely contextual.

Each of the four applications of justice will be clarified and enriched when we deal with the key defining features of each of the four spheres in coming chapters. For now, justice is a value we place in our toolbox to use in developing our vision for society.

Decision Influence: Self-Management

Society and its defining institutions affect the amount of say each person has in determining outcomes. What is our value for the level of say in decision-making that people should have?

Of course one wants good, insightful, caring decisions. Typically people say they want democracy, which is one-person-one-vote majority rule. Others might say that sometimes it is better to have autocracy—an elite, however small, deciding, because they know best. Another stance is that we should mostly all agree. Or, even if we don't precisely all agree, no one should be so distraught that they want to block a choice others agree on—and thus we should decide by consensus. And then there are combinations and variants, such as needing two-thirds or 60 percent or three-quarters in favor for some decision to be enacted. Variations also arise in how long deliberations should last, who should partake in deliberations and representation—and concerning issues of efficiency and how to locate and utilize expertise—and other factors, as well.

Our thinking, however, is a bit different. What do we want vis-à-vis decisions? What is the aim for how much say people should have? What is the appropriate level of that say?

Suppose I work with a bunch of people and I want to wear brown socks instead of black or green socks, or I want to wear no clothes instead of clothes. Or say I want to put up a picture of my mate on my wall, or I want to put a stereo on my shelf and play it very loud. Almost everyone would say I should get to decide alone about my socks and my mate's picture. No one else should have a say, just me. Most would say, however, that I can't decide to go nude and dictate that outcome alone—and certainly I can't decide to listen to loud music and dictate that outcome alone.

The difference is that some decisions affect just me—or nearly so. Other decisions affect other people not just me. About the former type of decision, we tend to say, go for it. About the latter type, we tend to say, hold on, others have to be allowed to influence that decision too.

The fact is that we spontaneously think that implies an underlying value that most of us largely share. People should have a say in decisions in proportion to the degree they are affected by them, or as near to that as we can manage without wasting time seeking a nonexistent and picky perfection. Let's call that value self-management.

With that value guiding us, we will use majority rules or two-thirds or consensus, not as a matter of principal but because one or the other best approximates self-management. Sometimes, as with the sock decision, we will opt for a dictatorial approach. Other times we will favor more inclusive modes of arriving at decisions.

The rejectionist will say that self-management dilutes the quality of decisions. The idea is that some people are better at decisions—the experts. So to get the best decisions we need to give experts disproportionate say based on their skills at decision-making, even when they are not most affected by the decisions.

We should be careful here. We do prefer good decisions to bad ones. And expertise is important when making good decisions. But what is often needed is expert knowledge of implications, and once we consult experts and have that information at our disposal, why should the experts be given more say than is warranted by how much they will be affected? This would only make sense if understanding the implications—even after they were clearly spelled out—required the expert's knowledge. Typically, it doesn't.

If the experts say the bridge will collapse if we make decision X, and the bridge will be fine if we make decision Y, we don't have to be able to replicate or fully understand how they arrived at their conclusion. We have to be able to judge if they are reliable, and we have to be sure the situation doesn't give them perverse motives.

There is another hole in the critic's case. While one component of deciding if we should or shouldn't do X is the implications of doing X, a second component is how I, you, and others feel about X's implications. And regarding our own preferences, each of us is the world's foremost expert. It follows that when discussing options it is very important to sufficiently consult those with special relevant knowledge. But when tallying opinions to settle on a decision, then paying attention to expertise means we must let each person determine their own preferences and register them. Hopefully, as we see self-management's implications for institutions, its merits will become obvious.

Relations to Nature: Stewardship

People and the environment exist entwined. There is us. There are our artifacts. And there is the rest. But, of course, nature impinges on and helps define us and we impinge on and help define nature—both to such an extent that viewed differently there is really only one highly entwined whole. Still, regarding what we broadly mean by nature, what is the value we would like to see a new society abide by and even foster?

The usual answer from virtually everyone who addresses this issue is sustainability. We should behave in ways that allow us to continue behaving, not in ways that disrupt nature so much that our behaving becomes no longer possible. Taken literally, sustainability says society should not commit suicide by way of environmental degradation. Well, yes, of course.

But can we go beyond this? We could say we want steward- ship. This word implies we are not only relating to the envi- ronment for the continuation our own future but also for the effect on us and on the environment insofar as it creates a new context at all. Does a proposed act's impact on the environment benefit or hurt human growth and development. If it benefits us, okay. If it hurts us, then there needs to be larger, offsetting benefits or we should desist.

Even more, however, the word *stewardship* conveys that humans are taking responsibility for the environment beyond considering nature's impact on us. Seeking to be good stew- ards opens the possibility that we seek to preserve, protect, and even nurture aspects of nature in their own right. What aspects? Well, that's a future decision. Perhaps it will be obvious at times. Perhaps it will be contentious. Maybe species. Maybe natural environments.

The point of the value is to say we recognize that change in the environment due to our actions rebounds on us, and we shouldn't commit environmental suicide. Indeed, we should try to affect the environment in ways beneficial for the human community. We also consider environmental, and particularly natural, forms and conditions. We act on behalf of the envi- ronment like we act on behalf of future generations—because neither can speak for themselves.

Internationalism

In one sense, our value for international relations can be said to be just the other values writ larger. But, to keep our eyes on the issue, which is what concepts are for, we give this value its own name and clarify it a bit. We call it internationalism, meaning each society should regard the world arena as its social context and should wish to be comfortable and benefit by its relations to other societies but also to have other societies do likewise.

To homogenize the world would be to rob it of its richness and suffer horrible loss due to diminished vicarious experiences and a cessation of experiment and exploration of alternatives. We need international diversity. We don't want hostility, we want sociality. We need solidarity. Fairness for anyone requires fairness for everyone, so we also need international justice. Surely people in the world should all have the same norm for degrees of influence over their own and world affairs. Thus we should favor international self-management. The ecology of the planet obviously requires the same attentiveness as the ecology within any one country—so we favor international stewardship.

Internationalism means each nation respects, learns from, and assists other nations so that there are steadily diminishing and then no new emergence of significant differences in per capita wealth, influence, or circumstances from nation to nation, yielding a condition of mutual aid, learning, and peace.

These international aims are familiar aspirations, posed and preached in many versions. Of course, wide allegiance to internationalism typically disappears whenever the self-interested domestic pursuits of any one nation can be advanced by imperial behavior toward others—most often as an outgrowth of domestic social structures. So the basis of internationalism is ultimately to (a) clean up the domestic front by achieving the values above in each society and to (b) establish not only a norm but also means of fulfilling those values internationally.

Where We Fit: Participation

When we come to examine the implications of implementing the above values throughout each of society's four spheres and two contexts, we will see that their establishment implies and requires the elimination of divisions of people into opposed sectors along kinship, community, political, or economic lines. This entails what we call feminism, intercommunalism, participatory politics, and participatory economics replacing sexism, homophobia, racism, ethnocentrism, classism, and other forms of cultural, gender, political, and economic oppression with the pursuit and fulfillment of solidarity, diversity, justice, and self-management.

How do we arrive at vision for all this? In the domain of society and history, if a particular set of institutions violates one's values in unjustifiable ways, especially if the violation is extreme and intrinsic, then those institutions are not worthy of support. To reject oppressive institutions is morally and logically consistent. Anything less is hypocrisy.

If I say that I value solidarity but I advocate social relations that produce antisociality, that means I am seriously confused, lying, or delusional. The same applies if I advocate diversity, justice, self-management, stewardship, or internationalism but support institutions that obliterate one or more of those values.

If we take this brief chapter seriously, we are all potential revolutionaries, because we reject the defining institutions of modern societies by the central, uncorrectable, and inexorable ways they violate our values.

CHAPTER 5

Parecon

> **"If all economists were laid end to end,
> they would not reach a conclusion."**
> —*variously attributed*

Dealing with economy means conceiving economic institutions for production, consumption, and allocation. We call our economic vision, which has come into being over the last twenty years or so, participatory economics, or parecon for short.

Parecon's Values
Translating the preferred values proposed in the last chapter into their meaning in the economic sphere will get us started toward arriving at an economic vision.

Solidarity
In capitalist economics, to increase your income and power you must ignore the horrible pain suffered by those left below or even help push them further down. This is the logic of the roles owner and worker and buyer and seller. "Greed is good" runs the mantra.

In contrast, a good economy should be a solidarity economy generating sociality rather than antisocial greed. A good economy's institutions for production, consumption, and allocation should, therefore, by the roles they offer, propel even antisocial people into having to address other people's well-being if they are to advance their own well-being. Getting ahead in a good economy should derive from and depend on others getting ahead as well. By virtue of acting to better our lot, we should become more solidaritous with others, rather than having to be hostile to others.

Interestingly, this first economic value is entirely uncontroversial. Who would argue that an economy would be better if it produced more hostility and antisociality in its participants than if it produced more mutual concern in its participants? Who would rather live in a hostile dystopian realm of nastiness than in a realm of mutual aid?

Diversity

Capitalist market rhetoric trumpets opportunity, but capitalist market discipline curtails satisfaction and development by replacing what is human and caring with what is commercial, profitable, and in accord with existing hierarchies of power and wealth. Market diversity excludes humane options. We get Pepsi and Coke, but we do not get soda that takes into account the well-being of soda producers, consumers, and the environment. The tremendous variety of tastes, preferences, and choices that humans naturally display are truncated by capitalism into conformist patterns imposed by advertising, narrow role offerings, and coercive marketing environments.

In capitalism, those who control outcomes seek the most profitable method instead of many parallel methods suiting a range of priorities. They seek the biggest, quickest, brightest of almost everything if that is what they can sell most widely and without undercutting hierarchies of power and wealth. This virtually always crowds out more diverse choices that would support greater and more widespread fulfillment and, most important, affect people's knowledge, skills, confidence, and ties in ways contrary to elite domination.

In the economy that we seek we instead want economic institutions that emphasize finding and respecting diverse solutions to problems. A good economy would recognize that we are finite beings who can benefit from enjoying what others do that we ourselves have no time to do, and that we are fallible beings who should not vest all our hopes in single routes of advance but should instead insure against damage by exploring diverse parallel avenues and options. Even when we think there is one best way most of the time, in fact, it is not the case. We should rarely, if ever, put all our eggs in one basket, shutting down all other options.

Equity

Not only should equitable economic institutions not obstruct equity, they should propel it. But what is equity? Well, it can't be equitable that due to having a deed in your pocket you earn a hundred, a thousand, or even more times the income some other person earns who works harder and longer. To inherit ownership—and by virtue of that ownership vastly exceed others in circumstance and influence—cannot be equitable.

And it also can't be equitable to reward power with income. The logic of the Mafia—which is the same as the logic of Wall Street, which is the same as the logic of the Harvard Business School—is that each actor should earn as remuneration for their economic activity whatever they are strong enough to take. If you have a monopoly on some assets that convey power, you can take more, if you don't, less. If your constituency suffers some denial in society—due to sexism, say, or racism—your power is lower, and you can take less. Since we are civilized, we reject Mafia economics.

What about output as a basis for income? Should people get back from the social product an amount determined by what they produce as part of that social product? Put differently, what could justify that we should get less than what we contribute? Someone taking part of the wealth I create? Or what could justify that we should get more than our own contribution? I take some of the wealth others create? Shouldn't we each get an income based only on the amount we produce?

This seems obvious to many caring people—including most anticapitalists throughout history. But is it morally or economically sound?

Suppose Jack and Catherine do the same work for the same length of time at the same intensity. If Catherine has better tools with which to generate more output, should she get more income than Jack, who has worse tools and, as a result, generates less output even though he is working as hard or harder? Some say yes. Others say no. All we can do to choose is to look at the implications of any proposed preference and decide what we do or do not like.

Should someone who happens to be employed producing something highly valued be rewarded more than someone who is employed producing something less valued? What if the latter is still socially desired? What if the less productive person works equally hard and equally long and endures similar conditions as the more productive person?

Similarly, should someone who inherited genes for big size, musical talent, tremendous reflexes, peripheral vision, or conceptual competency get rewarded more than someone who was genetically less lucky? Why, on top of the luck of your genetic inheritance, should economic institutions reward you with greater income as well?

A different view is that remuneration should be for effort and sacrifice in producing socially desired items.

In this view, if I work longer, I should get more reward. If I work harder, I should get more reward. And if I work in worse conditions and at more onerous tasks, I should get more reward. But I should not get more for having better tools or for producing something that happens to be valued more highly or for having innate highly productive talents. Nor should I get more even for the output of learned skills—though I should be rewarded for the effort and sacrifice of learning those skills. Nor, of course, should I get more for work that isn't socially warranted.

Some anticapitalists think that people should be rewarded for the overall volume of their output, so that a great athlete should earn a fortune since people in society highly value watching him or her play. A good doctor should earn way more than a hardworking farmer or a short-order cook, since an operation that saves a life is more valued than a dinner or some additional corn. A participatory economy, however, rejects that norm.

Participatory economic equity instead requires that assuming comparable intensity and duration of work, a person who has a nice, comfortable, pleasant, and highly productive job should earn less than a person who has an onerous, debilitating, and less productive—but still socially valuable and warranted—job due to the sacrifice endured. The participatory economy rewards effort and sacrifice endured producing socially valued labor. It does not reward property, power, or output. You have to produce socially valued output commensurate to the productivity of your tools and conditions, otherwise you are wasting assets and not benefiting society. You are not remunerated in accord with the value of your output, however, but in accord with the effort and sacrifice you expend generating that output.

Two other anticapitalist stances regarding remuneration claim many advocates, and we should consider those too. The first says work itself is intrinsically negative. Why should anyone thinking about a better economy think in terms of organizing or apportioning work? Why not just eliminate work?

This stance moves from the worthy aim of reducing debilitating work to suggesting that we should entirely eliminate work, which is obviously nonsense.

First, work yields results we can't do without. The bounty that work generates justifies the costs of undertaking it. In a good economy, people would desist from excess work rather than suffer only insufficient returns for it. We expend our effort and make associated sacrifices only up to the point where the value of the income we receive outweighs the costs of the exertions we undertake. At that point, we opt for leisure not for more work. I want some stuff, so I am going to work, but I don't want so much stuff that I will work myself at all hours, at a breakneck pace, or in odious conditions. Nor will I forget that it is desirable to change work to make it more pleasurable, less painful, more interesting, less boring and fragmenting, more sustainable, less pollutive, more productive, less wasteful.

In other words, we want to eliminate work that is onerous and debilitating, but we do not want to eliminate work per se. We need to keep work, partly because of the outputs but also partly because of the fulfillment that comes from the labor itself.

The second anticapitalist remunerative stance claims that the only criterion for remuneration ought to be human need. We should follow the advisory, "From each according to ability, to each according to need."

This stance says if a person can't work for reasons of health, surely we don't starve them or deny them income at the level others enjoy. Their needs, modulated in accord with social averages, should be met. If, likewise, someone has special medical needs, these should also be met. And so far, so good. The problem with rewarding need arises not when we are dealing with people who are physically or mentally unable to work, for which the advisory makes perfect sense, but when we try to apply the norm to people who can work but choose not to.

For example, can I forego work and still benefit from society's output? Can I forego work and consume as much I choose? If we say yes, then why won't people choose to work relatively little yet consume a whole lot?

Usually what those who advocate payment for need and people working to capacity have in mind is that each person will responsibly opt for an appropriate share of consumption and responsibly contribute an appropriate amount of work.

But how does anyone know what is appropriate to consume or to produce? And, more subtly, how does the economy determine what is appropriate?

It turns out that in practice the norm "work to ability and consume to need" becomes, for those who advocate it, work and consume in accord with the social averages unless you have a good reason not to. Advocates of the norm believe people will responsibly go over and under social averages only when it is warranted.

But when is deviating from the average warranted? Won't one person think it is okay for so and so reason, and another person think it isn't? And how does anyone even know what the social averages are? If we are all just working to the extent we choose and taking content to the extent we want, what way is there to measure either? How does the economy decide how much of anything to produce? How does anyone know the relative values of outputs if we have no measure of the value of the labor—or of other inputs involved in their production—or of the extent to which anyone wants the outputs? How do we know if labor—or other assets—are apportioned sensibly? Do we need innovations to increase output of some items or should we diminish output of others? How do we know where to invest to improve work conditions or to generate much-desired items rather than other items that are consumed but not much appreciated?

Whether one believes that remuneration for need and working to one's ability is a higher moral norm than remuneration for effort and sacrifice—and this is an open question that reasonable people can certainly differ about—the former is not practical unless there is a way to measure need and ability, a way to value different labor types, a way for people to determine what is warranted behavior, and an expectation that we will all only do what is warranted.

All these qualifying requirements are precisely what remunerating effort and sacrifice instead of need makes real, even as it also enables people to work and consume more or less as they choose and permits everyone to judge relative values in tune with true social costs and benefits. In other words, the desires behind the call to remunerate only need and to work up to ability are fulfilled most desirably and fully by remunerating for the duration, intensity, and onerousness of socially valued labor.

So we want a good economy to remunerate duration, intensity, and onerousness of socially valuable labor and when people can't work to provide income and health care as needed.

Self-Management

In capitalism, owners have tremendous say. Managers and high-level lawyers, engineers, financial officers, and doctors—each of whom monopolize empowering work and daily decision-making positions—are part of what we have called the coordinator class and have substantial say. But people doing rote and obedient labor rarely even know what decisions are being made, much less influence them.

In contrast, we want people to have control over their own lives consistent with others doing likewise. Each person should have a level of influence that won't impinge on other people's rights to have the same level of influence. We each affect decisions in proportion to how we are affected by them.

Imagine that a worker wants to place a picture of his daughter on the wall in his work area. Who should make that decision? Should some owner, a manager, all the workers? Obviously not. The worker whose child it is should decide alone, with full authority. Sometimes making decisions unilaterally makes sense.

Now suppose that a worker wants to put a radio on her desk to play loud, raucous rock and roll all day long. Who should decide? My office, my desk, my ears, I decide? Obviously not, because it isn't only my ears that will hear it. Instead, all those who will hear the radio should have a say, and those who will be more bothered—or more benefited—should have more say. The worker no longer gets to be a dictator, nor does anyone else.

We easily realize that we don't want a majority to decide everything all the time. We do not always want one person, one vote, with some percentage of voters deciding. We do not always want one person to decide authoritatively, as a dictator. Nor do we always want consensus or any other single approach to discussing issues, expressing preferences, and tallying votes. All the possible methods of making decisions make sense in some cases but are horribly unfair, intrusive, or authoritarian in other cases, because different decisions require different approaches.

What we hope to accomplish when we choose from among all possible institutional means of discussing issues, setting agendas, sharing information, and, finally, making decisions is that each person influences decisions in proportion to the degree they are affected by them. And that is our fourth participatory economic value, economic self-management.

Problems with Our Values?

Is there any problem with an economy generating solidarity among its actors? Well, someone could say it will make us uncritical, so that we interact with one another only with praise, only with flattery, and so on. But of course that isn't solidarity—which is instead premised on honesty, concern, empathy, mutual aid, and, in particular, at rock bottom, shared interests.

Diversity? Well, someone might say if you emphasize diversity you might add options ad infinitum, crowding out the excellent with the mediocre. True enough. Sort of like denying that vitamin C is good for you by noting that if you have a pound of it a day you won't last long.

Equity is another issue. Here reasonable people are going to have severe doubts. The argument goes like this. If you remunerate for duration, intensity, and onerousness, why would I become a surgeon? I can make as much—in fact I can make more—working in a coal mine. So I will opt for that or for something like that. And so will everyone who would have been a surgeon in a capitalist economy. As a result we will all die for want of medical care. Further, this critic says becoming a surgeon takes so long and is so difficult that I won't do it unless I get rewarded way more than for most other pursuits.

When speaking to all kinds of audiences all over the world this objection always comes up, always in virtually the exact same form, and always offered with absolute confidence. As response I offer a little thought experiment.

I point to two folks in the audience and say, okay, you (the first one) are just getting out of high school and going to work in a coal mine or something comparable for, let's say, $50,000 a year.

You (the second one) are also just getting out of high school but are going to go to college, then medical school, and then be an intern for a couple of years, and then be a surgeon—earning $500,000 a year.

What the critics of parecon's remuneration are telling us is that going to college and medical school and then being an intern is so much worse than being in the coal mine that after those years, for the next forty, the doctor needs to earn ten times what the coal miner earns. An advocate of our equity value says that instead the doctor earns more only because they can take more. The doctor doesn't need it as an incentive, or wouldn't, if things were arranged differently. So let's test which is the case.

I say to person two, suppose we drop your income as a surgeon to $400,000. Will you forego college, medical school, and being an intern, as well as then being a surgeon, to instead go into the mine or work on an assembly line or cook burgers or whatever? No?

Okay, how about $300,000, $200,000, $50,000, $40,000— and with every audience, not with most but every single one,

I get the same result. Person two asks, "What's the minimum I can survive on? I am going to be a surgeon or lawyer or engineer or whatever—not a coal miner or a short-order cook—down to whatever pay level I can manage to survive on."

The truth is, we need an incentive to do what is more oppressive, so we need an incentive to work longer, harder, or in worse conditions, rather than to do what we would prefer.

What about problems with self-management? Here too there is an almost universal objection. If all people—save, presumably, those in a coma or literally unable to cognitively function—have a say in proportion as they are affected, we will get horrible decisions says the critic. Decisions involve serious thinking and some people are much better at making decisions than others. If we are all making decisions, we will get bad decisions compared to if we have the experts decide.

In response: first, while critics may think they are just rejecting self-management, in fact it is instructive to point out that their complaint also rejects democracy, and even, arguably, makes a case for dictatorship. If Stalin happened to be the best decision-maker in society, then, by the critic's logic, why shouldn't Stalin decide everything? The point of this observation is to convey that while the quality of a decision is important, so is participation. We don't argue against having a dictator solely on the grounds that Stalin isn't omniscient or is malevolent.

We might also say to the critic that we agree that expertise is very important to good decisions. Asking the critic, "Who is the world's foremost expert regarding what your preferences are?" the reply is invariably that the critic is. And we then point out that by the stated logic that means that when it is time to consult people's preferences and to tally those preferences into a decision, each of us is the person to consult as the best expert in our own preferences.

Imagine we are a workplace. We are going to paint the walls and we need to decide which paint to use. There are three cans and one of them is lead-based. That, however, happens to be the one that most people like the look of. We agree that the impact of the paint on the wall on each is such that in this case majority rule makes sense. We are all very comparably affected. So we vote and the lead paint wins. In fact, only the expert chemist who knows about lead in paint—this is fifty years ago—votes against using that can. So we screw ourselves. What's the lesson?

We don't let the chemist decide for us, but we do consult the chemist. We don't let experts decide everything, but we do consult experts.

When people ask, "What do you want for the economy?" at this point in our discussion, we can reasonably say we want solidarity, diversity, equity, and self-management, but we need to be aware this doesn't fully answer their question. If we advocate institutions whose logic leads to outcomes contrary to those values—such as markets, corporate organization, and private ownership—what good is our rhetorical attachment to the fine values? Bill Clinton and Bill Gates would probably say they too like solidarity, diversity, equity, and maybe even self-management, but would add that reality requires some minor compromises—which, however, lead to wars, starvation, indignity, etc. for the rest of us, plus their personal enrichment and empowerment. So we need to advocate worthy values, but we also need to advocate a set of institutions that can make our worthy values real without compromising economic success.

Parecon's Institutions
Workers' and Consumers' Councils
Workers and consumers need a place to express their preferences if they are to self-manage their economic actions as our values advocate. Historically, when workers and consumers have attempted to seize control of their own lives, they have invariably created workers' and consumers' councils. In the parecon case, workers' and consumers' councils use

decision-making procedures and modes of communication that give members a degree of say in each decision proportionate to the degree they are affected.

Council decisions could sometimes be resolved by majority vote, three-quarters vote, two-thirds vote, consensus, or other possibilities. Different procedures could be used for different decisions, including involving fewer or more participants and using different information dispersal and discussion procedures or different voting and tallying methods.

As an example, a publishing house could have teams addressing promotion, production, editing, and the like. Each team might make its own workday decisions in the context of broader policies decided by the whole workers' council. Decisions to publish a book might involve teams in related areas and might require a two-thirds or three-quarters positive vote, including considerable time for appraisals and reappraisals. Many other decisions in the workplace could be one person, one vote by the workers affected or could require slightly different vote counts or methods of challenging outcomes. Hiring might require consensus in the workgroup that the new person would join, because a new worker can have a tremendous effect on each person in a group they constantly work with.

The point is that in groups of councils and teams workers make both broad and narrower workplace decisions, including about both the norms and the methods for decision-making, as well as about the day-to-day and more policy-oriented issues.

Those who consume the workplace's books, bicycles, or band-aids are affected and must, in turn, have some say. Even those who are unable to get some other product because energy, time, and assets went to the books, bicycles, or band-aids and not to produce what they wanted are affected and so must be able to influence the choice. And even those tangentially affected, such as by derivative pollution, also have to have influence, and sometimes collectively a lot of influence. But accommodating the will of the workers with the will of other actors in an appropriate balance is a matter of allocation not of workplace organization, so these matters will be addressed a bit later.

Remuneration for Effort and Sacrifice

Parecon's next institutional commitment is to remunerate for effort and sacrifice not for property, power, or even output. But who decides how hard we have worked? Clearly our workers' councils decide in a way that respects the broad economic norms established by all of the economy's institutions.

If you work longer and you do it effectively, you are entitled to more of the social product. If you work more intensely to socially useful ends, again you are entitled to more income. If you work at more onerous, dangerous, or boring—but still socially warranted tasks—you are entitled to more.

But you aren't entitled to more income by virtue of owning productive property or working with better tools or producing something more valued or even having personal traits that make you more productive, because these attributes don't involve effort or sacrifice but instead luck and endowment. Your work has to be socially useful to be rewarded, but the reward is not proportional to how useful it is. Effort, duration, and sacrifice expended producing outputs that aren't desired is not remunerable labor.

Greater output with less waste is appreciated, of course, and it is important that the means of accomplishing it are utilized, but there is no extra pay for greater output. Yes, my working longer or harder yields more output, and greater output can even be a revealing indicator of my greater effort. But while output is often relevant as an indicator, the absolute level of output is beside the point as a means of establishing the level of remuneration, other than helping indicate how long I worked or how hard and whether my work was socially useful.

If one is concerned with increasing each worker's output by offering incentives, one should remunerate effort expended in producing socially valued labor. Effort is the variable the worker controls that impacts output. It's as simple as that.

Some on the Left, however, continue to reject remuneration for effort and sacrifice on the ground that this is what we have now with capitalism. Workers rent themselves out to capitalists and are supposedly rewarded more for working harder and longer. When they hear parecon advocates proposing effort and sacrifice as fair criteria for remuneration, they feel that we have missed the point and will not transcend the rat race generated by the dynamics of capitalist economics.

This view is, however, incorrect. Capitalism does not remunerate for how hard or how long we work—although it can seem that way when we think in terms of hourly rates. Rather, capitalism remunerates for private ownership and for bargaining power. If you are a worker, your hourly rate will be determined by your bargaining power, which, in turn, derives from your job description, type of workplace organization, monopoly over skills or knowledge, etc. So, for example, doctors have more bargaining power than nurses due to having a monopoly on valuable knowledge and skills, and, as a result, get vastly better pay.

But what about the workplace as a whole? The way it works is pretty straightforward. The workplace has certain assets—building, equipment, workforce, inputs in the form of resources or intermediate goods, for example. For the work that is done in the workplace to be considered socially useful, those assets have to be wisely used. Suppose my workplace has assets such that with an average duration and intensity of work its output level should be X. Suppose instead its output level is 90 percent of X. We can't claim average income but only 90 percent of average income. How we divide that up internally depends on how long you worked, how long I worked, how intensely, and more. But the total amount we have for the workforce depends on the workplace using its assets well. The need for work to be socially valuable to be remunerated is what provides the whole workplace an incentive to use good equipment well, to organize and operate wisely, etc. The remuneration for effort and sacrifice for each person provides incentive for needed labor. The whole calculus follows our values. It is equitable, yet it also elicits desirable behavior that makes effective use of equipment and the talents of workers.

Both morally and in terms of incentives, parecon does what makes sense. We get extra pay when we deserve it for our sacrifice at work. The economy elicits the appropriate use of productive capacities by providing incentives to the whole workplace to properly utilize technology, organization, resources, energy, and skills, so that the work that is done is all socially useful.

Balanced Job Complexes

Suppose that, as proposed, we have workers' and consumers' councils. Suppose we also believe in participation and self-management. And we have equitable remuneration. Now, also suppose that our workplace has a typical corporate division of labor as our institutional way of apportioning tasks. What will the roles associated with a corporate division of labor do to our other aspirations for our workplace?

Roughly 20 percent at the top of the corporate division of labor will monopolize daily decision-making positions and the knowledge essential to comprehending what is going on and what options exist. These folks—who we call the coordinator class—will set agendas. The decisions these managers, engineers, lawyers, doctors, and other empowered actors make will be authoritative. Even if workers lower in the hierarchy have formal voting rights and the whole population is, in principle, sincerely committed to self-management, still, rote workers' participation is only to vote on plans and options put forth by the coordinator class. The will of this coordinator class will decide outcomes, and in time this empowered group will also decide that it deserves more pay to nurture its great wisdom. It will separate itself not only in power but in income and status.

It isn't enough to have workers' and consumers' councils that seek to implement self-management and remuneration on the basis of effort and sacrifice if, on top of those features, we have a division of labor which imposes a coordinator class of empowered employees above a working class of disempowered employees. In that case, even with the councils and commitments, our greatest hopes will be dashed against the structural implications of our job design.

So what do we do to have a better situation?

Well, imagine you are visiting another planet. You go to a few workplaces and you see the same thing in each. One in every five workers has way better conditions and income and dominates all decisions. You also notice that before each workday the one-fifth who dominate eat a chocolate bar and the others don't. You assume that is just another privilege they have, but then you investigate and discover that on this planet eating chocolate gives one knowledge, skills, information, confidence, and more. In fact, the one in five dominate precisely because they eat the chocolate and the rest do not. The chocolate empowers them. So what do we need to do in the workplaces on this planet to avoid a fifth of the participants dominating four-fifths? Share the chocolate, of course.

Well, the same thing applies to dealing with the corporate division of labor. Instead of combining tasks so that some jobs are highly empowering and other jobs are horrible, so that some jobs convey knowledge and authority, while other jobs convey only stultification and obedience, parecon says let's make each job comparable to all others in its quality of life and even more importantly in its empowerment effects. We don't have to share chocolate, we have to share empowering tasks.

In a parecon with balanced job complexes, each job must contain a mix of tasks and responsibilities such that the overall empowerment effects of work are comparable for all.

In a parecon there won't be someone doing only surgery and someone else only cleaning bedpans. Instead, people who do surgery will also help clean the hospital and perform other tasks so that the sum of all that they do incorporates a fair mix of conditions and responsibilities, and likewise for the person who used to only clean bedpans.

A parecon doesn't have some people in a factory who only manage production relations and other people who do only rote tasks. Instead, people throughout factories do a balanced mix of empowering and rote tasks.

A parecon doesn't have lawyers and short-order cooks or engineers and assembly-line workers as we now know them. All the tasks associated with these jobs get done as needed, of course, but in a parecon the tasks are mixed and matched very differently than they are in capitalist workplaces.

Each parecon worker does a mix of tasks that accords with their abilities but that also conveys a fair share of both rote and tedious and interesting and empowering conditions and responsibilities.

Our work doesn't prepare a few of us to rule and the rest of us to obey. Instead, our work comparably prepares all of us to participate in collectively self-managing production, consumption, and allocation.

Three objections always arise. The logic always follows the same path. If surgeons have to clean bedpans, we will have way less surgery done. We will have eliminated class division and the obstacle that class division poses for self-management and equity, but we will have done so at the cost of essential output—in this case surgeries and in other fields, poems, calculations, research, legal work, and so on.

A parecon advocate must admit that in one respect the complaint is exactly right. To make it simple, suppose current surgeons work a forty-hour week doing nothing but surgeries and suppose it wound up that in a parecon the work week got shorter (which it quite predictably would) and after balancing off surgery with other less empowering tasks, the forty-hour a week surgeon in the old economy only did fifteen hours a week of surgery in the new one. Well, that is a dead loss, looking at that one person, of twenty-five hours a week, or five-eighths of all the surgery by that person. And it would be true for all surgeons, so the previous surgeons would only be doing three-eighths as much as they were doing before. And, indeed, we would all be screwed if that was the end of the story, especially given that it would also be true for engineers, scientists, artists, managers, accountants, and so on. But the calculation overlooks a very important point. We don't settle for the drop in empowered work. Instead, those who previously were doing no empowered work now do their share and make up the deficit. Many folks hear this and tend to go more or less berserk. Impossible, they say, because nurses and custodians can't do surgery, law clerks and typists can't be lawyers, and so on.

To answer, one might offer the following thought experiment. Imagine it is fifty years ago. You take all the surgeons in the U.S. and put them in a very big stadium. What do you see that is striking?

They are all men. Yes, and every one of those male surgeons would have said that women aren't in the stadium with us because women can't do surgery. Five decades later we, of course, recognize that as gross sexism, not only because we are sensible, but also because students at medical schools in the U.S. are currently, for example, a bit over 50 percent women.

The advocate of balanced job complexes can then explain that what makes people think those not now doing any empowering tasks are incapable of doing any empowering tasks is classism, quite analogous to sexism. Instead of realizing that the reason people are unable to do certain things is that they are not only denied the training but, even more, are forcefully robbed of the initiative, confidence, and access, while we attribute the failing to their inadequate capacity. This is precisely analogous to the sexist explanation of the absence of women surgeons decades ago.

Of course it takes time and training, but a random set of twenty people chosen from workers and a random set of twenty chosen from the coordinator class have pretty much exactly the same general capacity to do empowering work of one kind or another, a claim we have come to understand about women as compared to men and about various racial and cultural communities as compared to others, and now we need to come to understand it about working people, as well.

"But wouldn't it be inefficient to have to train so many more doctors, lawyers, engineers, etc.," rejoins a critic? To the contrary, getting all we can from everyone is the opposite of inefficient. To have a tool lie fallow is inefficient. The same holds for a person. We should also point out that even if total output would drop—though, in fact, on the contrary, it would climb dramatically due to new contributions from more people, not to mention the gains that accrue from not having an elite defending its privileges and having those below recalcitrant about cooperating—we should favor the changes.

Our values said nothing about maximizing output. Rather, the aim was to conduct economic life to meet needs and develop potentials, while advancing solidarity, diversity, equity, and self-management. And balanced job complexes would do all that plentifully, even if they were not more productive of desirable final goods and services—which they would be.

But what happens if we have a new economy that has workers' and consumers' councils, self-managed decision-making, remuneration for duration, intensity, and onerousness of productive labor, plus balanced job complexes—but we combine all that with markets or central planning for allocation. Would the sum of all those components constitute a good economy?

Allocation: Markets and Central Planning
Suppose we hook up our fledgling firms with each other via market competition. First, markets would immediately destroy

the remuneration scheme because markets reward output and bargaining power instead of effort and sacrifice.

Second, markets would force buyers and sellers to try to buy cheap and sell dear, each fleecing the other as much as possible in the name of private advancement and market survival. Markets, in other words, would generate antisociality not solidarity.

Third, markets would explicitly produce dissatisfaction because it is only the dissatisfied who buy again and again. As the general director of General Motors' Research Labs, Charles Kettering, who introduced annual model changes for GM cars, put it: business needs to create a "dissatisfied consumer"; its mission is "the organized creation of dissatisfaction." The idea was that planned obsolescence would make consumers dissatisfied with the cars they already had.

Fourth, prices in a market system don't reflect all social costs and benefits but instead take into account only the impact of work and consumption on the immediate buyers and sellers (mediated by their power) but not on those peripherally affected, including those affected by pollution or, for that matter, by positive side effects. This means markets routinely violate ecological balance and sustainability, not to mention stewardship. They subject all but the wealthiest communities to a collective debit in water, air, sound, and public availabilities.

Fifth, markets also produce decision-making hierarchy not self-management. This occurs not only due to market-generated disparities in wealth translating into disparate power, but because market competition compels even council-based workplaces to cut costs and seek market share regardless of the ensuing implications. To compete, even workplaces with self-managing councils, equitable remuneration, and balanced job complexes have no choice but to insulate some employees from the discomfort that cost cutting imposes—so that those people can then figure out what costs to cut and how to generate more

output at the expense of worker (and even consumer) fulfillment but not their own.

In other words, to cut costs—and otherwise impose
market discipline—there would emerge, due to market logic,
even with councils and balanced job complexes, a coordinator class located above workers and violating our preferred
norms of remuneration, as well as accruing power to themselves and obliterating self-management and equity.

That is, under the pressure of market competition, any
firm I work for must try to maximize its revenues to keep up
with competing firms. If my firm doesn't do that, then we lose
our jobs. So we must try to dump our costs on others. We must
seek as much revenue as possible—even via inducing excessive
consumption. We must cut our costs of production—including
reducing comforts for workers and unduly intensifying labor.

To relentlessly pursue all these paths to market success,
however, requires freedom for the managers from suffering
the pains their choices induce. So even a firm that is initially
committed to self-management and balanced job complexes, if
it must operate in a market context, will over time impose on
itself a necessity to hire folks with appropriately callous and
calculating minds like those that business schools produce. It
will then have to give these new callous employees air-condi-
tioned offices and comfortable surroundings. It will have to
say to them, "Okay, cut our costs to ensure our livelihood in
the marketplace."

In other words, it will have to impose on itself a coordinator class, not due to natural law and not due to some internal
psychological masochism but because markets will force it
to subordinate itself to a coordinator elite it must accept and
welcome lest its workplace lose market share and revenues and
eventually go out of business.

There are those who will claim that all these market failings
are not a product of markets per se but of imperfect markets
that haven't attained a condition of perfect competition. This is

a bit like saying that the ills associated with ingesting arsenic occur because we never get pure arsenic but only arsenic tainted with other ingredients.

On the one hand, calling for perfect markets ignores that in a real society there is literally no such thing as frictionless competition, so of course we will always get imperfect markets. But even more important, it also ignores the fact that the harmful effects of markets we have highlighted do not diminish when competition is made more perfect—they intensify. And all this is not just true in our thought experiment but also in past practice.

Historically, the closer economies have come to a pure market system—without state intervention, with as few sectors as possible dominated by single firms or groups of firms, and with as few unions as possible—the worse the social implications have been. For example, there have rarely, if ever, been markets as competitive as those of Britain in the early nineteenth century, yet, under the sway of those nearly perfect markets, young children routinely suffered early death working in the pits and mills of the time. The point is, well-functioning markets get various economic tasks done but otherwise do not promote excellence in any form. They do not resist—they even facilitate—cultural and moral depravity. As a result, seeking an economy fulfilling our values means rejecting markets as a tool of allocation.

Moreover, the same broad result of market allocation destroying the benefits sought via councils, including destroying equitable remuneration and balanced job complexes, has historically held for central planning allocation as well, though for different reasons. Central planning elevates central planners and their managerial agents in each workplace, and then, for legitimacy and consistency, it elevates all those actors in the economy who share the same type of credentials.

In other words, the central planners need local agents who will hold workers to norms the central planners determine.

These local agents must be locally authoritative. Their credentials must legitimate them and must reduce other actors to relative obedience. Central planning, thus, like markets, also imposes a coordinator class to rule over workers, with the workers, in turn, made subordinate—not only nationally but in each workplace.

The allocation problem that we face in trying to conceive a good economy is therefore that (as could be seen in the old Yugoslavia and Soviet Union) even without private ownership of means of production, markets and central planning subvert the values and structures we have deemed worthy. They obliterate equitable remuneration, annihilate self-management, horribly misvalue products, impose narrow and antisocial motivations, and impose class division and class rule.

This is precisely the kind of thing our overarching theory attunes us to. It is a case of particular institutions—markets and central planning—having role attributes that violate our aims. The same held for the corporate division of labor, discussed earlier, and for private ownership of productive assets. The associated roles of those institutions obstruct, in fact, actually obliterate, the values we favor. That is why we had to transcend them. And now we see the same implication for markets and central planning.

Allocation is the nervous system of economic life. It is both intricate and essential. To round out a new economic vision we must conceive a mechanism that can properly and efficiently determine and communicate accurate information about the true social costs and benefits of economic options, while giving workers and consumers influence over choices proportional to the degree they are affected.

"True social costs and benefits." What is that? Well, suppose we make a car. What does it cost? What are the benefits? If we don't know, how can we decide it is a good idea to make the car instead of something else? If we don't know, how can we decide if we need more cars or fewer? The costs we take into account go beyond those that the current capitalist owners of automobile plants consider. They want to maximize profits while retaining the rights to accrue those profits to themselves. We want to advance our values while meeting needs and developing potentials of all those involved. Very different.

They take into account the amount they have to pay for resources, intermediate goods, technologies employed, rent, electricity, and wages—as well as whether there are any significant effects on their balance of power and their ability to keep taking their preferred giant share of revenues.

We take into account the costs of producing, transporting, and consuming cars, including the impact on the environment, workers, consumers, bystanders, and communities. We also take into account the benefits for those same affected constituencies—both individual and collective. So true social costs and benefits are an accurate measure of the gains and losses associated with the production and consumption of the car: in social relations, in the material, moral, and psychological condition of workers, communities, and consumers, and in the environmental impact.

Desirable means of allocation must allocate resources, labor, and the products of labor in a flexible manner that is able to realign in case of unexpected crises or shocks. It must not homogenize tastes but instead abide diverse preferences, preserve privacy and individuality, engender sociality and solidarity, and meet the needs and capacities of all workers and consumers. Desirable allocation must operate without class division and class rule, but instead with equity and classlessness, and it must operate without disproportionate influence for a few people, but instead with self-management for all. Finally, in deciding what to do with any particular asset—whether people's labor or a resource like oil or copper or some technology—it needs to take into account the true and full material and ethereal social and environmental effects of the contending options.

Self-management of allocation is clearly no small ambition given that virtually everyone is, to at least some degree, affected by each decision made in an economy, so that in any institution—whether a factory, university, health center, or whatever—many interests ought to be represented in decision-making. There is the workforce itself, obviously affected by their actions each day. There is the community in which the workplace is located—polluted, for example, or uplifted. And there are the users of its products or services, presumably benefitting by their consumption or losing out because ingredients were not put to a different use that they would have preferred. If society is making cars instead of public transport, I may gain from having a car, but I will also lose due to the lack of public transport. To have self-management entails structures that eliminate any influence by private owners of the means of production and resources by ensuring that that type ownership no longer exists—but that also consult all affected parties appropriately in determining outcomes.

In other words, while private ownership is disastrous in its effects on economic outcomes, the deeper and arguably even deadlier villains, as we have all too briefly indicated above, are markets and central planning. We not only need "directly democratic" workers' and consumers' councils, but we also need allocation connections between workers and consumers that preserve and enhance informed, insightful, self-managed decisions.

Participatory Planning

Suppose in place of top-down allocation via centrally planned choices, and in place of competitive market allocation by atomized buyers and sellers, we instead opt for informed, self-managed, cooperative negotiation of inputs and outputs by socially entwined actors who:

- each have a say in proportion as choices affect them;
- each have accurate information to assess;

- each have appropriate training, confidence, conditions, and motivation to develop, communicate, and express their preferences.

This choice of allocation attributes—if we could conceive institutions able to make it real—would compatibly advance council-centered participatory self-management, remuneration for effort and sacrifice, and balanced job complexes. It would also provide proper valuations of personal, social, and ecological impacts and promote classlessness.

Participatory planning is conceived to accomplish all this. In participatory planning, workers' and consumers' councils propose their work activities and their consumption preferences in light of continually updated knowledge of the personal, local, and national implications of the full social benefits and costs of their choices.

What does it look like?

Workers and consumers cooperatively negotiate workplace and consumer inputs and outputs. They employ a back and forth communication of mutually informed preferences using what are called indicative prices, facilitation boards, rounds of accommodation to new information, and other participatory planning features which permit people to express and refine their desires in light of feedback about other people's desires.

Workers and consumers indicate in their councils their personal and group preferences. I say I want such and such. My workplace settles on a proposal that we wish to produce. We learn what preferences others have indicated, just as they learn ours. They, and we, alter and resubmit our preferences—keeping in mind the need to balance a personally fulfilling pattern of work and consumption with the requirements of a viable overall plan. Each participant worker and consumer seeks personal and group well-being and development, but each is able to improve their situation only by acting in accord with more general social benefit. New information leads to new submissions in a sequence of cooperatively negotiated refinements, until settling on a plan.

As in any economy, consumers deciding on what they want for their share of the social product take into account their income (earned via the duration, intensity, and onerousness of their socially valued labor) and the relative costs of available products they desire. This occurs not only for individuals deciding personal consumption but also for households, communes, neighborhoods, and regions, up to the cumulative demand put forth by all of society. Workers in their workers' councils similarly indicate how much work they wish to do in light of requests for their product and their own labor/leisure preferences. While workplace proposals are collective, they are arrived at with input from each individual in the workplace.

In a participatory economy, even if I could set some false, inflated price for what I was selling, my income would not climb, as income doesn't depend on overall sales revenue. And the same goes for somehow getting people to buy what they don't really need. In fact, why would I want to produce anything—taking my time and energy—that wasn't actually going to benefit folks? I wouldn't, not in a participatory economic institutional setting.

Individuals and units do not advance by way of beating others in any manner. Rather, motives are simply to meet needs and to develop potentials at whatever level turns out to be preferred without wasting assets. We seek to produce what is socially acceptable and useful, while compatibly and cooperatively fulfilling our own as well as the rest of society's preferences. This is true not because people are suddenly saints but because cooperation is lucrative for all. Merciless fleecing simply has no place in a parecon because there is neither means to do it nor gains to be had from doing it.

Preferences for desired production and consumption are communicated by means of special mechanisms developed for the purpose. Negotiations occur in a series of planning rounds. Every participant has an interest in most effectively utilizing productive potentials to meet needs because everyone gets an equitable share of output that grows as overall social output for all grows.

Each person also favors workplaces—and all of society— making investments that reduce drudge work and that improve the quality of the average balanced job complex, because this is the job quality that everyone, on average, enjoys.

Plans for the economy are continually updated and refined. It isn't that there are no errors or imperfections in the day-to-day and year-to-year operations of a participatory economy. It is that such deviations from ideal choices as occur arise from ignorance or mistakes and not from the system intrinsically causing such deviations. Mistaken choices and deviations don't snowball or multiply in a manner that continually benefits some (in a ruling class, for example) to the detriment of others.

There is no legitimate choice that one can make in a parecon that would accrue what other members of society would deem unjust power, wealth, or circumstance.

Summing Up

In a parecon I can get better work conditions if the average job complex improves. I can get higher income if I work harder or longer with my workmates' consent or if the average income throughout society increases. I not only advance in solidarity with others, I also influence all economic decisions in my workplace—and even throughout the rest of the economy—at a level proportionate to the impact those decisions have on me.

Parecon not only eliminates inequitable disparities in wealth and income, it attains just distribution. Parecon doesn't force people to undervalue or violate other people's lives but produces solidarity. Parecon doesn't homogenize outcomes or even underlying preferences but generates diversity. Parecon doesn't give a small ruling class tremendous power while burdening the bulk of the population with powerlessness but produces appropriate self-managing influence for all.

More, parecon claims that the combination of workers' and consumers' self-managed councils, remuneration for duration, intensity, and onerousness of socially valued labor, balanced job complexes, and participatory planning eliminates class difference.

The first step in checking this claim is to ask: Is there an owning class and a class that doesn't own? Parecon passes this first test.

The second step is to ask: Is there a coordinator class above a working class—the one empowered and high stepping, the other disempowered and low slung?

The most direct cause of the existence of this division is eliminated root and branch by incorporating balanced job complexes. The next most direct avenue to this type of division is eliminated by adopting self-managed decision-making and equitable remuneration. And finally, most subtly, the only known indirect source of this division—the presence of an institution chosen simply to distribute labor goods and services that by its role implications subverts self-management and equitable remuneration, and even enforces the reinstitution of a coordinator/worker division of labor—is eliminated (in both its market and central planning variants) by adopting participatory planning.

We want classlessness because with classes, and class rule, our values will be violated. To get classlessness we must reject private ownership of productive property and the corporate division of labor. If we reject those but retain markets or central planning, they will overthrow our intentions and certainly reimpose the corporate division of labor. Thus, we must adopt, on top of our other commitments, participatory planning.

CHAPTER 6

Parpolity

"I swear to the Lord
I still can't see
Why Democracy means
Everybody but me."
—*Langston Hughes*

Current times make a loud argument, by example, that contemporary political structures are decrepit and redundant. Every day hammers home the realization. The U.S., for example, arguably has one of the most democratic political systems now operating. Yet, even if there weren't huge concentrations of corporate wealth and power dominating political outcomes, even if media didn't constrain and manipulate information to distort political preferences, even if the two parties weren't two wings of a single corporate party, even if there weren't diverse, idiotic, and at best anachronistic structures like the electoral college, even if elections weren't winner take all affairs in which upwards of half the voting population have their desires ignored (as do most of the other half, but that's another matter), and even if elections weren't easily hijacked by outright fraud, clearly modern electoral and parliamentary democracy would still diverge greatly from a system that maximally facilitates participation, elicits informed opinion, and justly resolves disputes.

So, what do we want instead of current political systems? When activists take to the streets in the Middle East, Africa,

Asia, Europe, and even America—protesting governments that range from dictatorships to "democracies"—what, beyond indignation, fuels their tenacity? What do they want? What do we want?

With polity encompassing legislation of shared rules or laws, implementation of shared programs and pursuits, and adjudication of contested claims, including violation of rules and laws—our task is to determine our values for the political sphere of life, and, more particularly, a set of institutions able to actualize our values.

Positive political vision has not yet been as fully spelled out, explored, and challenged as the participatory economics presented in last chapter. But the U.S.-based activist and political scientist Stephen Shalom, among others, has at least begun the process in his preliminary presentation of participatory polity (parpolity). In this chapter, we lean heavily on Shalom's work, as his parpolity is a political vision that seeks to further the same values as parecon.

The Need for Political Vision

One thug with a club can disrupt even the most humane gathering. Thugs with clubs, in all variants—whether aroused by liquor, jealousy, arrogance, greed, pathology, or some other antisocial attribute—won't disappear from a good society.

Likewise, even in the best of environments a dispute that has no means of resolution will often escalate into a struggle that vastly transcends the scope of its causes, whether the escalating dispute occurs between the Hatfields and McCoys, northern and southern states, rural and urban areas, France and Germany, or Pakistan and India.

What prevents social degradation as a result of thugs? What prevents escalating disputes? More generally, if we lack agreed upon social norms, people will have to repeatedly start social projects from scratch. We won't be able to benefit from a set of previously agreed upon responsibilities and practices.

We will have to repeatedly negotiate to the point of never implementing.

In a good polity, will we have known responsibilities we cannot violate or will everything we do be up for grabs with each new day? In the former case, we might attain civilized existence. In the later case, we would have only chaos. To have social success, in other words, we need political structures. Roles certainly eliminate some options, but they also fantastically facilitate others. When options that are precluded are all harshly harmful and options that we embrace are all desirable, the limitations and facilitations of institutional roles benefit us.

Put differently, it is true that even the most desirable mutually agreed upon roles and responsibilities will, to some degree, limit our range of options. Laws restrict what we are permitted to do. So do conventions, norms, and agreements. In fact, for any role, role-violating behavior disappears, typically even as an option. In return, desirable mutually agreed upon roles make the range of all options available to us vastly larger and more attainable by facilitating their accomplishment. Having red and green lights at intersections constrains our driving options since we must stop at red and go at green, but this also keeps us alive to do all else we might choose, not to mention facilitating driving through intersections without crashes and jams halting our motion. More generally, having diverse collectively established rules that we all abide by permits us each to operate far more effectively and diversely than if we had no such rules, even as having rules also narrows our choices in some contexts. If our political institutions limit options agreeably, and if they facilitate options desirably, then the coherence and ease of interactive activity that institutional norms bring will more than outweigh any limitations they impose.

If I violate my previously agreed upon roles and responsibilities, it will likely disturb and perhaps completely disrupt other people's expectations, actions, and options. We don't want everyone to be free to kill. We don't want everyone to be free to drive through red lights. Nor do we arrive at our rules every day anew. We establish them. We want the kind and level of freedom whose exercise facilitates further freedom and the means to enjoy it. We do not want the kind and level of freedom whose exercise curtails additional freedom and the means to enjoy it. We want to escape needless restrictions, but we want to do this only in a way consistent with others having the same freedoms we have, while also preserving previously agreed upon role responsibilities.

The anarchist desire for freedom from constraint imposed on the population by a state operating from above it is apt and accurate. But when this sometimes morphs into a claim that any effort to accomplish political functions is doomed to be oppressive, it goes too far. Accomplishing legislation, adjudication, and collective implementation by way of lasting institutions is not itself a problem. The problem is doing this in ways divorced from the will and needs of the populace. We must not have states existing above people if we are to attain our values, yet we must still collectively accomplish needed political functions. Thus, we confront the same type of problem as we addressed in the last chapter. What institutions can fulfill the functions of the polity while also fulfilling our overall social values?

Failed Political Visions
One failed answer comes from the perspective called Marxism-Leninism. As history has verified, the "dictatorship of the proletariat," even when sought for worthy reasons, translates virtually seamlessly into the dictatorship of the party, the politburo, and, in the worst case, the beneficent, or worse, the megalomaniacal, dictator. That this trajectory could ever have been equated with a desirable form of political life will always be a horrible blemish on the political history of "the Left." Outlawing all but a single "vanguard" party ruled by

"democratic centralism" fundamentally subverts democracy, not to mention self-management.

Democratic centralism systematically impedes participatory impulses, promotes popular passivity, nurtures fear, and breeds authoritarianism, and it does all this even against the far better aspirations of many Leninists. To routinely outlaw external opposition and suppress or manipulate internal dissent by transferring members who become critical between branches does not engender democracy.

Western-style electoral democracy is another answer to the political vision question, but it is nonetheless a far cry from participatory democracy. Highly unequal distribution of wealth stacks the deck before the political card game even begins. Citizens choose from preselected candidates screened for compatibility by society's corporate elites. And even if we remove private ownership of productive assets to overcome money-related problems within a Western-style democracy, participatory democracy requires more than infrequently voting for a representative to carry out political activity that is largely alienated from popular will and often contrary to popular interests.

The incorrect claim of some anarchists in reaction to oppressive government is that polity per se is oppressive. Anything goes should be the watchword. The correct claim of still more anarchists is that a polity which exists above the populace, imposing on the populace, not reflecting the informed will of the populace, is oppressive.

While electing representatives is, for certain situations, a plausible and perhaps even an essential part of a true participatory democracy that promotes deliberation and exploration, frequent and regular referenda on important political propositions and policies at every level of political organization accompanied by a full airing of competing views would presumably be at least an important addition to voting for candidates. The question that arises, however, is: Can we conceive mechanisms that would permit and promote engagement, deliberation, and participatory decision-making, give all citizens appropriate say, whether directly or when desirable through representatives, and preserve essential rights while serving justice?

Parpolity

The first important thing to realize is that political life will not disappear in a desirable society. This might seem utterly obvious, but some who approach the problem of envisioning a better future miss this key point.

Politics will no longer be privileged groups perpetuating their domination. Nor will oppressed constituencies battle an unjust status quo. But having a desirable polity doesn't mean having universal agreement about social choices. If we assume universal agreement, not only is there little to discuss, but we will also be operating in an ugly delusion. Homogenized minds is not an apt image upon which to build liberated circumstances.

While the goal of social diversity dictates that competing ideas should be implemented in parallel whenever possible, many times one program will have to be implemented at the expense of others. Even more, since a desirable society will promote our participatory impulses, in a good society debate will sometimes heat up rather than cool down, whether about pornography, prostitution, deep ecology, drug legalization, multilingualism, children's rights, allocation of expensive or scarce medical resources like heart transplants or cloning, surrogate motherhood, euthanasia, single-sex schools, or religious freedom when the religions violate other important societal values like gender equity, or whatever else. As Shalom summarizes, "In short, even in a society that had solved the problem of economic exploitation and eliminated hierarchies of race, class, and gender, many controversies—many deep controversies—would still remain. Hence, any good society will have to address issues of politics and will need some sort of political system, a polity."

Broadest goals are well understood and enunciated. A truly democratic community insures that the general public has the opportunity for meaningful participation in the formation of social policy. A society that excludes large areas of crucial decision-making from public control, or a system of governance that merely grants the general public the opportunity to ratify decisions taken by elite groups hardly merits the term democracy. But what institutional vehicles can guarantee the public truly democratic opportunities?

One condition of real democracy is that groups with competing opinions can effectively communicate their views. Democratization of political life must include democratization of the flow of information and commentary.

Participatory democracy requires not only democratic access to a transformed media and the possibility for people to form and utilize single-issue political organizations to make their views known but also, at least in all likelihood, a pluralism of political parties with different social agendas. In other words, there is no reason to think that having a society means that people won't disagree about major matters in ideological ways. An absence of class, gender, and racial hierarchy doesn't imply an absence of all difference and dispute. What can we offer by way of political vision beyond general intimations of possible achievements of a desirable polity?

Values

Surely a polity should produce solidarity and generate diversity. These two economic values transfer easily and directly into politics, though they are rarely implemented. The former means political actors should each advance via the advance of all. The latter means that political institutions should be protecting and celebrating dissent and diversity as much as possible—not seeking one right mind or one right path.

For polity, the analogue of economic equity is justice, which addresses the distribution of rights and responsibilities, including the need to redress violations of social agreements. This does not mean vengeance or retribution. Justice is about fairness of outcomes over time, including redress of past imbalances and preventing future imbalances.

Self-management is arguably even more a political value than an economic one, both in its origins and its logic, and is therefore certainly a worthy political aim. Politics should facilitate actors having influence on decisions in proportion as those decisions impact their lives.

So for politics we have as guiding values solidarity, diversity, justice, and self-management. And, unsurprisingly, achieving these values implies achieving other more familiar political values, including liberty and tolerance, without which we will have the violation of diversity and solidarity, and most of particularly participation, which is a prerequisite to all four aims.

Institutions

A desirable polity must accomplish legislation, adjudication, and collective implementation. For legislation seeking self-management, Shalom's parpolity vision advocates "nested councils" where "the primary-level councils will include every adult in the society" and where, Shalom suggests, "the number of members in these primary-level councils might plausibly be somewhere between 25–50."

Everyone in society is in one of these basic political units. Some folks are elected to higher-level councils since "each primary-level council will choose a delegate to a second-level council" where "each second-level council would again be composed of 25–50 delegates." And this would proceed for another layer, and another, "until there is one single top-level council for the entire society." The delegates to each higher council "would be charged with trying to reflect the actual views of the council they came from." On the other hand, "they would not be told 'this is how you must vote,' for if they were, then the higher council they were attending would not be a deliberative body."

Shalom suggests that "the number of members on each council should be determined on the basis of a society-wide decision, and perhaps revised on the basis of experience, so as to meet the following criteria: small enough to guarantee that people can be involved in deliberative bodies, where all can participate in face-to-face discussions; but yet big enough so that (1) there is adequate diversity of opinion included; and (2) the number of layers of councils needed to accommodate the entire society is minimized."

Surprisingly, it turns out that "a council size of 25, with 5 layers, assuming half the population consists of adults, can accommodate a society of 19 million people; a council size of 40, again would need 5 layers to accommodate 200 million people; a 50-person council could accommodate 625 million people by the fifth level. With a sixth level, even a 25-person council could accommodate a society of about half a billion people."

What happens in these proposed political councils?

Legislation is enacted, which is to say voting on norms and collective agendas takes place. The councils are deliberative and public. The idea is to utilize them to approximate as much as possible, within a sensible time frame and in accord with the importance of particular issues, self-managed decision-making. Sometimes higher-level councils vote and decide. Sometimes they deliberate and report back to lower-level councils that vote and decide. The exact combination of voting at the base versus voting in higher-level councils, of procedures for presenting, debating, and tallying viewpoints, and of how council members are chosen (among many other features) are all degrees of political detail we don't have to address in an overview discussion like this, or perhaps in any discussion at all, before experimentation and experience provides information to guide choices.

Suppose we are choosing between one person, one vote majority rule and consensus for decisions at some level on some type of issues. Or we are determining the mandates of representatives and their responsibilities. Or we are settling on the procedures of debate and evaluation, the means of voting, tallying, and then reconsidering. How do we arrive at a preference for one approach compared to another at particular levels and for particular types of decisions? The answer is that we try to achieve self-management, facilitate arriving at wise calculations, protect and pursue diversity, maintain solidaritous feelings and practices, and get things done without serious delays.

To what extent do we build in diversity by protecting it in spirit and in practice? The former, of course, without limit. But regarding practice, sometimes policies must be undertaken pretty much by all affected in the same manner. For example, you can't do allocation by markets for some folks and by participatory planning for others—both would fail to make any sense unless done for all. Similarly, you can't decide a dispute or arrive at a law using different procedures for some folks than for others if all are involved in the same situation. Yet, even in such cases, it is possible to experiment with keeping alive alternative methods that claim to be better than those predominantly preferred. And a parpolity would by mandate, and presumably by structures, do just that.

But what if some choices and gains, if fully pursued, tend to compromise the pursuit of others? Well, that is the conundrum of politics and values generally. It is when reasonable people can disagree not only due to seeing facts differently or because some people calculate incorrectly, while others do so more accurately—it is simply due to having different priorities or intuitions about complex implications. The trick of legislative structure, methods, and all of politics is to have a system that allows self-managed choices, with everyone agreeing that the choices reached are fair for all and are flexibly subject to review, even while alternative choices, as much as there remains interest in them, are still explored. This is what the nested council system—guided by commitment to self-management, solidarity, and diversity—seeks to achieve.

What about shared executive functions?

Having a participatory economy takes care of a lot of what we typically know as executive functions in contemporary politics and, in doing so, helps pinpoint the remaining political elements. Think of delivering the mail, investigating and trying to limit outbreaks of disease, or providing environmental protection. All of these pursuits involve a production and allocation aspect handled by the structures of participatory economics, including balanced job complexes, remuneration for effort and sacrifice, and participatory decision-making. The workers' council delivering mail would in these respects not be particularly different from the workers' council producing bicycles, nor would the center for disease control workers' council be very different in these economic aspects from a typical hospital, and likewise for the Environmental Protection Agency and a typical research institute.

But in another sense the three examples are different from their parecon counterparts. The Post Office, CDC, and EPA operate with the sanction of the polity and carry out tasks that the polity mandates. Particularly in the case of the CDC and EPA, executive agencies act with political authority that permits them to investigate and sanction others where typical economic units would have no such rights and responsibilities.

It follows that the executive branch would be largely concerned with establishing politically mandated functions and responsibilities—typically carried out according to the norms of the participatory economy insofar as they involve workplaces with inputs and outputs—but with a political aspect defining their agendas and perhaps conveying special powers. This overlap between polity and economy is more or less analogous to the overlap between culture and economy visible when churches function in the economy for their inputs and perhaps some of their outputs but do so with a cultural/religious definition. The change in economics to a parecon instead of capitalism is part of what makes a polity or culture or family or other aspect of society new in a new society, but the heart of their alteration is the change in their intrinsic logic.

Presumably the means for an executive branch to politically mandate its agendas and establish lasting mechanisms to oversee them would be through the deliberation and votes of a legislative branch, on the one hand, and economic planning, on the other hand, including establishing empowered entities with their own rules of operation like the CDC and other politically empowered agencies.

What would be the role of a judiciary in a parpolity?

As Shalom asserts, "Judicial systems often address three kinds of concerns: judicial review (are the laws just?), criminal justice (have specific individuals violated the laws?), and civil adjudication (how are disputes between individuals resolved?)."

For the first, Shalom offers a court system that would operate more or less like the Supreme Court does now, with hierarchical levels adjudicating disputes arising over council choices. Is this the best approach we can imagine, and can it be refined or transformed to further enhance self-management? I don't know. It certainly merits close consideration.

For criminal matters and civil adjudication Shalom proposes a court system modestly different from what we have now, plus a police force that would, of course, have balanced job complexes and enjoy remuneration for effort and sacrifice.

Regarding having a police function and associated workforce in a desirable society—which is actually for many people more controversial than matters of judicial courts—I agree with Shalom and don't really see any alternative or any intractable problems. There will be crimes in a good society, sometimes violent and sometimes even horribly evil, and the investigation and capture of criminals will be serious matters requiring special skills. It seems obvious that some people will do that kind of work, with special rules and features to ensure they do it well and also consistently with social values—just as some people will spend some of their work time flying airplanes or treating patients or doing other difficult jobs that require special skills and have special rules to ensure they are done well and consistently with social values.

The contrary idea that policing would be unnecessary in a humane system is, at best, not realistic. Sure, in a good society many reasons for crime would be eliminated and criminal acts would be far fewer, but that doesn't mean there will be no crime at all. And the idea that policing can be done on an entirely voluntary basis makes no more sense than saying flying planes or doing brain surgery can be done entirely on a voluntary basis. It fails to realize that policing, and especially desirable policing, like flying planes or doing surgery, involves special skills and knowledge. It fails to recognize the need for training and likely also for disciplined attention to special rules to avoid misuse of police (or transport or medical) prerogatives. So the proposal often put forward that in a postrevolutionary society social order will be maintained by some kind of "people's militia" is rejected for good reason. That said, the concerns typically raised relating to police roles being open to abuses of power are legitimate and must be taken into account.

Beyond the powerful implications of pareconish workplace structure and decision-making for police motivations and for preventing police or any other workers from accruing undue benefits, might there be a special limited duration for police work due to its particular pressures and requirements? Might there be empowered community review mechanisms to oversee specific rules of police operations and evaluation? Sure. And such things might exist for various other jobs as well. Will the different approaches of a good society in determining guilt or innocence and administering punishment and rehabilitation impact police functions differently than the old approaches they replace? The answers are all very likely yes, of course.

Why does the above formulation inspire outrage in some very sincere leftists who desire a better society? The usual answer is police very often act in ways that hurt rather than help all but narrow elites. This being so, we must, in a new society, do away with police. If this formulation said we must do away with police as we now know them, it would be fine. But it doesn't say that. It says and it means we must do away with institutional solutions for all police functions. This is the problem. Going from rejecting what is vile to rejecting underlying functions and all possible institutional means to accomplish those functions—which are not only not vile but in fact essential to viable and worthy social life—is not desirable but suicidal.

Consider a parallel argument. Many anarchists say that government serves the narrow interests of the elite while working against the interests of those below. So it follows, they argue, that we must get rid of all political/government functions. This has the same logic. Or an ecological activist might say workplaces often spew pollution and in doing so hurt rather than help all but a few elites. Or someone might argue that families, cultures, and schools all impose on people horribly restrictive and destructive habits and beliefs, so we ought to get rid of any institutional structures for addressing nurturance, socialization, education, celebration, and communication.

The problem in all these examples is going from a rightful rejection of contemporary means of accomplishing some function to rejecting any institutional means of addressing even refined versions of the function. Ironically, the person who reasons this way is actually agreeing with Margaret Thatcher that "there is no alternative." Thatcher, of course, never meant by TINA that you literally couldn't do things any other way than they were currently being done. She only meant all other ways were worse. And the person rejecting institutional means of dealing with social functions is, in fact, saying, like Thatcher, that the only way to accomplish these functions is our current way or an even worse way, so we have to reject structurally addressing the functions at all. The only difference with Thatcher is that she took for granted that no one would seriously argue the efficacy of doing away with all institutions—not realizing, I guess, how far one can be driven by hatred of what exists.

Returning to the judiciary, the advocate model in which lawyers work on behalf of clients—regardless of guilt or innocence—makes considerable sense. We don't want people having to defend themselves so that those who are good at it have a tremendous advantage over those who are not good at it. We therefore need well-trained lawyers and prosecutors available to all disputants.

We also want these advocates to try hard, of course. But the injunction that prosecutors and defense attorneys should seek to win favorable verdicts—regardless of their knowledge of the true guilt or innocence of the accused and by any means that they can muster—because that approach will yield the greatest probability of truthful results strikes me as about as believable, in certain respects, as the injunction that everyone in an economy should seek selfish private gain as the best means of benefiting society as a whole and engendering sociality. Of course the ills of the competitive legal methodology are incredibly aggravated by role structures in which benefits and losses are a function of gaining sought-after verdicts, regardless of justice. Even when those involved in jurisprudence are bound by equitable incomes, the pursuit of worthy justice will still entail many alterations from current practices. But we have no good ideas about how to adapt or replace the combination of courts, judges, juries, and aggressive advocacy with different mechanisms (other than concerning matters of new norms of remuneration and job definition that economic innovations indicate and that would certainly be highly beneficial in curbing antisocial motivations and outcomes).

The state of shared political vision on the Left, whether for legislative, executive, or adjudicative functions, is still modest and incomplete and needs to be developed further to justify powerful and committed advocacy, perhaps largely by experiment, but perhaps also by careful analysis of options based on current experiences.

CHAPTER 7

Feminism

"In my heart, I think a woman has two choices:
either she's a feminist or a masochist."
—*Gloria Steinem*

In discussing visions for gender relations we have in mind a good society's procreation, nurturance, socialization, sexuality, and organization of daily home life, with a special eye on three dimensions: relations between women and men, between homosexuals and heterosexuals, and between members of different generations.

Kinship Vision

Our values imply that accomplishing kinship functions should enhance solidarity among the involved actors, preserve diversity of options and choices, apportion benefits and responsibilities fairly, and convey self-managing influence—taking into account issues of age, etc.

So with that set of broad desires, will there be families as we now know them? Will upbringing diverge greatly from what we know now? What about courting and sexual coupling? How will the old and young interact?

Fulfilling our values will require removing the features that produce systematic sexism, homophobia, and ageism, plus gaining an array of positive improvements we can only guess at until we have experimented with more complete proposals for visionary kinship institutions.

Even in a wonderful society, we can confidently predict that there will still be unrequited love. Sex will not lack turmoil. Rape and other violent acts will occur, albeit far less often than now. Social change can't remove the pain of losing friends and relatives to premature death. It can't make all adults equally adept at relating positively with children or with the elderly or vice versa.

What we can reasonably require, however, is that innovations eliminate the structural coercion of men and women, of heterosexuals and homosexuals, and of all adults and children into patterns that have for so long preserved systematic violations of solidarity, diversity, equity, and self-management.

But what will the institutions defining a vastly better kinship future look like? In contemporary societies, sexism takes overt form in men having dominant and wealthier conditions. It takes more subtle form via longstanding habits of communication and behavioral assumptions. It is produced and reproduced by institutions that differentiate men and women, including coercively, as in rape and battering, but also more subtly via what seem to be mutually accepted role differences in home life, work, and celebration. It also includes the cumulative impact of past sexist experiences on what people think, desire, and feel, and on what people habitually or even self-consciously do.

If we want to find the source of gender injustice, we need to determine which social institutions—and which roles within those institutions—give men and women responsibilities, conditions, and circumstances that engender motivations, consciousness, and preferences that elevate men above women.

One structure we find in all societies that have sexist hierarchies is that men father but women mother. That is, we find two dissimilar roles which men and women fill vis-à-vis the next generation, with each role socially defined but in only a very minor sense biologically fixed. One conceptually simple structural change in kinship relations would be to eliminate this mothering/fathering differentiation between men and women.

What if instead of women mothering and men fathering, women and men each parented children? What if men and women each related to children in the same fashion, with the same mix of responsibilities and behaviors (called parenting), rather than one gender having almost all the nurturing as well as tending, cleaning, and other maintenance tasks (called mothering) and the other gender having many more decision-based tasks, with one gender being more involved and the other more aloof, and so on?

This particular idea comes from the work of Nancy Chodorow, most prominently in a book titled *The Reproduction of Mothering* (Berkeley: University of California Press, 2nd edition, 1999). The book made a case that mothering is a role that is socially not biologically defined and that as mothers women produce daughters who, in turn, not only have mothering capacities but a desire to mother. "These capacities and needs," Chodorow continues, "are built into and grow out of the mother-daughter relationship itself. By contrast, women as mothers (and men as not mothers) produce sons whose nurturant capacities and needs have been systematically curtailed and repressed." For Chodorow, this has implications: "The sexual and familial division of labor in which women mother and are more involved in interpersonal affective relationships than men produces in daughters and sons a division of psychological capacities which leads them to reproduce this sexual and familial division of labor."

So perhaps one feature of a vastly improved society regarding gender relations will be that men and women will both parent, with no division between mothering and fathering.

Another structure that comes into question when thinking about improved sex/gender relations is the nuclear family. This has to do with whether the locus of childcare and familial involvement is very narrow, resting with only two biological parents, or instead involves an extended family or friends, community members, and more.

It seems highly unlikely that members of a good society would have to live alone or in pairs or in groups in any single or even in any limited number of patterns. The key point is likely to be diversity, with each frequently chosen option embodying features that impose gender equity rather than gender hierarchy.

While we don't feel equipped to describe such possible features, we can say that the men and women that are born, brought up, and then themselves bear and bring up new generations in a new and much better society will be full, capable, and confident in their demeanor and will also lack differentiations that limit and confine the personality or the life trajectories of either gender.

The same can be broadly said about sexuality and intergenerational relations. We don't think we know or, arguably, even have a very loose picture of what fully liberated sexuality will be like in all its multitude of preferences and practices, or what diverse forms of intergenerational relations adults and their children and elders will enter into. What we can say, however, is that in future desirable societies no few patterns will be elevated above all others as mandatory, though all widely chosen options will preclude producing in people a proclivity to dominate, to rule, to subordinate, or to obey based on sexual orientation, age, or any other social or biological characteristic.

A good society will eliminate oppressive socially imposed definitions so that everyone can pursue their lives as they choose, whatever their sex, sexual preference, or age. There will be no nonbiologically imposed sexual division of labor, with men doing one kind of work and women doing another simply by virtue of their being men and women, nor will there be any hierarchical role demarcation of individuals according to sexual preference. We will have gender relations that respect the social contributions of women as well as men and that promote sexuality that is physically rich and emotionally fulfilling.

It is likely, for example, that new kinship forms will overcome the possessive narrowness of monogamy while also allowing preservation of the depth and continuity that comes from lasting relationships. New forms will likely destroy arbitrary divisions of roles between men and women so that both sexes are free to nurture and initiate. They will likely also give children room for self-management, even as they also provide the support and structure that children need.

Obviously women must have reproductive freedom—the freedom to have children without fear of sterilization or economic deprivation and the freedom not to have children through unhindered access to birth control and abortion. But feminist kinship relations must also ensure that child-rearing roles do not segregate tasks by gender and that there is support for traditional couples, single parents, lesbian and gay parenting, and more complex, multiple parenting arrangements. All parents must have easy access to high quality daycare, flexible work hours, and parental leave options. The point is not to absolve parents of child-rearing by turning over the next generation to uncaring agencies staffed mainly by women (or even women and men) who are accorded low social esteem. The idea is to elevate the status of child-rearing, encourage highly personalized interaction between children and adults, and distribute responsibilities for these interactions equitably between men and women and throughout society.

Feminism should also embrace a liberated vision of sexuality respectful of individual's inclinations and choices, whether homosexual, bisexual, heterosexual, monogamous, or nonmonogamous. Beyond respecting human rights, the exercise and exploration of different forms of sexuality by consenting partners provides a variety of experiences that can benefit all. In a desirable society that has eliminated oppressive hierarchies, sex can be pursued solely for emotional, physical, and spiritual pleasure and development or, of course, as part of loving relationships. Experimentation to these ends will likely not merely be tolerated but appreciated.

We need a vision of gender relations in which women are no longer subordinate and the talents and intelligence of half the species is free at last. We need a vision in which men are free to nurture, childhood is a time of play and increasing responsibility with opportunity for independent learning not fear, and in which loneliness does not grip as a vise whose handle tightens as each year passes.

A worthy kinship vision will reclaim living from the realm of habit and necessity to make it an art form we are all capable of practicing and refining. But there is no pretense that all this can be achieved overnight. Nor is there reason to think a single kind of partner-parenting institution is best for all. While the contemporary nuclear family has proven all too compatible with patriarchal norms, a different kind of nuclear family will no doubt evolve along with a host of other kinship forms as people experiment with how to achieve the goals of feminism.

Parecon and Parpolity's Impact
In parecon, reproduction of sexist relations emanating from a patriarchal sex/gender system disappears. It isn't just that a participatory economy works nicely alongside a liberated kinship sphere. It is that a parecon also precludes or at least militates against nonliberated relations among men and women. Parecon unravels sexism.

A parecon will not give men relatively more empowering work or more income than women because it cannot provide such advantages to any group relative to any other.

Balanced job complexes and self-management need and seek adults able to engage in decisions and to undertake creative empowering labor, regardless of gender or any other biological or social attribution. If kinship relations press for other results, there is a contradiction and either kinship or economy must give way to the other.

There is no process of a parecon that is functioning properly that would abide hierarchies born in gender relations because there are no hierarchies in a parecon that can abide it. Women cannot earn less than men, have less-empowering jobs, or have less say in decisions.

But what about household labor? Many feminists will ask, "Parecon claims to remove the differentiation at work and in income required by contemporary sexism, but is household labor part of the economy?"

We can imagine a society that treats household labor of diverse types as part of its participatory economy, and we can imagine one that doesn't. Neither choice is ruled out or made inevitable purely by the logic of parecon.

Beyond that logical openness, however, we tend to think household labor shouldn't be organized as mainly part of the economy.

First, nurturing and raising the next generation is not like producing a shirt, stereo, scalpel, or spyglass. There is something fundamentally distorting to our thinking if we conceptualize of childcare and workplace production as the same type of social activity.

Second, the fruits of household labor are largely enjoyed by the producer him/herself. Should I be able to spend more time on household design and maintenance and receive more remuneration as a result? If so, I would get the output of the work and I would get more income too. This is different than other work, and it seems to us that changing the design of my living room or keeping up my garden is more like consumption than production.

Suppose I like to play the piano or build model airplanes or work on my car. The activity I engage in for my hobby has much in common with work, but we call it consumption because I do it solely under my own auspices and for myself. What we call work, in contrast, is what we do under the auspices of workers' councils to produce outputs that are enjoyed by people other than just ourselves.

Is there a problem with saying that because caring for and raising children is fundamentally different in kind than producing cars or screwdrivers or that maintaining a household is different in its social relations and benefits than working in a factory we shouldn't count household labor as work to be remunerated and to occur under the auspices of parecon's workplace institutions?

If we think it is impossible to have a transformation of sex/gender relations themselves, then there is a problem, yes. If the norms and structures of households and living units are highly sexist, and if a parecon doesn't incorporate household labor as part of the economy and subject it to parecon's norms, then household labor may be done overwhelmingly by women and will, as a result, reduce their leisure or their time for other pursuits relative to men.

But why assume that? Why shouldn't it be that transformed norms for household labor are produced by a transformation of sex/gender relations themselves, rather than by calling household labor part of the economy?

Take it in reverse. If this were a book about feminism and the rest of society, and if I had mapped out a feminist sex/gender vision, I don't think many people would ask whether we can count the workplace as a household so that it gets the benefits of the innovative relations that new families and living units have. We would assume instead that there would need to be a revolution in the economy not just in kinship, and we would rely on the former for the chief redefinitions of life at work, even as we also anticipated and required that the economy abide by and even abet the gains in kinship, and even as we worked to ensure that the gains of each meshed compatibly with the other.

In any event, clearly a parecon mitigates sexism because, on the one hand, it would have no reason to and even could not incorporate sexist hierarchies, and, on the other hand, because it empowers and remunerates women in a manner that precludes their being easily subordinated in any other realm.

The situation with polity is even more simple and straightforward. Of course legislative and other structures would not favor one gender over the other. And laws would be consistent with feminist kinship, as feminist kinship must nurture and socialize people capable of participatory self-managing political relations. So the polity will have laws, constitutional and otherwise, guaranteeing the character of political relations is consistent with and even reproductive of the feminist benefits of new kinship relations and vice versa.

Perhaps it is the paucity of our understanding showing, but other than in direct analogy to the above discussion, we honestly don't see a deeper relation of economics or politics and sexuality. If there is homophobia or other sexual hierarchies in a society, and if the economy is capitalist, then the economy will—to the extent owners are able to do so—exploit whatever differentials in bargaining power they are handed. A typically top-down polity will also at least reflect and often exacerbate those differentials. Beyond this, however, the capitalist economy and any authoritarian polity may also incorporate gay and straight behavior patterns into economic roles and consumption patterns. With parecon and parpolity, however, no exploitation of sexual difference is even possible—much less enacted in the economy—because there is one norm of remuneration and one logic of labor definition that applies to everyone, which, by their very definition, foreclose options of hierarchy, while the polity derives from and thus reflects and protects the will of men and women schooled by feminist relations.

What about intergenerational conflict? Capitalism will always exploit age differentials for profit via diminished remuneration for the young and old due to these constituencies' reduced bargaining power. For exploitative reasons, it will take advantage of different capacities related to age for exploitative divisions of labor and will rush premature labor entry or enforce slower than warranted labor withdrawal. A parecon, however, will not only promote humane behaviors as being in every participant's interests—and, in any event, the only effective way of being—but will make violations impossible, given that they are contrary to defining parecon norms and structures. In a parecon, there is no way to exploit age-based differences because there is no way to accrue advantage. Similarly a parpolity will likewise protect and incorporate the will of people of all ages, as self-management permits nothing less.

Societies will decide the role of the elderly, including retirement age, and likewise determine the point of young people's entry into economic and political responsibility as part of parpolity decision-making. While family and other extra-economic intergenerational relations will certainly not be governed solely by economic or political structures and will arise instead due to a host of variables, including new kinship and gender forms, the fact that a parecon and a parpolity require developed and fully participatory and self-managing actors imposes on life more generally a respect for all actors and gives all actors material equality and behavioral wherewithal and habits contrary to any kind of subordination emanating from any other of society's institutions.

CHAPTER 8

Intercommunalism

**"Segregation is the adultery of an illicit
intercourse between injustice and immorality."**
—Martin Luther King Jr.

As we discussed in developing our overall conceptual toolbox,
humans tend to create diverse communities bound by shared
cultures that differ from one another in their artistic, linguis-
tic, and spiritual allegiances and preferences. The problem of
cultural communities is not this diversity per se but that cultural communities can exploit one another, attack one another,
or even obliterate one another. In a good society, presumably
this type of largely one-way or sometimes mutual intercommunity assault and destruction would be eliminated.

What kinds of cultural relations would we like to have in
a good society?

Community Vision
We will not be magically reborn in a desirable society, free of
our past and unaware of our historical roots. On the contrary,
our historical memory, sensitivity to past and present social
process, and understanding of our own and of our society's
history will all very likely be enhanced during the process of
reaching a desirable society. Rather than our diverse cultural
roots being submerged on the road to a better world, they will
grow in prominence.

Instead of homogenizing cultures, in the transition to a better world the historical contributions of different communities should be more appreciated than ever before with greater means for their further development, without destructive mutual hostilities.

Trying to prevent the horrors of genocide, imperialism, racism, jingoism, ethnocentrism, and religious persecution by attempting to integrate distinct historical communities into one cultural niche has proved almost as destructive as the nightmares this approach sought to expunge.

"Cultural homogenization"—whether racist, fundamentalist, or even leftist—ignores the positive aspects of cultural differences that give people a sense of who they are and where they come from. Cultural homogenization offers few opportunities for variety and cultural self-management and is self-defeating in any event, since it heightens exactly the community anxieties and antagonisms it seeks to overcome.

In a competitive and otherwise mutually hostile environment, religious, racial, ethnic, and national communities often develop into sectarian camps, each concerned with defending itself from real and imagined threats, even waging war on others to do so.

But the near ubiquitous presence of racial and other cultural hierarchies throughout society and history no more means we should eliminate cultural diversity than the existence of gender, sexual, economic, or political hierarchies means we should eliminate diversity in those realms. The task is to remove oppression and achieve liberating conditions not to obliterate difference.

Racism often has a very crass and material component. Consider Desmond Tutu commenting on the South African experience: "When the missionaries came to Africa they had the Bible and we had the land. They said 'Let us pray.' We closed our eyes. When we opened them, we had the Bible and they had the land."

But theft is not always the dominant theme of cultural violation, and even when it is highly operative, it is generally only one part of the whole cultural picture. Most of racism, ethnocentrism, nationalism, and religious bigotry is based on cultural definitions and beliefs pushing and extending beyond material differences.

Dominant community groups rationalize their positions of privilege with myths about their own superiority and the presumed inferiority of those they oppress. But in time these often materially motivated myths attain a life of their own, often transcending material relations. The effects are brutal. For the oppressed, in the American novelist Ralph Ellison's words, "I am an invisible man. No, I am not a spook like those who haunted Edgar Allan Poe; nor am I one of your Hollywood-movie ecto-plasms. I am a man of substance, of flesh and bone, fiber and liquids—and I might even be said to possess a mind. I am invisible, understand, simply because people refuse to see me."

Some sectors within oppressed communities internalize myths of their inferiority and attempt to imitate or at least accommodate dominant cultures. Others in oppressed communities respond by defending the integrity of their own cultural traditions, while combating as best they can the racist ideologies used to justify their oppression. But as W.E.B. Du Bois notes, "It is a peculiar sensation, this double-consciousness, this sense of always looking at one's self through the eyes of others, of measuring one's soul by the tape of a world that looks on in amused contempt and pity."

Cultural salvation does not lie in trying to obliterate the distinctions between communities but in eliminating racist institutions, dispelling racist ideologies, and changing the environments within which historical communities relate so that they might maintain and celebrate difference without violating solidarity. An alternative is, therefore, what we might call "intercommunalism," which emphasizes respecting and preserving the multiplicity of community forms by guaranteeing each sufficient material and social resources to confidently reproduce itself.

Not only does each culture possess particular wisdoms that are unique products of its own historical experience, but the interaction of different cultures via intercommunalist relations enhances the characteristics of each culture and provides a richness that no single approach could ever hope to attain. The point is: negative intercommunity relations must be replaced by positive ones. The key is eliminating the threat of cultural extinction that so many communities feel by guaranteeing that every community has the means necessary to carry on its traditions and self-definitions. In accord with self-management, individuals should choose the cultural communities they prefer, rather than elders or others of any description defining their choices for them, particularly on the basis of prejudice. And while those outside a community should be free to criticize cultural practices that, in their opinion, violate humane norms, external intervention that goes beyond criticism should not be permitted except when absolutely required to guarantee that all members of every community have the right of dissent, including to leave the community, with no material or broader social loss.

Until a lengthy history of autonomy and solidarity has overcome suspicion and fear between communities, the choice of which community should give ground in disputes should be determined according to which of the two is the more powerful and therefore, realistically, the least threatened. The more powerful community that has less reason to fear domination would be responsible for unilaterally beginning the process of de-escalating the dispute. When needed, oversight and enforcement could occur by way of an intercommunal legal apparatus specializing in conflict resolution and including balanced job complexes and equitable remuneration.

Given the historical legacy of negative intercommunity relations, it is delusional to believe this can be achieved overnight. Perhaps even more so than in other areas, intercommunalist relations will have to be slowly constructed, step by step, until a different historical legacy and set of behavioral expectations are established. For example, it will not always be easy to decide what constitutes the "necessary means" that communities should be guaranteed for cultural reproduction or what development free from "unwarranted outside interference" means in particular situations. The intercommunalist criterion for judging different views on these matters seems likely to be that every community should be guaranteed sufficient material and communication means to self-define and self-develop its own cultural traditions and to represent its culture to all other communities in the context of limited aggregate means and equal rights to those means for all—just as all of its members, by virtue of participatory economic, political, and kin relations, are equitably remunerated and self-managing.

Race in a Participatory Society

If a parecon exists in a society that has cultural hierarchies of race, religion, and other communities, what does it contribute? If it exists within a society that has desirable communities without hierarchies, what then? In general, does a parecon's needs regarding economic life impose any constraints on cultures? Does a participatory polity or kinship sphere?

If we change the U.S. economy, for example, to a parecon without altering the racial, religious, and ethnic landscape, there will be sharp contradictions. Existent racial and other dynamics in this hypothetical society will pit groups against one another and give people expectations of superiority and inferiority. The participatory economy, however, will provide income and circumstances inconsistent with residual cultural hierarchies. It will tend to overthrow the cultural hierarchies by the empowerment and material means that it affords to those at the bottom of any and all hierarchies.

People in a participatory economy won't—and indeed can't—systemically economically exploit racism and other cultural injustices. Individuals in a parecon could try to do this, of course, and they could also harbor horrible attitudes, but there are no mechanisms for racists to accrue undo economic power or wealth—even as separate individuals, much less as members of some community.

Whether you are black or white, Latino or Italian American, Jewish or Muslim, Presbyterian or Catholic, southerner or northerner—regardless of cultural hierarchies that may exist in the broader society—in a parecon you have a balanced job complex and a just income and self-managing power over your conditions. There just isn't any lower position to be shoved into.

Lingering—or even continually reproduced—racism or other cultural injustices could perhaps penetrate a parecon in the role definitions of actors, but they could not do so in a manner that would bestow economic power, material wealth, or economic comforts unfairly. Thus blacks, Latinos, Asians, and many more in a transformed U.S. might have statistically different characteristics in their balanced job complexes, but the differences could not violate the balance of those complexes. Such disproportionately distributed job features might have otherwise denigrating attributes, it is true, though one would think that if they did the self-managing dynamics of the economy would tend to undo those injustices too.

Indeed, one can imagine that in a parecon members of minority communities in workplaces would have means to meet together in (what are typically called) caucuses to assess events and situations, precisely to collectively guard against racial or other denigrating dynamics—or to fight against those that are present as residues from the past or as outgrowths of other spheres of social life. This would seem to be about the best one can ask of an economy regarding intrinsically obstructing cultural injustices.

But what about a participatory economy and desirable cultures in a desirable society? There is no reason why cultural norms established in other parts of society cannot impact economic life in a parecon, and we can predict that they will. The daily practices of people from different cultural communities could certainly differ not only in what holidays their members take off from work, say, but in their daily practices during work or consumption, including arranging periods of prayer or disproportionately engaging in particular types of activity that are culturally proscribed or culturally preferred. There could be whole industries or sectors of the economy that members of a community would culturally avoid, as with the Amish in the U.S., for example.

One possibility, for example, is that in more demanding cases it might make sense for members of a workplace to nearly all be from one community so that they can easily have shared holidays, workday schedules, and norms about various daily practices that others would find impossible to abide. Self-management doesn't preclude such arrangements and may sometimes make them ideal.

Alternately, a workplace may incorporate members of many diverse communities, as will larger (and sometimes also smaller) consumer units. In such cases, there may be minor mutual accommodations—some members celebrate Christmas and others celebrate Hanukkah or some other holiday, and schedules are accorded. Or perhaps there are more extensive accommodations having to do with more frequent differences in schedule or with other practices affecting what type of work some people can undertake.

The point is, parecon's workplaces, consumer units, and planning processes are very flexible infrastructures whose defining features are designed to be classless but whose details can vary in endless permutations—including accommodating diverse cultural impositions due to people's community practices and beliefs.

Finally, do the needs and requirements of the roles of worker, consumer, and participant in participatory planning in a parecon put limits on what practices a culture can elevate in its own internal affairs?

The answer is in some sense, yes, they do. Cultural communities in a society with a parecon cannot, without great friction, incorporate internal norms and arrangements that call for material advantages or great power for a few at the expense of many others.

A culture could exist, say, that would elevate some small sector of priests or artists or soothsayers or elders or whoever else and require all other members to obey them in particular respects or to shower them with gifts. But the likelihood that such a cultural community would persist alongside a parecon for long would be quite low.

That is because the people involved will be spending their economic time in environments that produce inclinations for equity, solidarity, and self-management, as well as diversity, and that "teach" them to respect but not passively obey others. Why would they submit to inequitable conditions and skewed decision-making norms in another part of their life?

Assuming that in a good society people will be free to leave cultures—since people would have both the economic wherewithal, education, and disposition to manage themselves—we guess that many would exercise that freedom to leave any cultural community that denied them the fruits of their labors or denied them their self-managing say.

This could also be expected for the connection between a parpolity or kinship and a culture. The analysis is completely parallel. These other parts of a desirable society, just like its economy, will also impose only equity and self-management and solidarity on culture and will take from cultures that which is compatible with those values. There are no means for oppressive cultural relations to be legitimately and naturally manifested in kin or political relations because the roles available do not include ones seriously subordinate or superior to others. Similarly, while the details of a set of participatory kinship relations or parpolity relations would likely reflect the cultural commitments of participants—with a different mix of features in light of different cultural commitments—these refinements would not undo or restrict the key defining attributes of these spheres of life.

CHAPTER 9

Participatory Ecology

"Keep a green tree in your heart
and perhaps a songbird will come."
—*Chinese proverb*

Society and Ecology

When asking about the implications of participatory society regarding the ecology, the main issue is economics, since it is via production and consumption that by far the largest social impact on ecology occurs. Economies add new contents to the environment, such as pollutants, deplete natural contents from the environment, including resources, and alter the arrangement and composition of attributes in the environment—or the way in which people relate to the environment—by, for example, building dams or creating changed patterns of human habitation. Each of these and other possible ways an economy can affect the environment can, in turn, have ripple effects on nature's composition and, via those changes, back again on people's lives.

For example, an economy can add economic byproducts to the environment by exhaust spewing from cars or smokestacks accumulating chemicals in the atmosphere. These effluents can impede breathing or alter the way the sun's rays affect atmospheric temperatures. Both of these economic implications can have ripple effects on people's health or on air currents which then impact sea currents, affecting polar ice caps, and then altering weather patterns, sea levels, and crop yields.

Or an economy can use up oil, water, or forests, leading to people having to reduce their use of depleted resources, affecting the total level of both production and consumption around the world, the availability of nutrients essential to life, and of building materials needed for creating dwellings.

Or an economy can alter the shape and content of the natural environment's dynamics—for example, by reducing forests we reduce the supply of oxygen they emit into the atmosphere or by increasing the number of cows and affecting their eating patterns (to produce tastier steaks for ourselves) and increasing the methane they expel, again leading to greenhouse effects that alter global weather patterns. Or economies can alter human living patterns, and thus transportation patterns and other consumption patterns and attitudes, in turn affecting people's ongoing relations to mountains, rivers, air, and other species.

In the above cases and countless others, what we do in our economic lives affects either directly—or by a multistep process—how we environmentally prosper or suffer in our daily lives, as well as how the environment itself adapts.

In other words, economic acts have direct, secondary, and tertiary effects on the environment, and the changed environment, in turn, has direct, secondary, and tertiary effects on our living conditions.

Sometimes these effects are horrifying, as in seas rising to swallow coastal areas and low-lying countries—or in crop, resource, or water depletion that causes starvation or other extreme widespread deprivations. Or maybe the effects are slightly less severe but still horrific, as in tornados, hurricanes, droughts, and floods devastating large populations or inflated cancer rates caused by polluted groundwater or escalated radiation cutting down large numbers of people early in life or dams eliminating whole towns or villages due to their footprint. Or maybe the effects are limited to smaller areas suffering loss when natural environments are paved over or when noise pollution arises from loud production or consumption.

It follows from all these possibilities that the relation of an economy to the surrounding natural environment is deadly serious and that to fail to regard this relation to the environment, even if succeeding on all other criteria, would be a damning weakness for any proposed economic model for new society.

Capitalism and Ecology

Capitalism fails miserably regarding the environment. First, capitalism's market system prioritizes maximizing short-term profit regardless of long-term implications. Second, markets ignore environmental effects and have built-in incentives to violate the environment whenever doing so will yield profits or, for that matter, consumer fulfillment at the cost of others. And, third, there is the capitalist drive to accumulate regardless of effects on life and all other variables.

In other words, markets create incentives to violate the environment and anything else external to the buyer and seller whenever doing so will enhance the producer's profit.

Sellers will, for example, use production methods that spew pollution, damage groundwater, or consume more resources but cost less than clean methods and technologies. To reduce production costs or induce more purchases, they will build into products secondary effects that consumers who buy the product won't directly suffer but others will.

And it isn't only that in each transaction the participants have an incentive to find the cheapest, most profitable course of production and the most personally fulfilling course of consumption, it is that markets compel the absolute maximum of exchanges to be enacted. There is a drive to buy and sell even beyond the direct benefits of doing so, because each producer is weighing not the benefits of a little more income versus a little more leisure due to working less but instead the benefits of staying in business versus going out of business. That is, each actor competes for market share to gain surpluses with which to invest to reduce future costs, pay for future advertising, etc. These surpluses must be maximized in the present lest one is outcompeted in the future.

The race for market share becomes a drive to continually amass profit without respite, which means to do so even beyond what the greed of owners might otherwise entail. The guiding philosophy is grow or die, regardless of contrary personal inclinations. This not only violates attentiveness to sustainability of resources but also produces a steadily escalating flow of garbage and pollution. Transactions multiply, and in each transaction the incentive to pollute and to otherwise violate the environment persists. We get an economy spewing into, using up, and damaging the environment on a massive scale. We get an economy turning communities into dump sites, making cities sick with smog, polluting ground waters that in turn escalate cancer rates, and causing global warming that threatens not only raging storms but even vast upheavals of ocean levels and agriculture.

Parecon and Ecology

Will a participatory economy be any better for the environment than capitalism? Yes, for a number of reasons.

First, in a parecon there is no pressure to accumulate. A producer is not compelled to expand surplus in order to compete with other producers for market share. Instead, the level of output reflects a true mediation between desires for more consumption and desires for a lower overall amount of work.

In other words, in a parecon we each face a choice between increasing the overall duration and intensity of our labor to increase our consumption budget or working less to increase our overall time available to enjoy labor's products and the rest of life's options. And since society as a whole faces this exact same choice, we can reasonably predict that instead of a vir-tually limitless drive to increase work hours and intensity, a parecon will have no drive to accumulate output beyond levels that meet needs and develop potentials. This will, therefore, stabilize at much lower output and work levels—say thirty hours of work a week to produce socially useful products—and eventually, even less.

The second issue is one of valuation. Participatory plan-ning doesn't have each transaction determined only by the people who directly produce and consume the items trans-acted, nor do these participants have a structural incentive to maximize purely personal benefits regardless of the broader social impact. Instead, every act of production and consump-tion in a parecon is part of a total overall integrated economic plan. The interrelations of each actor with all other actors and of each action with all other actions are properly accounted for by parecon's decision-making.

Production or consumption of gas, cigarettes, and other items with either positive or negative effects on people beyond the buyer and seller take into account those effects. The same holds for decisions about building a dam, installing wind tur-bines, or cutting back on using certain resources. Projects are amended in light of feedback from affected councils at all levels of society.

By eliminating the market drive to accumulate and to have only a short time horizon and the market-compelled ignorance of economic effects that extend beyond buyers and sellers (such as on the environment)—and the consequent market mispricing of items—parecon properly accounts for costs and benefits and provides means to sensibly self-manage environmental impacts.

It isn't that there is no pollution in a parecon. And it isn't that nonrenewable items are never used. You can't produce without some waste, and you can't prosper without using some resources. Rather, when production or consumption generates negative effects on the environment or depletes resources that we value and cannot replace, we should not transact unless the benefits outweigh the detriments. And we should not transact unless the distribution of benefits and detriments is just.

This is what parecon via participatory planning accomplishes ecologically, and this is really all that we can ask an economy to do by its own internal logic. We don't want the economy to decide by the pressure of its institutional dynamics results that humans have no say in. We want a good economy to let people who are affected make their own judgments with the best possible knowledge of the true and full costs and benefits by bringing to bear appropriate self-managing influence. If the economy presents this spectrum of possibility and control to its actors, as parecon does, what is left to assess is what people will then likely decide. Parecon provides for people to be free and self-managing, and simultaneously ensures that the logic of the economy is consistent with the richest possible human comprehension of ecological connections and options.

Similarly, we can ask of the rest of society—its culture, its kinship relations, and its polity—that these too, by their roles, not bias people against the environment or future generations. This means a polity manifests people's will and has no institutional bias regarding ecology. It means kinship occurs in context of the environment and is attuned to husbanding it. And the same for culture. This last can take many forms, but, in any event, it means there will not be disdainful—much less polluting—attitudes and inclinations within cultural norms.

CHAPTER 10

Internationalism

"War does not determine who is right, only who is left."
—*Bertrand Russell*

Parecon and the World

Current international market trading overwhelmingly benefits those who enter today's exchanges already possessing the most assets. When trade occurs between a U.S. multinational and a local entity in Guatemala, Kenya, or Thailand, the benefits do not go more to the weaker party with fewer assets, nor are they divided equally—they go disproportionately to the stronger traders who, thereby, increase their relative dominance.

Opportunist rhetoric aside, capitalist globalizers try to disempower the poor and the weak and to further empower the rich and the strong. The result: of the one hundred largest economies in the world, over half aren't countries, they are corporations, and tens of millions throughout the world starve to death or die of preventable disease each year.

Similarly, international market competition for resources, revenues, and audience is most often a zero-sum game. To advance, each market participant preys off the defeat of others so that capitalist globalization promotes a "me first" attitude that generates hostility and destroys solidarity between individuals, corporations, industries, and states. Public and social goods are downplayed, while private ones are elevated. Businesses, industries, and nations augment their own profits while imposing losses on other countries and even on most citizens of their own country. Human well-being is not a guiding precept.

Capitalist globalization swamps quality with quantity. It creates cultural homogenization, not diversity. Not only does Starbucks proliferate, so do Hollywood images of women and minorities and Madison Avenue styles, elevating greed, self-centeredness, and violence. Anything indigenous, noncommercial, gender-equitable—much less feminist—must struggle to even survive. Diversity declines.

Only political and corporate elites are welcome in the halls of the capitalist globalizers. Indeed, the point of capitalist globalization is precisely to reduce the influence of whole populations, and even of state leaderships, save for the most powerful elements of Western corporate and political rule. Capitalist globalization imposes corporatist hierarchy not only in economics but also in politics and culture—and because it carries the seeds of patriarchy, in gender relations as well. Authoritarian and even fascistic state structures proliferate.

So, what is the alternative to capitalist globalization?

Supporting Global Justice

What do antiglobalization activists propose to put in place of the institutions of capitalist globalization?

So far, not much, but why not look forward and have new (not merely reformed) institutions that work to attain equity, solidarity, diversity, self-management, and ecological balance in international financial exchange, investment, development, trade, and cultural exchange?

Why not try to ensure that the benefits of trade and investments accrue disproportionately to the weaker and poorer parties involved? Why not prioritize national aims, cultural identity, and equitable development?

Why not enhance domestic laws, rules, and regulations designed to further worker, consumer, environmental, health, safety, human rights, animal protection, or other interests that do not prioritize profit?

Why not subordinate the desires of centralized multinationals and large economies to the survival, growth, and diversification of smaller units?

Why not assist countries to identify health, environmental, and other risks and help them guard against their ill effects?

Why not facilitate governments advancing environmental interests, worker rights, and other noncommercial purposes?

Why not outlaw brutalizing child labor, the exposure of workers to toxins, and the lack of regard for species protection?

Why not have international institutions be open, democratic, transparent, participatory, and bottom-up, with local, popular, and democratic accountability?

Why not restrain runaway global corporations, capital, and markets by regulating them so people in local communities can control their own economic lives?

Why not promote equitable trade that reduces the threat of financial volatility and meltdown, expands democracy at every level from the local to the global, defends and enriches human rights for all people, respects and fosters environmental sustainability worldwide, and facilitates the economic advancement of the most oppressed and exploited groups?

Such choices would encourage domestic economic growth and development, advance standards for the regulation of financial institutions by national and international regulatory authorities, and promote a shift of financial resources from speculation to useful and sustainable development.

These new institutions would also work to get wealthy countries to write off the debts of impoverished countries and to create a permanent insolvency mechanism for adjusting debts of highly indebted nations.

They would use regulatory institutions to help establish public control and citizen sovereignty over global corporations and to curtail corporate evasion of local, state, and national law.

Beyond all the above, antiglobalization activists also advocate a recognition that international relations should not derive from centralized but rather from bottom-up institutions. Why not have the structures mentioned above gain their credibility and power from an array of arrangements, structures, and ties enacted at the level of the citizens, neighborhoods, states, nations, and groups of nations on which they rest. Having these more grassroots structures, alliances, and bodies defining debate and setting agendas would also be transparent, participatory and democratic, and guided by a mandate that prioritizes equity, solidarity, diversity, self-management, and ecological sustainability and balance.

The overall idea is simple. The problem isn't international relations per se. The problem is that capitalist globalization alters international relations to further benefit the rich and powerful.

In contrast, activists want to alter relations to relatively weaken the rich and powerful and empower and improve the conditions of the poor and weak. Anti–corporate globalization activists know what we want internationally—global justice in place of capitalist globalization.

Parecon and International Relations

What are parecon's implications for international relations?

First, there is no drive to accumulate per se, and there is no tendency to endlessly expand market share or to exploit international profit-making opportunities, because there is no profit-making. The sources of imperialism and neocolonialism, not merely some of their symptoms, are removed.

If the whole world has participatory economies, then nothing structural prevents treating countries like one might treat other locales—neighborhoods, counties, states—within countries. And, likewise, there is no structural obstacle to approaching the production side similarly, seeing the world as one international system.

Whether this would occur or not, or at what pace, are matters for the future and are also affected by other dimensions of social life. A participatory polity writ large into international relations leads toward equitable and participatory international adjudication and legislation. Intercommunalism and feminism writ large into international relations tends to mitigate and remove the traffic in women and racial and ethnic bases for nation attacking nation. It certainly seems that the natural and logical international long-term extension of domestic advocacy of participatory economics, kinship, polity, and community would favor internationalism over imperialism. If balanced job complexes, self-management, justice, feminist, and intercommunalist relations are morally, economically, and socially sound choices in one country, why not across countries? Likewise, if it makes sense to plan each country's economic life in a participatory manner and to govern its polity in a self-managing way, why wouldn't it make sense to do these things from country to country?

Of course, even with the structural obstacles emanating from capitalist relations of production gone, and even assuming cultural and political forms would also welcome internationalism, and even extending the logic of domestic parecons and participatory societies to a worldwide participatory economy, there remains the difficulty of the magnitude of the gaps between nations that would need to be overcome. One cannot sanely equilibrate income and job quality between a developed and an underdeveloped society without massive and time-consuming campaigns of construction, development, and education. Moreover, if there are some parecons and some capitalist economies, the situation is still more difficult, with gaps in development and social relations.

So as countries adopt participatory economies and become participatory societies domestically, what happens to their trade with and other policies regarding countries that remain capitalist?

A good answer seems to be implicit in the earlier discussion of international global policies. The idea ought to be to engage in trade and other relations in ways that diminish gaps of wealth and power, while respecting cultural integrity and adjudicating and legislating in a self-managing and just manner.

One proposal is that a parecon trades with other countries at either market prices or parecon prices depending on which option does a better job of redressing wealth and power inequalities.

A second proposal would be that a parecon engage in a high degree of socially responsible aid to less well-off countries.

A third proposal would be that a parecon supports movements seeking to attain participatory economic relations elsewhere.

There is every reason to think that the workers and consumers of a parecon would have the kind of social solidarity with other people that would drive them to embark on just these kinds of policies, but such actions would involve a future choice and would not reflect an inexorable constraint that is imposed on society by a systemic economic pressure.

The long and short of this discussion is that seeking just international relations leads rather inexorably toward seeking just domestic relations and vice versa. A participatory society fulfills both agendas.

CHAPTER 11

Conclusion

"Will the people in the cheap seats clap?
And the rest of you, if you'll just rattle your jewelry."
—*John Lennon*

In talking about a vision for a future society, one could go into far more detail than we have provided. Indeed, we have been minimalist in addressing only a few institutions in each sphere, and, even regarding those few, we have only addressed broad attributes.

There are four reasons why we restrain ourselves.

1. To delve much further into visionary details is to risk the idiocy of arrogant excess. The future is not an open book but will be a complex product of choices and conditions no one can fully know in advance.

2. There are few if any singularly right details to know. A future society will opt for many different choices regarding its detailed features. Saying what those choices will be now not only ignores that what they will be will depend on lessons learned in the future but also ignores the way that in different places and different communities there will be different choices, not only due to lessons we haven't learned but also due to different tastes.

3. We wish to avoid a slippery slope that leads beyond arrogant excess to stultifying rigidity. The more visionary details one offers—even if such details could be confidently known, which they can't, and even if such details

wouldn't vary from place to place and time to time, which they will—the more one is likely to see a vision as some fixed, finished, final, and complete result, and thus the less likely one is to be flexible about assessing, improving, adapting, and refining it. To get overly detailed is a fool's errand, not only because it will yield gross errors, and not only because there are no universal details to foresee, but because it risks corrupting the whole process by rigidifying attitudes.

4. The details of vision are not our concern. The task we face is to provide future generations with a society whose institutions facilitate their making their own decisions. Our task is to provide a societal setting consistent with human well-being and development for all, without specifying the shapes people opt for within that freedom. The actual choice of policies and details in future settings is, in other words, for future people to decide. For us to act like those choices are our province would violate self-management (for them) and is a slippery slope toward us dictating for others how they will live.

So we have been and we need to remain minimalist in projecting institutional commitments for a better future. But our minimalism regarding institutional proposals does not mean we don't aim high. To deliver a society that is without oppressive class, race, gender, and power hierarchies, and in which just outcomes, diversity, solidarity, and self-management are produced by society's institutions, even as those institutions also facilitate people fulfilling and developing themselves and others as the highest priority, is no small goal.

The relatively few institutions we advocate are a minimal list, yes. But they are a minimal list essential to accomplishing the maximal goal of carrying out society's core defining functions in a manner that allows future citizens to self-manage their own choices in a solidaritous, diverse, and just setting.

PART THREE: OUR METHODS

"Revolution is not a one-time event."
—*Audre Lorde*

CHAPTER 12

Strategy Is Central

"'Incapacity of the masses.' What a tool for all exploiters and
dominators, past, present, and future, and especially for
the modern aspiring enslavers, whatever their insignia."
—*Voline*

No Strategy Means No Victory

One of the first things we learn from any serious teacher about
any conflictual game—for example, chess or football—is that
to have a prospect of winning we must have a plan. No choice
we make should be disjointed from all other choices. Choices
should not be a spontaneous or unplanned reaction (which is
almost universal for most players' choices in typical cases) but
instead a carefully chosen part of a clear and flexible scenario
we have in mind for attaining our desired goal—which is, presumably, to win, hopefully with our integrity intact.

On the one hand, any contest involves many conflictual
moments or brief spans of active engagement. Each separate
set of a few actions is rarely conclusive. Rather, the separate
acts or small sets of acts combine into a larger whole.

The point is, there are temporary tactics which might
recur in similar positions fairly often or that might be replaced
by others. Such tactics are not themselves strategy. Strategy is
instead a hoped-for pattern of actions including sought-after
gains and broad methods to pursue those gains that finally
culminates into your ultimate aims.

Our first observation about strategy is that it is very rare that strategy remains unchanged from the beginning to the end of an endeavor. After all, you have an opponent. And particularly in trying to change the world, you also have a very complex context in which you operate. Your opponent makes changes. Your context changes. Aspects of your strategy often have to change as well.

In trying to change the world, anything and everything might change—the field, the players, and even your goals as you attain new insights. In fact, even the rules can change, including being intentionally changed as part of a strategy for altering society's institutions.

"No strategy, no victory" means if you act pretty much without aim or pattern by just reflexively reacting each time your opponent acts, without conceiving what you are doing in terms of a plan to steadily improve your situation, you are very likely to lose.

Let's say we have two sets of people who are committed to battling for liberty. The first group reacts reflexively without plans that extend into the future. The second group develops coherent long-term goals and formulates ideas about how to marshal their abilities and energies into patterns that can accrue gains that create sufficient advantages to win their goals. They also periodically refine their strategy in light of continually changing circumstances. The first set is likely doomed, while the second set has very good prospects.

Strategy enhances our likelihood of achieving what we desire. While it is doubtful that anyone would disagree with the observation, nonetheless almost everyone fights injustice with very little, if anything, in the way of a flexible, guiding strategy.

If you want to travel, it helps to know where you want to go. If you hope to get where you want to go, it helps to have a plan for what vehicle and fuel to use to get there.

Inflexible Strategy Means No Victory

If one side is a virtual behemoth compared to the other side, the former is unlikely to ever have to make a new plan. In more realistic contests, however, and especially in trying to win a better world, things are far more complex. The most basic elements of strategy—such as who to reach out to and organize, what broad focuses to have, and many other aspects we will explore as we proceed—might go pretty much unaltered. But there will certainly be many other aspects that will have to change as conditions alter, not least when the forces seeking to block winning a new world engage in surprising choices.

If you have an inflexible strategy, then you lose if you make a mistake at the outset in conceiving it, since being inflexible means you are stuck with your error. If you have an inflexible strategy, it also means you lose if the forces arrayed against you behave dramatically differently than anticipated, since you will be stuck with a conception that no longer works. If you have a setback or a success that was unexpected, again, you will be stuck with a plan that no longer fits your new reality.

Having a flexible, sensible strategy opens the possibility of victory. Not having a flexible, sensible strategy pretty much closes that possibility. Inflexible strategy means no victory.

The Composition of Strategy

It is perhaps easiest to think of strategy as a flexible conception of how to go from one condition or situation to another.

Strategy begins with a flexible conception of current conditions and is later updated as times change. Generating the concepts for our analysis of current and future conditions was what Part One was about.

Strategy ends with reaching the conditions we are seeking to win. Generating the concepts for conceiving and steadily refining our vision of a desired future is what Part Two was about.

Strategy mainly involves amassing tools for seeking change and utilizing them to win change. A key component, for example, is increasing the number of people on the side of winning change and strengthening their abilities to fight for it. You can't alter society without involving people in sufficient numbers. We will call this consciousness-raising and commitment building. The issues central to consciousness-raising and commitment building are which people to attract and how to retain and enlarge those people's informed and sustained commitment.

At the outset of a campaign to win a new society, consciousness-raising and commitment building are foremost. They are not the sole initial priorities, but they are certainly the dominant ones, since they create a foundation of support necessary for all future efforts.

Additionally, consciousness-raising and commitment building remain important focuses right up to and even through the time of winning a new society, because the foundation of popular support for the new society must be continually strengthened. While initially consciousness-raising and commitment building are the core of strategy, as time passes consciousness-raising persists but becomes less central. So, what grows in relative importance?

Once there is sufficient support for change to marshal energies and resources to begin winning some victories, winning those victories becomes another element of strategy. Contestation over demands steadily climbs in importance to become the central aspect of the process, in turn contributing to—and always also needing—further growth in support and commitment, even as the victories regarding demands alter existing relations to favor change.

Alongside contestation, however, there is also construction. Movements not only fight for victories—contesting opponents who want to ward off change—they also construct new relationships and, when possible, new institutions of their own that enhance both consciousness-raising and contestation, as well as lay the groundwork for the structures of a new society. Thus movements develop organization locally and globally and build new projects. We can call this construction.

Taking this view, strategy has three primary, mutually supporting, and mutually dependent aspects, each always operative but also altering in their centrality as time passes.

First, consciousness-raising and commitment building are paramount, while even in the early stages there is also some contestation and construction.

In a second stage, consciousness-raising continues and construction keeps growing, but contestation becomes the most central and dominant aspect.

Finally, while both consciousness-raising and contestation continue, as one gets steadily closer to winning a new society, construction becomes steadily more central, finally becoming most important in the literal creation of the core institutions of the new society—no longer only within the interstices of the old, and no longer only as beachheads and inspiring models, but literally as the infrastructure of the new world.

It follows that while strategy can be seen—as it most often is, as we established earlier—as a path composed of combinations of tactical steps plus larger-scale programs, it can also be seen as a set of preferred conceptions bearing on consciousness-raising, commitment building, contestation, and construction. Indeed, in the rest of this volume, we will circle in on a viable strategic conception by utilizing both of these angles of approach.

CHAPTER 13

Strategy Is Complex

"Everybody knows the boat is leaking
Everybody knows that the captain lied
Everybody got this broken feeling
Like their father or their dog just died."
—*Leonard Cohen*

In this chapter, we focus on seven areas of strategy with nearly universal applicability:
- the size of movements;
- the types of demands movements need to develop;
- the efficacy of institutional construction;
- issues of power;
- the value of spontaneity;
- the organizational composition of movements;
- the necessity of organization at all.

Agents of Revolution

Who will be on the side of change? Who will oppose change? If we said left-handed people are likely on the side of change, it would mean we thought there was something about being left-handed that gave people interests, inclinations, desires, and beliefs that would make them more often receptive to seeking change, so that overall we would find most left-handers seeking change once a movement for change was visible, serious, and growing. The movement would organically and naturally appeal to left-handers. If left-handers, as is undoubtedly the case, had no such shared propensities due to being left-handed, then, as a group, their favoring social change would instead occur like it would for any random cross-section of the whole population.

Suppose we do identify a group that is a likely agent of change or of reaction. It doesn't mean that everyone in the group aligns automatically one way or the other. It means only that there is a good probability of aligning one way or the other. If we orient our movements to inviting, welcoming, and empowering a constituency that is a likely agent, our effort will have considerable promise.

Once identifying a constituency that by its roles in society's institutions has a high probability of liking a movement's aims, we have good reason to investigate what that constituency's priorities, hopes, and agendas are, to listen to it, to work in solidarity with any efforts it already has underway, to welcome it to participate, and to empower it to lead.

Additionally, since we are seeking to find likely potential agents of revolution because they are the constituencies we should most powerfully relate to, we should not adopt manners, behaviors, values, and practices that intrinsically and needlessly alienate such constituencies but ones that welcome and empower them.

So, who are they?

In this book we believe that society rests on the entwined relations of four spheres of social life—economy, kinship, culture, and polity. We don't know a priori which, if any, of these four is more dominant than the others in defining social relations and possibilities at any moment. They all could be centrally critical, including each sphere being capable of reproducing the old characteristics of itself and the other three, even if the rest were temporarily changed.

We also believe that each of the four spheres demarcate—by the implications of the roles they offer—contending groups in society which are arrayed in class, gender, community, and political hierarchies. In the event of mutual co-reproduction of the four spheres, or even short of that, in the event the dominant and dominated groups in the various hierarchies have sufficient interests and inclinations to act together and abet or disrupt efforts at change, we feel there are many agents of change—those at the bottom of the hierarchies of power and wealth of the four spheres. A strategic insight emerges, the potential likely agents of revolution are the groups arrayed at the bottom of society's central class, gender, political, and cultural hierarchies.

The Numbers Game: Without Outreach, No Victory

Consciousness-raising and commitment building entail communication with people who could become participants in social change. How many members must a movement for a participatory society have? How many members must become not only committed to the movement but very capable participants in its agendas? How many must understand its shared vision and strategy well enough to contribute to both? How many must energetically engage in associated actions and projects?

At the very least, one can surely say that the more folks movements reach, the better. The more folks movements involve, the better. The more folks movements welcome to energetically contribute, the better.

If a movement for participatory change isn't constantly applying energy and insight to communicating with more people in ways likely to enhance their comprehension and commitment *it is not a serious movement*. To have a small number of supporters with growing commitment and insight is not enough. To have growing numbers of supporters whose commitment and insight are not enlarging is also not enough.

There is a slogan, "better fewer but better." It is right, and it is wrong. Of course you need "better"—meaning more conscious and more committed. But the idea that a few high quality members are sufficient is an abysmal mistake.

Wherever you are building a movement—on a campus, in a workplace, in a community, in a whole country—a handy, albeit rough, rule of thumb is that one-third of the affected population needs to be seriously committed, informed, and involved if the movement is to be a really serious vehicle for lasting transformation of basic defining relations. Recruitment doesn't stop at a third, but reaching a third puts one in a comfortable position to continue on and win. A movement with a third support is moving from the stage that might best be called predominantly consciousness-raising and commitment building to the stage that continues with those efforts but becomes predominantly contestation.

It follows that as a movement develops it must conceive methods of outreach, training, and commitment building that can successfully engage a third of the associated population. That is no small number. And it is a rare effort in today's world that has as its aim to seriously engage at least a third, despite the fact that aiming for less is pretty much settling for a movement that will not win a participatory new world.

As an example, let's consider a campus movement—but it could also be a workplace movement or a neighborhood movement. Suppose the campus has ten thousand people. Suppose the movement reaches four hundred members. That's a big meeting. It feels powerful. There is a justified sense of community and of accomplishment. To get to that point people have worked hard, going room to room, person to person, talking, agitating, spreading literature, having gatherings, and more. At four hundred participants, meetings can be held. Projects can be undertaken. Demonstrations can be called. We like our group. We stop reaching out as our foremost priority and start enjoying our community of like-minded activists. Now comes the bad news. Four hundred people is just 4 percent of our campus. If we only organize 4 percent, we are not serious about our task. That might sound harsh, but it is true. The absolute priority needs to be enlarging our group for some time to come. Perhaps at around three thousand people, while we still want to keep growing more, our foremost focus might become fighting for gains that are conceived to a considerable degree to further the growth of our community.

You can't get to one-third serious, committed, and informed membership without dramatically altering the consciousness of lots of people who would otherwise not be relating. At the outset, maybe a handful join, and maybe another 1 percent are amenable. Getting beyond that means, first and foremost, communicating with folks with whom one doesn't ordinarily communicate. Put differently, getting a nice but proportionately very low number and then acting in light of the views of that number but no one else—and even acting in ways that will alienate others—is a recipe for disaster.

Without Stickiness, Defeat

Suppose we create a movement and do terrific outreach to new people of diverse backgrounds using whatever approaches work well where we are. And suppose as a result the number of participants is growing, as are the insights of the people joining. We seem to be succeeding.

But what if those who are leaving the movement equal, or even exceed, those who are joining the movement?

If we open a faucet to fill a tub, but we have an open drain simultaneously emptying the tub, the volume of water retained reflects a contest between the entry and exit speeds.

The same holds for movements as for bathtubs. If movements aren't sticky—a movement where once people join and become involved they overwhelmingly remain involved—then even the most effective outreach won't be enough for continual growth. Worse, when exit is faster than entry, we would have steady depletion ending in total defeat.

But why should a movement that is trying to make the world a better place have a significant exit of old members at all, much less have old members leaving faster than new members join? After all, a movement trying to make the world a better place is composed of caring and committed people trying to fight injustice. If members have developed mechanisms for reaching out to their rightful constituencies and are successfully doing that as a foremost priority, why would they simultaneously suffer from even greater numbers of members leaving?

The first thing to realize is that this is not a paranoid fantasy. This happens over and over with social movements and organizations to such an extent that it is by some accounts the chief reason for the demise of movements.

As evidence, think about the number of people who have become at least somewhat involved with or entwined with or impressed by movements against various wars, green movements for ecological sanity, no nukes movements, movements against racism and for civil rights, movements against sexism and for women, labor movements, gay and lesbian movements, and neighborhood and consumer movements, among others, since, say, 1965. Add to that people who have taken courses from movement faculty, who have lived with movement members, and so on. In the past fifty years, such movements, projects, living units, school classes, and the like have very conservatively involved, at least to some degree, fifteen million people in the U.S. alone and similarly large numbers in other countries. Suppose that nearly all of those people—let's say twelve million in the U.S. and comparable proportions elsewhere— once having gotten into the vicinity of social movements were firmly and continuously attracted so that they became steadily more involved and committed. How would that matter?

At this moment, if our movements were all sticky, then not only would most to the fifteen million people in the U.S. and the comparable numbers elsewhere currently still be active in movements with a very high level of experience and commitment, but there would also be the effects of their work since they were first involved, in many cases decades ago. Thus, they would have been attracting others who would have also have become seriously committed, likewise attracting others. Thinking about this picture makes it obvious that the problem of people leaving movements is, and always has been, paramount to prospects for societal change.

Whether we are talking about movements initially not doing the work needed to increase their tally of new participants or not doing what is necessary to prevent a steadily rising tally of ex-participants, the discussion is critical because the movement tub needs to be constantly filling. We need to open the spigot, but we also need to close the drain.

Think of the progressive/left community as a team fighting against both apathy and outright support for the status quo. Call it Team Change. To win Team Change needs to emanate a force field that involves potential team members ever more strongly the closer it attracts them. First a person hears about some facet of Team Change. There is an attraction, however slight it may be. As the person is drawn closer the attraction must increase to offset pressures telling him or her to avoid Team Change. Otherwise, the person will drift off. As many people orbit more closely, the force should increase in accord. Once people join Team Change, the attraction they feel should sustain permanent membership.

Is this Team Change's actual character, or is this stickiness a goal we are far from attaining? To decide we can look at (1) the historical experience that Team Change has had with potential recruits in the past and (2) the characteristics of Team Change to see whether its attractive force escalates as people get closer to full commitment.

If you think in terms of a year or two, then the outreach problem certainly seems paramount. How do we get beyond the choir? But even with our limited means of outreach, if you think about a decade—and certainly two or three decades—it is the stickiness problem that really demands attention. Look at our history and ask what the biggest problem is that we have to correct if our movements are to succeed. Our movement's stickiness, or lack thereof, jumps out.

We can come at the situation from another angle. Why should someone, once involved in the logic and dynamics of the progressive/left community, broaden and deepen their opposition stance and stick with it? And, conversely, why should people feel steadily less attachment for their opposition stance as time passes, only to finally return to the mainstream?

Well, think of a person getting more and more involved with progressive ideas and activity. Does this person merge into a growing community of people who make her feel more secure and appreciated? Does she get a growing sense of personal worth and of contribution to something valuable? Does she enjoy a sense of accomplishment, with regular uplifting feedback? Does she have her own needs better met than before? Does her life get better? Does it seem that she is making a contribution to improving other people's lives?

Or, conversely, does this person meet a lot of other people who continually question her motives and behaviors, making her feel insecure and constantly criticized? Does she feel diminishing personal worth and doubt that what she is doing is making a difference for anyone? Does she suspect there is little accomplished and have no daily, weekly, or monthly evidence of progress? Does she have needs that were previously met but are now unmet and few new ones that are addressed? Is her life getting more frustrating and less enjoyable? Does it seem she is only bothering other people and rarely doing anything meaningful on their behalf?

Our Team Change has no coach and needs to be participatory and democratic, so being self-critical is everyone's responsibility. But Team Change must play to win. And that means we need to reassess how we organize ourselves, the culture of our movements, what we learn as we become more committed, how we interrelate, and what benefits and responsibilities we have due to our political involvements.

The alternative to doing much better regarding "movement stickiness" is another long season—two or three decades worth—which means hundreds of millions of lives unnecessarily stunted and terminated for want of our greater success and final victory.

Being right about what's wrong with society, and even being able to convey our insights to wide audiences, is essential but not enough. Movements that can win need a degree of clarity about goals and strategy if they are to retain a sense of purpose, confidence, identity, and integrity in the face of criticism. But they also have to be organized and function both in ways that not only enlarge but retain membership and in ways that not only contribute to change but do so clearly in all members' eyes. Movements have to not only attack problems but also meet needs for members and populations more broadly, and they have to not only win victories that meet needs but also victories that create the conditions for winning still more victories. The absence of all this is our stickiness problem.

So, again, regarding closing the drain that empties our movement, why might people leave a social movement, even after having become involved and thus agreeing with that movement's stated aims?

Here are some key reasons.

Oppression Frustration

Of course a key reason people join movements is their horror at the existing oppressions they or other people suffer. Movements exist to fight injustice. People join movements with that aim.

Maybe it is an experience with sexism, heterosexism, racism, classism, or authoritarianism that causes a person to join. Maybe it is outrage at the pain around one of these issues—or perhaps most often around a combination of these issues. But here is one reason movements tend to not be sticky but repulsive. Movements too often saddle members with the same frustrating, depressing, and outraging personal situation that propelled them to join in the first place.

Suppose I am outraged at patriarchal sexism and I join a movement that claims to oppose it. Suppose I then experience within that movement levels of sexism that approach or even exceed those I had experienced in society at large. I may try to endure this depressing condition. Maybe I am also for ending some war so strongly that I try to rationalize and otherwise alibi or ignore the sexist setting I have to occupy—which is made all the more painful by the hypocrisy of its claiming to be what it isn't. But, for most people, a time comes when we are worn down and we exit. The attractiveness of being opposed to injustice in name, and even in some deeds, is overcome by the repulsiveness of being a party to injustice—perhaps racism, sexism, classism, authoritarianism—in our own daily existence in a movement that claims to be so much better.

One can be eager to diminish and eliminate oppressive dynamics and structures inside one's movement on moral grounds to avoid hypocrisy, and no doubt for many other reasons as well. The point here, however, is that one must reduce and eliminate oppression inside movements or those movements will not be sticky—and therefore will not win.

The Class Problem

When the women of Bread and Roses, an early feminist organization in the U.S. in the sixties, said to the antiwar movement, "Clean up your act or you won't succeed," they were right. When the Black Power component of the civil rights struggle said to the antiwar movement, "Clean up your own house or you won't succeed," they were right. We are for ending racism and sexism in society. We have learned that we must also persevere to reduce and finally end racial and sexual hierarchies inside our movements since otherwise:

- we are hypocritical and uninspiring;

- we suffer the ills of these oppressions ourselves;
- our movements will not attract, much less empower, women, people of color, and other oppressed groups;
- we won't retain our broader antiracist and antipatriarchal priorities.

This is the race and gender instance of the more general oppression frustration problem mentioned above.

We are also for ending economic injustice and class hierarchy in society. And so we also need to patiently, calmly, and constructively restructure our movements so that they no longer replicate corporate divisions of labor, corporate hierarchies of decision-making, and market norms of remuneration. This must become a patient but unrelenting priority if we are to avoid class-centered hypocrisy, become economically inspiring, not suffer class alienation ourselves, attract and empower working people in our efforts, and retain our economic justice priorities.

Class, which at various times in history has wrongly crowded race, gender, and sexual identity off our agendas, now needs to be re-highlighted in ways that address not only the ills of capital but also the ills of coordinators who monopolize decision-making and the positive needs of labor.

For the moment, instead of battling these ills, many of our movements are often largely "coordinatorish." They don't attract and hold working people nearly as effectively as they need to for the same reason that movements disdainful of gender or race don't attract and hold women and members of minority cultural communities nearly as effectively as they need to.

For many years, the issue of class and social change was seen as just a matter of us versus them. We were on the side of labor. They were on the side of capital. Each side might have members coming from the other side by background (Engels was an owner who opposed capital; cops are workers in the aid of capital) but the two sides were the only really important class teams that one could join. Of course, individual people weren't personally homogenized into two precise positions, as locations on the class map were much more varied at the personal level. But collectively, when thinking in terms of overall prospects, class was bipolar.

The message of our new class analysis is that we need to reject a two-class formulation. And it isn't just that there is a third consequential group. Anyone can see further distinctions among the people labeled capital and among the people labeled labor. There are big capitalists and little ones, industrial and financial ones, and so on. There are organized workers and unorganized ones, employed ones and unemployed ones, skilled and unskilled ones, and so on. Rather, it is that a movement could advocate on behalf of capital, could advocate on behalf of labor, or could instead advocate on behalf of a third class between those two, the coordinator class. There exists, as such, an economy elaborating the interests of each of the three classes as its central logic not only an economy for two of them. The strategic problem is to develop a movement whose program, structures, and practices lead toward a truly classless future, rather than toward a coordinator-dominated future.

It isn't enough that many people want classlessness. Most of the rank-and-file in every past revolution wanted classlessness. Rank-and-file activists in the Soviet Union wanted classlessness. Attaining classlessness must be built into the logic of what people do and what they construct not just into their rhetoric. This requires not only that we create movement institutions in accord with classlessness—they also must have a more personal dimension.

If we questioned many typical activist audiences—with obvious exceptions, of course—we would often find widespread disdain for religion and for most sports. Try asking campus activists (in the U.S.), for example, about NASCAR or bowling, or for that matter football, and watch the incredulous, dismissive reaction. Activists also disparage most TV shows and generally disdain country and western music, as well as most restaurants where working people eat and most newspapers that working people read.

The fact that many leftists adopt daily preferences that are not only different from but that routinely disparage working people, with nary a nod toward comprehension of other people's choices, is no accident. There are additional factors, case by case, but overall not seeing that these attitudes are significant derives from our having not yet comprehended that coordinator elitism is as prevalent and as vile as capitalist, racist, or sexist elitism.

We need to understand how people trying to carve out reasonably fulfilling situations in tightly constrained settings can highly value commodities and practices that other people living in different situations utterly disdain.

It is partly that sometimes many options are excluded by costs or accessibility and that some options are made highly accessible or even essential. Why, for example, do many young black boys, and now often black girls too, think that playing basketball makes more sense than reading books? Is this genetic? Obviously not. It is due to structural channeling, and those who are channeled are not doing anything stupid in making their choices, nor are they merely being tricked. They, in fact, see reality and act reasonably in light of what they see.

Why do leftists decry mainstream newspapers like the *New York Times* as horrendous lying machines, and then pore over them for hours each day—ridiculing those who instead opt to read only a tabloid's sports section, which is the one section that doesn't lie? Is this wisdom? Or is it self-delusion?

Once we open our eyes to seeing how a classist movement can make working people feel alienated, just like a racist or sexist movement can make blacks, Latinos, or women feel alienated, the relation of all this to the stickiness problem is obvious. If a movement doesn't attract and hold enough working people, it is typically because its projects, organizations, and campaigns are not welcoming and empowering for working people. They instead embody coordinator-class tastes, values, behaviors, and structures.

Imagine an antiracist movement mimicking the structure and culture of a southern slave plantation and ask yourself, would that be sticky for blacks? Extrapolate to class and the way some movement institutions mimic mainstream divisions of labor and distributions of circumstance, income, and power. The good news, however, is there is a clear path forward.

Ignoring Our Own Positive Needs

The needs of people inside movements are not confined solely to not being oppressed by forms of injustice that are common throughout society. If people join a movement that talks about liberation, freedom, and fulfillment, but they feel no better than they felt before they joined, what does it say about the movement's capacity to deliver a better life?

Movements often rightly focus their attention on the needs and potentials of oppressed constituencies in the broader society. So far, so good. But they also often pay little or no attention to the needs and potentials of their own members. Members often do not find their lives enriched due to being part of the movement. They often do not enjoy more and deeper friendships. They often do not enjoy a greater sense of dignity and mutual aid. They often find more time for struggle but not for well-being. Indeed, they often do not have a better sex life, more intimacy, more caring, less hostility.

If you joined a club that was supposed to make people happier, more expansive, and more creative, and your life became less fulfilling, expansive, creative, and happy, what would you do? Well, unless you were a masochist, you would leave the club.

People leave movements not only because the movements feel hypocritical in not addressing internally what they say they will address externally but also because members just feel crappy too much of the time. Their needs are rhetorically and intellectually aroused, but they often aren't doing anything creative and engaging. They often aren't getting any respect. They often aren't enjoying deeper and better friendships. They are even lonely. They give up. Ignoring our own needs is a ticket to movements not being sticky.

The alternative to ignoring our own needs, of course, is to build movements that pay serious attention to the well-being of their members, providing services and means for socializing, learning, playing. A movement becoming a medium for mutual aid, rather than a den of disparagement.

This doesn't mean we simply say that having such things would be nice. It means that we give time and energy to making such things happen in a sustained way, structurally, as part of movement policy and program.

TINA *Syndrome and Hopelessness*

The belief that "there is no alternative" (TINA) enunciated perhaps most famously by Margaret Thatcher in the UK but trumpeted over and over through the decades limits our numbers in two ways. On the one hand, absence of vision, absence of a belief that our movements can actually win a new world, causes people to not join. On the other hand, people who do join in time feel a growing unease. Why am I doing this? It leads nowhere.

If we don't know what we want, we can't have a very good plan of how we are going to achieve it. If we don't have compelling vision, we can't have good strategy. How can movements lack worthy and workable vision? Shouldn't everyone know what critics of capitalism want?

We need vision that is disseminated publicly and also subject to continual refinement. What else can promote real participation?

We need vision about economics, politics, law, families, kinship, culture, ecology, and international relations. What else can respect society's complexity?

Activists have the mental faculties to propose vision. Activists have experiences from history and from our own lives to ground vision. Activists have mental and material means to test vision. Activists could, if we wished, invent, evaluate, refine, and, if need be, reinvent vision.

Drawing upon our diverse and often revamped phases of recent activism, not to mention assessing earlier history, surely we have created a store of experiences sufficient to inform credible, inspiring vision.

So why is it that among the many brilliant leftists who have tackled all kinds of problems so few have generated, or even tried to generate, truly inspiring, easily accessible, factually and logically compelling, operationally worthy, and widely shared vision? Two hundred years of struggle and we have no widely shared institutional vision. It must be that we lack vision not because vision can't or shouldn't exist, but because we haven't brought it into being—despite being able to. Our vision problem is of our own making.

Consider the following thought experiment. Imagine we made a pile from the past forty years of all the public talks, interviews, essays, articles, movies, songs, stories, and books that have been about what is wrong with modern society. How high would that pile climb? To the moon? Only to the top of Mount Everest? In any event, it would reach very high.

Next, imagine that instead we made a pile from the past forty years of all the public talks, interviews, essays, articles, movies, songs, stories, and books about new institutions we want to have in a new society. How high would that pile climb? Fifty feet? Twenty feet? To our knees? In any case, not very high.

Yet when an activist talks with someone not on board the movement train, very often the first major query the person has is, "What do you want?" And the prospective ally doesn't mean, "Do you favor justice, do you favor freedom?" They mean, "What new institutions do you want that would make life seriously different for everyone?"

We don't have vision not because vision is impossible and not because it isn't needed, but because—despite being both possible and needed—we haven't given time to conceiving, sharing, and improving it. Huge numbers of people know that the basics of contemporary society are broken, or, more accurately, that they never worked humanely in the first place. But they don't know, and often don't believe, there is any alternative worth fighting for.

When we keep explaining how bad our society is and how powerful the agents of reaction are, ironically we are largely telling people what they already know and, worse, we are feeding a main reason for their not lining up on behalf of change—the belief that change is impossible.

More, and Better Too

If we have good outreach, new people joining, and our movement retains members, have we solved the numbers game? Almost, but not quite. We will have dealt with growing membership, but we also want membership whose quality keeps improving. Instead of Better Fewer but Better, we want Better More and also Better.

But what is a better member? Put differently, if Sue or Sam is a member, what changes make Sue or Sam a better member over time?

Once Sue develops a greater understanding of the theory, vision, and strategy of the organization—not simply as someone who can repeat it, but as someone who really understands and can evaluate it, apply it, and improve it—she becomes a better member.

Once Sam develops stronger ties to others in the organization and becomes more deeply involved in various aspects of the organization, as his life permits, he becomes a better member.

When a person joins, they shouldn't just dangle in the wind with no ties and no implications. There should be a

MICHAEL ALBERT

process that uplifts their knowledge, confidence, capacities, involvements, and connections.

Like meeting members' needs with social programs, similarly enlarging members' ties and capacities by way of serious and careful training and welcoming involvements must be a priority. It doesn't require deep analysis to understand this point. Historically, however, there does seem to be a serious level of commitment and clarity needed if a project, movement, or organization is to act on it. Thus, it is advisable to have structured means to welcome new members, to share ideas with new members, to involve new members in decisions, events, and projects, to have programs of enrichment and development. All of this should be systematically undertaken as a priority. Then we will have growing numbers of members, each of whose level of involvement becomes steadily better.

Dealing with Difference

Around the world activists argue that we should show that "another world is possible." We should be internationalist. We should generate solidarity. We should reduce racial, gender, sexual, political, and economic hierarchies. We should seek ecological sustainability. We should demand peace and justice.

But activists report, "We are fragmented. We are less effective than our cumulative size, energy, and wisdom warrant. People repeatedly, naggingly, and divisively dispute vision, strategy, and tactics with one another."

Two values we all universally favor, solidarity and diversity, can speak to this problem.

Solidarity celebrates entwinement—we will both benefit if you and I empathize and act on behalf of one another. But solidarity also embraces the idea that we disinterestedly respect one another's plights and possibilities out of a sense of human community. We all act on this considerably already, but to the extent that our natural empathetic inclinations have been worn down by vicious market competition—something that has certainly happened to one degree or another to everyone in modern societies—we can consciously nurture them back into prominence. A proviso, however, is that we should not pursue solidarity to the point of disallowing sober critical evaluation. Solidarity isn't blind allegiance or unquestioning support of one another, but we should certainly put a high burden on refusing to offer aid and logistical support to other radical and progressive actors. Informed and reasoned solidarity is mutual aid.

Diversity means that in pursuing our own agendas we also pay attention to preserving and exploring options that others favor, even when we have doubts about their logic or efficacy. We shouldn't put all our eggs in one basket, lest we misjudge, and having explored no other options leave ourselves powerless, disarmed, and otherwise inadequately prepared to redress our error. Whether individually or in organizations, we should celebrate differences and, when possible, we should keep alive varied approaches so that everyone benefits from the lessons and accomplishments others attain. That is, we understand an "insurance" logic to favoring diversity to ward off making grave errors. We also understand an "exploratory" logic to seeking diversity, so that we gain benefits from many more paths explored than we can ourselves embark on. We shouldn't diversify into microfragmentation, but we should pursue diversity well beyond homogenized unity.

We understand the immense benefits of mutual aid. We need to transcend the dehumanizing ills of aloof individualism.

We understand the gains of avoiding uniform approaches. We need to welcome the positive educational and vicarious implications of advocating varied explorations.

Can we massage these insights into explicit ways to deal with movement difference?

Focus

One kind of difference that plagues movements is about focus. Prioritize race. No, prioritize gender. You are both wrong, prioritize class. Authority? No, I prefer sustainability. War and peace? No, I prefer gay liberation. For every major area there are folks who think it is primary. They think everything else should be understood in reference to it. If you don't see things their way, then you aren't their ally. Advocates of different focuses butt heads. Why? And what's the solution?

People butt heads this way because we live in a multidimensional world in which different aspects of life profoundly and very differently impact our possibilities. Some people identify primarily via their roles and circumstances in one part of life. Others situate themselves primarily in reference to another part. We get feminists, nationalists, labor organizers, peace workers, environmentalists, gay activists, disability activists, and so on. This partitioning of priority for individuals is not going to go away. And, in fact, this partitioning of priorities for individuals is desirable because individual people have different priorities due to their different life experiences, conditions, and insights. They are experientially attuned to address different aspects of life with their organizing energies. In any event, regardless of whether we like this or not, there is no point bemoaning it. It will not cease.

There are two widely proposed solutions to the ensuing fragmentation, but in practice it turns out that they are not solutions at all.

The first approach to unifying is for someone to say, hey, the conflicts are no problem. We should all do our own thing, but we should all also recognize that one thing (and it always turns out to be the speaker's thing, of course) is above the rest. My thing is the organizing principle, the heart of the matter, the core concern. We may each address everything, that's fine—or only part of it all, that's fine too—but we should all do whatever we prefer in light of the defining, foundational priority that I espouse and which you all need to agree with me on.

And then the speaker says this central priority that should contour how we understand everything else should be smashing the state. Or perhaps the speaker says it should be uprooting patriarchy. No, it should be transcending capitalism or attaining peace or winning multiculturalism or sustainability, says the speaker.

The idea of marching behind one banner that elevates one focus—even as everyone can also focus on their own personal priorities—doesn't work because every constituency wants its domain to be the elevated one. Worse, people in each constituency rightly realize that the minute some other focus than theirs is elevated, theirs will be subordinated. Passions run high. Unity will not emerge via even the most broadminded exaltation of one focus above all others.

The second approach to unifying disputing actors is called coalition building. We do not get behind the banner of one school of thought and practice—not even if we each retain our own autonomy and focus but must always prioritize another's conceptual and programmatic priorities above our own. No, we all instead get behind one tiny morsel of thought and practice that we can all enthusiastically support. We join hands for ending a particular war or for pursuing some other mutually acceptable short-term aim that we can all agree on, and we are silent—when in each other's presence—regarding everything else. We avoid rocking the coalition boat. We practice lowest common denominator politics. The aim we all share, we steadfastly share. The rest we studiously ignore. It isn't that coalitions are worthless. It is that coalitions on their own don't produce lasting, mutually supportive unity. In fact, to a considerable extent, they institutionalize separation.

Here is an alternative to trying to get folks to accept one overarching banner or to only celebrate a lowest common denominator coalition. We build a bloc.

We take the Left, the whole broad Left—and we will see how we can define that in a moment—and we call it a bloc. If your group wants to be in it, fine, it has to assent to providing people power and other support for the bloc's overall agenda, while also autonomously developing and pursuing its own focused agenda. The same holds for my group. The same holds for every other group. The peace movement pursues peace and supports the whole bloc. Movements against racism, patriarchy, poverty, and homophobia pursue their agendas and support the bloc agenda as well. And what is the agenda of the whole bloc? It is the sum of the agendas of all its components. It is their greatest common sum—not lowest common denominator—including all the differences.

This is not as odd as it might at first seem. It is precisely what a society is, the totality of all its components, differences and all. In our case, we just add that the totality's components must be mutually respectful and supportive, even about their differences. The resulting bloc is the active Left. Maybe some people or groups think they are part of the Left but just can't abide being part of the bloc. Okay, you are in the bloc or you aren't, and the bloc is, or aspires to be, the active Left. Maybe some people or groups aren't welcome. Their commitments are clearly contrary to the bloc's central allegiances. Fine. It happens.

Those in the bloc operate as an encompassing combination of components: a movement of movements. The antiracists get aid and benefit from the energies and assets of the gay liberationists and the peace activists. The peace activists get aid and benefit from the energies and assets of the environmentalists and the anticapitalists. And so on, around and around, for all those in the bloc, each getting mutual aid from all others in the bloc. In contrast, those outside go it alone, which gives them a big incentive to join, of course.

The leadership for the emergence of agendas in each facet of life comes from the people most affected by that facet of life, which means from those most attuned to it, those most focused on it—not individuals but large and representative movements. Everyone appends the insights of the rest of the bloc to their own insights in the totality of their thinking. Friction is abided. Difference is part of life and of activism too. Unity of this broad type is deemed so beneficial that attaining it dwarfs worries about differences—save for the most egregious. And at the same time, differences aren't confused, ignored, or made either subterranean or put destructively in the forefront. They are instead treated to serious, informed, and often vigorous debate and abided in their place.

Is there a mind-set that can sustain such commitments among folks with different priority focuses? We think there are at least two.

The first will most likely be held by only some folks, but we strongly advocate it and would like to see more people adopt it. In accord with the concepts in this book, it says, for example, that society is a product of the impact of different spheres of institutions and contexts—economy, polity, culture, kinship, international relations, ecology—each powerfully influencing all our life prospects while dividing people into different and often opposed constituencies. There is no a priori assertion of the importance of one focus as compared to any other—of economy as compared to polity, culture, or kinship, or vice versa—but instead their relative effects on life and their centrality to efforts at change are determined only in practice. In societies like the U.S., the evidence is seen as overwhelmingly indicating that all these spheres of life and their influences are fundamental and that all of them generate defining influences and pressures that mold the rest of society and contour possibilities so greatly that to dramatically transcend the limits of any one of these phenomena requires that we address them all. With this attitude, the need to combine autonomy and solidarity in our organizations and movement building seems self-evident. We have no choice. We arrive at the bloc.

Luckily, a second viewpoint exists that could support this bloc approach and which can be held even by people who themselves continue to believe that one particular sphere of influence is fundamental. This second view can be held by people who believe that women in homes should address kinship, prioritizing implications for class struggle, or that workers in firms should address pay scales, firstly prioritizing women's liberation, or that peace activists should address wars, with prioritizing attending to race, or vice versa, each favoring one sphere above all others as the central focus for strategic calculation, whichever the operationally dominant focus might be.

The mitigating view is to realize that solidarity without a preferred prioritization—be it around class or gender or race or whatever—is vastly superior to seeking universal prioritization around a preferred focus and failing miserably to attain that prioritization.

If I think patriarchy (or capitalism or racism or war or whatever) should be the main underlying organizing focus, even on other issues—and if I have the additional understanding—it doesn't matter to my attitude toward being part of a bloc. I understand that not everyone is going to agree with me about prioritization, so that requiring that everyone must agree with me in my prioritization of one sphere of life above all others as the only route to solidarity will not yield solidarity.

It doesn't matter if I think that were we to get solidarity based on my prioritization we'd be in better shape, because I know it isn't going to happen. And, likewise, I know that while forming coalitions will sometimes have merit, coalitions will not yield full solidarity either. So I should argue for my beliefs when people are interested in discussing such matters, but I should prefer that people with other views help each other and help me, and that I, in turn, help them as they help each other—rather than that we all compete. This type of thinking can, if sincere, support the bloc approach.

One of the things that can prevent such insights from becoming majoritarian is that typically an advocate of prioritizing class or race or any other particular focus not only thinks they are right, which is fair enough, but actually wants to be right and wants others to be wrong more than they want to win change. This desire is what breeds real trouble.

We should all want a better world. If you say the route to a better world is by way of paying priority attention to class, and she says, no, we should prioritize gender, and he says, no, it ought to be race, and so on . . . still, we should all want some approach to succeed way more than we want our own viewpoint to be advocated if it isn't succeeding.

Supposing that more than anything else we all want to succeed, isn't the best way forward to insure against the error of all adopting one wrong approach? Therefore, shouldn't we advocate an overall design that preserves and explores many approaches, even as we personally argue the benefits of whatever one we most favor?

In other words, it turns out that even if I think a single-focus approach would be intellectually best, so long as I am sufficiently humble to respect the possibility that I could be wrong about my favored sphere's priority, then I ought to favor the bloc approach. In any event, if I am remotely realistic, I ought to advocate the bloc approach because the real world alternative to the bloc is not my preferred idea of unity behind my banner, which simply won't happen whatever banner I may favor, but no unity at all.

Reform or Revolution
Still, the above isn't an end to all causes of sectarianism. Different activists can pursue different ultimate aims or visions not just different priorities, and we might reasonably intuit that this too would be a primary source of differences that can cause conflict.

For the moment, the only serious dividing line over what we want for these areas is typically over whether we seek to ameliorate the ills of existing institutions while taking their permanence for granted (therefore being reformist) or whether we seek to replace existing institutions with new ones that accomplish needed functions in fundamentally new ways (therefore being revolutionary).

Some feminists and gay rights activists want new institutions for socialization, nurturance, and family life. Others think modest variations of the existing family, marriage, and living arrangements—plus changes in mind-sets—will be sufficient.

Some antiracists feel that new community structures are required to eliminate root causes of oppressive cultural relations. Others feel some new laws and changed mind-sets within the rubric of existing defining relations will relieve suffering as much as it can be relieved.

Similarly, some argue that our government institutions for adjudication, legislation, and collective implementation of shared aims are corrupted by the ills of other spheres of life and need only some revisions and corrections to be optimal. Others argue that we need new ways of accomplishing essential political functions that in their underlying logic propel rather than trample our most impassioned values.

Some say we have to treat the ecology differently within the rubric of existing structures. Others say that treating the ecology differently requires new structures.

In short, some want to patch up society while maintaining its defining features. Others want to transcend society's defining features to attain a new structure. Is this difference an unbridgeable chasm or can the two camps constructively interact?

It depends.

If the reformists are intent upon preserving existing relations on behalf of existing elites and are only interested in ameliorating suffering when doing so is consistent with enlarging the continued benefit of those elites, then their conflicts with honest revolutionaries will be hard to bridge. The revolutionaries will rightly repudiate the reformists' elevation of the rights of elites to primary position and reject this type of bottom-line callousness to the conditions of the poor and oppressed.

If the reformists sincerely believe that ameliorative change can eliminate harsh ills and are intent on accomplishing that without regard for preserving elite advantages—thinking only that the preservation of elite advantages is likely but not favoring it—then it should to be possible to work together and have mutual respect. These types of reformists and revolutionaries should each respect the other's honest concern and informed opinions and seek gains when possible together, and, quite importantly, the reformists should not want to be right but should instead hope that it will turn out that more desirable changes than they anticipate are possible.

Likewise, if the revolutionaries seek fundamental changes without attention to the impact on those most afflicted, and if they are callous to short- and mid-term gains, then their conflicts with honest and caring reformists will be hard to bridge. The reformists will rightly repudiate this type of revolutionary's callousness to fighting to improve the immediate conditions of the poor and oppressed. But if the revolutionaries sincerely believe in the possibility and desirability of fundamental change but also respect and seek immediate gains for those suffering most now—trying to bring both agendas into mutual accord but never losing track of the immediate needs of the downtrodden—then it should be possible to work together with mutual respect and benefit.

Worthy revolutionaries want near-term higher wages, better working conditions, affirmative action, a shorter workweek, immigration reform, equal access to quality education, legal reform, free childcare, free health care, paid maternity and paternity leave, new housing, clean air, climate sanity, peace, a change in the rules of international exchange, and so on, and so forth, just as do well-meaning reformists.

The difference is that when the reformist fights for such gains it is not as part of a project to transform defining institutions. The reformist feels that to seek fundamental change is futile or unnecessary, or even worse, that it would disrupt interests of elites held in high priority. But the sincere reformist who believes fundamental change is not on the agenda but who would certainly celebrate if it were achieved should, of course, not be scared that others pursue such change and should not pray for their failure. And similarly, the sincere revolutionary should not disdain reforms per se, and should not pursue fundamental change in a manner callous to the immediate potentials of people suffering the ills of today's policies and institutions. If these conditions are met on both sides, then even though the differences in outlook and aims are profound, mutual work and mutual dialogue ought to be possible. If the conditions aren't met, then mutuality is unlikely, and rightly so.

What makes it possible for reformists and revolutionaries to meet these conditions?

- First, the necessary humility of those on each side to respect that, after all, they could be wrong.
- Second, the recognition of each side that, in fact, the other side really is also motivated to reduce injustice and to increase fulfillment.

What will be the nature of operational differences?

- Reformists will consider it a misuse of energy to talk about basic institutional dynamics and to advocate their replacement. They will feel that talking about revolution will reduce energies for seeking truly possible change and perhaps even obstruct some folks' allegiances to efforts at needed change.
- Revolutionaries will talk not only about an immediate goal but also about basic institutions and will offer a long-term vision and try to develop lasting infrastructure to pursue continuing gains leading to larger and larger movements. They will feel that to forgo these focuses not only reduces the likelihood of long-term revolution, but even undercuts prospects for immediate reforms. That is to say that revolutionaries will deny that the application of energies to future aims as well as to immediate ones

distracts from winning gains now, and will instead feel that without hope for continuing trajectories of change all the way to a new society, most people will be unlikely to join campaigns limited to immediate gains, feeling that even if such campaigns are won they will in time be rolled back as underlying defining relations reassert themselves. Is this difference intractable?

An advocate of the ideas developed in this book would not only advocate for higher wages or a shorter work week or peace but would also develop consciousness of underlying structural causes of associated ills, plus allegiance to inspiring visions, hope and desire for fundamental changes, awareness of long-term strategy, and increases in movement organization and infrastructure.

In contrast, the honest reformist would put all his or her energies solely into describing a reform and building activism on behalf of the immediate change to benefit those suffering.

The differences are intractable at the level of ideas, values, and even aims, but they are not so intractable that each activist has to regard the other as an enemy. Each can welcome the extent of the other's contribution. Each can avoid arrogantly suggesting that the other should not even exist.

Visionary Sectarianism

Okay, but beyond differences over reform and revolution, what about the existence of different visions of what institutions we should have in the future? When there are different visions, with different advocates for each, is that a difference we can handle constructively?

There is no universal answer. The issues are to what extent two different visions yield two different short-term agendas. And to what extent do the differences represent different understandings of how to attain essentially the same just conditions of fulfillment, or to what extent do they represent different definitions of what fulfillment is, and even about who to fulfill?

As an example, suppose an advocate of market socialism says, "I seek markets, councils, remuneration for output, public ownership of productive property, and workers' control, all on behalf of equity, diversity, solidarity, and self-management, including classlessness."

In contrast, an advocate of participatory economics, as per this book, says, "I seek participatory planning, councils, remuneration for effort and sacrifice, collective ownership of productive property, balanced job complexes, and worker and consumer self-management on behalf of equity, diversity, solidarity, and self-management, including classlessness."

The former says of the latter that she strives for more than is possible, giving up too much output and risking incursions on privacy, etc. The latter says of the former that he seeks contradictory aims, settling for institutions that fall short of his values.

This is an honest disagreement. It can be intense, of course, but there is no reason for it to yield unbridgeable hostility. It can occur regarding economy, as in this example, or regarding any other dimension of social life. Different visions that arise to attain essentially the same state of grace via different institutional allegiances can compete for support and validation through partial implementation via their direct appeals and, of course, by their logical arguments.

A person advocating one such visionary approach should not be upset if it turns out that the values she seeks to attain require another's institutional recommendations. Our values are principled. Institutions are means to ends. Conflicting visionaries, while the issue of which vision is to be implemented is undecided, will seek many and varied short-term gains, and these will overlap greatly, affording the possibility not only of debate but also cooperation.

Suppose instead of the above happy situation, the advocate of what he calls market socialism pursues the stated institutions on behalf of elevating those who have a monopoly on training, education, empowering tasks, and the levers of day-to-day decision-making power—what we call the coordinator class—to a dominant position in the economy. This advocate of "market socialism" wants to eliminate capitalist rule to replace it with coordinator-class rule.

The advocate of participatory planning, in contrast, wants to eliminate not only the source of capitalist rule but also the source of coordinator rule. For the market socialist, the economic vision serves firstly managers, engineers, and others who monopolize decision-making skills and levers, and then serves other workers secondarily. For the pareconist, the economic vision serves all who work, with no class differentiation. This is a different kind of disparity than favoring different institutions with the same values in mind. It is more basic than a dispute over what institutions can achieve shared values. In this more intractable case, difference is rooted in the underlying values themselves not in different understandings of the logic of particular institutions or aims for attaining shared values. It isn't analysis that is in question but rather values, and specifically class allegiances.

It would be delusional to deny that this second kind of visionary difference constitutes big trouble for unity. But so it should. Dealing with difference doesn't mean papering over disputes about our defining, central values. Those differences have to be admitted and, when intractable, they should be labeled as such. We can still communicate rationally, rather than in some kind of verbal joust mode. We can still address evidence and logic, rather than constructing personal assaults. But what is unbridgeable is . . . unbridgeable.

Many differences among activists are about what we should be doing in the present or over some span of time leading to a better future. Such differences are about activist strategy and tactics not about vision.

- Strategy is our view of the broad process of gathering support for change and developing means of manifesting that support to win a sequence of alterations in society and to finally attain new defining institutions. Part of strategy is deciding our focus—not just the issues but the constituencies to organize. Another part of strategy, however, is deciding on organizational structure, whether to operate locally or nationally, whether to work in electoral arenas or not, and so on.

- Tactics are the methods we employ to attain short-term aspects of strategy. Tactics include demonstrations, strikes, leafleting, modes of presentation and communication, conferences, polling or get-out-the-vote methods, civil disobedience, and so on.

Confusing the issue further, people who have a different focus or vision may agree about aspects of strategy and tactics. On the other hand, people who agree on the vision and focus can disagree about strategy or tactics. Regrettably, when differences over strategy and tactics exist, they often become debilitating. Our own strategic commitments will emerge as we proceed with the rest of this book. Still, for the purpose of addressing sectarianism, we will raise some strategic matters and related concerns immediately below—albeit without much supporting discussion.

Strategy and Tactics

For example, suppose we have two activist camps. They each advocate the same values—let's say those outlined in this book—and they also advocate the same long-term institutions to attain these values. Regarding what they ultimately want, they are united.

One camp, however, says that in fighting against the mental and behavioral dictates of current structures and to overcome opposition, it is essential—even though they wish it wasn't—to utilize what they call democratic centralism, an approach to organization which in practice bears a huge resemblance, as they admit, to the organizational structure of the Ford Motor Company. They say we need to use this ugly methodology to win, otherwise we will be disjointed and easily fragmented and trampled. They don't worship this type of organization, they just think conditions make it necessary.

The other camp instead argues that such hierarchy is not a powerful aid to winning classless goals and will also be uncongenial to and disempower working people, as well as instilling the wrong values and inclinations in our movements. Contextually it is a loser, in addition to having damaging side effects, says this advocate of the second approach.

In other words, there is a dispute over what is called Leninist organization. It could be a debate over goals—if one side thought this structure was good for the long haul—but, as noted in the case indicated here, it could also be solely about means. One side says the means will subvert the end. The other side rejects the idea that the means will subvert the end. We have to use it and aggressively prevent it from trampling our aims. What do we do?

We think the answer is dictated by reality. We explore both options. Trying both will be the reality, since both inclinations strongly exist, so we might as well celebrate trying both. Two camps, two approaches. The key thing is that we should all hope that one works. We should see which works by trying both. It is that simple. There is no reason for either side to want to be right, to feel it is important that they be right. What matters is to find out what is, in fact, right. If both sides are being honest, both should hope that an approach which avoids the use of authoritarian structures will prove viable and effective. After all, both views want a society without such structures. If both sides are honest, both should agree that if a new world can't be attained without using interim authoritarian structures, at least to a degree, then such structures will have to be utilized—with their ills carefully guarded against. On two sides of this divide, people feel very strongly. But that doesn't mean they can't be mutually respectful. If the difference is strategic, as in the case when there are shared long-term aims, there is no reason to be anything but respect. Of course, if the difference is really over vision, then we may be back to an intractable situation.

Take another example. Do we choose in our demonstrations violent confrontations, civil disobedience, or peaceful legal displays without any conflict at all? These alternatives do not reflect abiding principles. With very few exceptions, everyone agrees that all of these approaches could make sense in some cases but might not make sense in others.

We have a strike. We picket. Scabs arrive. It may make sense to block their entry to the firm by nonviolently clogging up routes of access, or perhaps even to block them forcefully. Very few leftists think that to advocate such choices reveals oneself to be unworthy. Likewise, very few think that someone who argues that such an approach is unwise in a given context because it overextends our means, invites repression that we can't ward off, and will alienate potential allies is unworthy for thinking such thoughts. The matter is contextual not universal. That's what characterizes tactics. There can be a large onus against a certain option on the grounds that the option has intrinsic qualities that typically tend to be counterproductive. But ultimately each issue is, nonetheless, its own issue.

What if there is a disagreement? For example, what if there is to be a large demonstration and some people want violent confrontation, some want active civil disobedience, some want passive civil disobedience, and some want peaceful legal marching? Then what? The issue isn't what single way of thinking about such choices is right. The main issue is to realize that diverse ways of thinking are going to exist, and thus to determine what attitude is most constructive in light of that diverse reality.

And the answer is what it has been throughout this discussion. We understand solidarity. We understand diversity. We know the price of fragmentation. We know the price of all eggs in one broken basket. So we all agree that celebrating different strokes for different folks makes more sense than seeking homogeneity—whether we like all the strokes that folks might opt for or not.

On the other hand, your stroke shouldn't trump my stroke or vice versa. The goal is to manifest our energies in ways that build a movement and raise social costs able to win sought-after ends. If we all agree on that, we may disagree on how any particular tactic contributes to or even hurts the cause. But the idea that one approach should imperially displace others that are also highly valued and supported should be obscene to everyone, even those favoring that particular approach.

One stroke for all violates diversity just as surely as ruling out options from the top violates diversity. So we can all easily see that we have to have a multitactic movement, just as we have to have a multifocus movement. There is no other route to significant unity. Multitactic doesn't mean, however, that we all choose what we like with no attention to the implications our choice has for others. If my choosing tactic X would preclude your choosing tactic Y, which you prefer, then we need to negotiate so that I can do X and you can do Y and the two undertakings can not only both occur but, to the extent possible, can be mutually beneficial.

Of course, negotiating like this can be difficult, but, as a first step, agreeing that we ought to do so can't hurt and may well lead to the obvious insight that actions can occur at different times, in different places, with different preparations.

Different Perceptions

Other types of difference may be more difficult to reconcile. You look out the window and see blue and green. I look out the same window and see maroon and yellow. We are trying to describe for the same audience what we see out there.

For example, you look and see Slobodan Milošević, Saddam Hussein, and Muammar Ghaddafi as relatively good guys, or even heroes, plus you also see grotesque U.S. violence and intervention. I look out and see Milošević, Saddam, and Ghaddafi as awful thugs, plus I see grotesque U.S. violence and intervention. We want to address the same audience about the Balkans, Iraq, or Libya. What makes the problem big? You think calling Milošević, Saddam, and Ghaddafi thugs plays into the hands of attacking their countries. I think denying the evil of these folks, much less extolling them, undercuts the legitimacy of the antiwar movement and thereby hurts efforts to prevent attacks on their countries.

Big problems over different perceptions of what is going on arise when different activist camps see reality in ways that are so at odds that each camp thinks the other's way of talking about reality is incomplete, confused, and even obstructs political awareness and progress. The part the two camps more or less agree about may even lead to similar desires about what they should be doing—for example, what demonstrations to be calling or what broad organizing to be doing. But the part they disagree about may lead to very different and sometimes even incompatible ways of pursuing the similar ends—what to say at the demonstrations, who to have speak, what to demand.

As long as the world appears so dramatically different to us, our messages will be dramatically different, and much else is likely to be dramatically different, as well. Is there any hope for civil, much less cordial, relations? Maybe.

Again there is a crucial condition. For any kind of civility to emerge despite the differences, it must be that we are both more interested in making progress than we are in having been right about our analysis. We should each be far happier if the other is right and great progress ensues than if we prove correct and slow or no progress ensues. If we have our motives clear in this respect, and again if we also have even the most minimal degree of humility, then an obvious if somewhat difficult way of operating arises. We live and let live, even as we also argue as forthrightly as we can for the views we think are correct.

Rather than waste time assaulting one another, instead we each face the whole population. We bring them our different messages and we see what happens. We don't try to stop the contrary advocate from presenting their case in exchange for them not trying to stop us. We each realize that it is better for both to proceed without each attacking the other than for both to waste energy in mutual attack and for all broader communication to be hurt by the overarching mutual hostility. If we can at times join together, we do so. If we can't, we don't. Debate is fine. Mutual aid is fine. Mutual or one-way assault isn't.

Sectarianism?

We all know sectarianism when we see it—at least in folks other than ourselves. But defining sectarianism is not so simple. Some might say sectarianism is feeling some view or value really strongly. Or that it is holding strong views without sufficient evidence. Or that it is being willing to strongly argue one's views or to say that others' views are wrong, dumb, or harmful. But sectarianism obviously can't be any of those features. We all believe various things strongly. We all believe some views are wrong, dumb, or even harmful. Everyone sometimes turns out to have believed something without sufficient evidence. We are all happy to argue for our beliefs. None of this in itself implies that we are sectarian.

Some say sectarianism is solely a political phenomenon. Others say it is only a phenomenon of a particular ideology. But we know that all kinds of folks can be sectarian, not only diverse political types—Leninists, anarchists, feminists, and more—but also religious folks, or economists, and so on.

Maybe sectarianism is another name for religion. But it can't be because we know that being sectarian doesn't mean that one is religious nor does being religious mean that one is inevitably sectarian. The same goes, by the way, for any political persuasion. Some in each persuasion are sectarian, some aren't. As a matter of fact, the same person can be sectarian sometimes yet the height of flexible sobriety other times.

We know that when a person is sectarian, logic, evidence, reason, empathy, mutual regard, and respect become only weakly operative, if present at all. What is symptomatic of sectarianism is, instead, inflexibility, dogmatism, and imperious disregard.

So, again, what is sectarianism? Perhaps sectarianism occurs when a person comes to feel a subset of their views to be their identity. We get sectarian mostly about views that do double duty as views and also as our identity. When we take our views to be who we are, any criticism of our views feels like an attack on our essence. Someone says I think your view of the need for Leninist organization or to prioritize gender or on behalf of absolute nonviolence or against markets or for small-scale organization or in favor of consensus or whatever . . . is dead wrong and even harmful. If we feel the view in question is a core feature of our very identity, is part of the essence of our being, is a component of our integrity and who we are— then we tend to perceive in the criticism of our views not just words of disagreement about ideas but a deadly attack on our personhood. We promptly assume the posture appropriate to warding off a deadly attack, and we strike back. Our rebuttal likely includes some harsh rejection of the critic's "defining" views. Now our critic feels assaulted, just as we did, and prepares for further verbal, if not physical, conflict.

This observation suggests that the spiral of defensive/ aggressive behavior characterizing sectarian conflict stems largely from perceiving disagreement with our views as an assault on our identity. It isn't only that we believe deeply. It isn't only that we argue strongly. It isn't only that we think some other views are wrong, dumb, or harmful, nor is it just that we might be wrong. If someone tells me the population of the U.S. is less than the population of Chile, I don't get berserk about it even though I hold my contrary view strongly and think their view is nonsense. If someone tells me a view upon which I premise my identity is wrong—berserk is what I may become. In sectarian exchange we aren't really arguing about ideas and evidence so much as we are protecting our identity and even our very existence.

It is pretty easy to come to this conclusion when you watch a particular brand of sect members redefine themselves to the point of dressing and talking like one another and in the imagined manner of their politically preferred deity, whether that is Lenin, Trotsky, Mao, or even, sad to say, Bakunin. The sects in question have all the earmarks of cults, but at the same time they are ultimately built around what was once a reasoned adherence by each member, for however short a time, to actual values, views, and aims—views that may even have had great validity and been meritorious. The increasing identification of the values, views, and aims with members' personal definitions of self, however, seems to jettison reason and augur the rise of inflexible, arrogant, dismissive, defensive, aggressive, out of touch, and sometimes drunkenly psychotic sectarianism—even against people's better judgment. We have very likely all drifted into it, at least to some extent, at some time or other, and so we all know the phenomenon personally. Some, however, are stuck in it—with a vengeance.

A remedy for this is to try to look inward to de-link our identity and our beliefs. We accomplish this not by reducing how passionately we hold our beliefs but by understanding that our beliefs are, after all, contingent, and that we are at all times more than our contingent beliefs, and that we should never want to cling to contingent beliefs at the cost of reality, effectiveness, and our true, and even deeper, identity.

What we are suggesting is that we try to defuse unproductive sectarian confrontations by attempting to draw a very clear distinction between another person's ideas, values, and aims that we wish to question and the identity and worth of the actual person who we are engaging with. On paper, it appears very simple. It appears to be platitudes, really. But nonetheless, achieving this partitioning between person and beliefs will help reduce or even eliminate needless division, infighting, and sectarianism—which is, in turn, part of attaining a movement that people stick with.

Paralysis of Analysis or Action Faction Subtraction

There is often a tendency to overthink things to the point of interfering with getting things done. More, the extra thought itself is, in such cases, typically fruitless. Long after what can be assessed is on the table and debated, people bring up disputes about matters that cannot be fully known or details that transcend need to know or byways of debate that reflect academic extrapolation, anything other than the serious attention to what needs doing and how to do it. We all know this happens, but what does it actually imply we should do instead?

First, the solution is obviously not to forego thinking, which is just the flip side of analysis paralysis. The world is a mess, we must act. Stop all the palaver, get on with it, and do so before anyone has any chance to offer any assessments at all. Act on impulse. Forego thought.

What do these mirror image problems have to do with the numbers game? It is simple. Movements lose members when participation in them seems either a useless pastime due to endless intellectual debate without action or due to perpetual action without taking the time to assess, plan, and choose wisely. Sensible people see the first dynamic as a waste of their time and, at least if they manage to give it even a little thought, see the second as unlikely to chart useful paths forward.

But where does overanalysis or underanalysis come from? There are numerous factors but one, in particular, is insecurity.

There is an old Chinese saying, "Dare to Struggle, Dare to Win." What does that mean? Why would one have to dare to win, or even to struggle (other than fear of losing)? The answer is "fear of error." It feels like a massive responsibility to struggle for change and to take steps instituting change—and morally sound people feel trepidation.

Fear of error can and often does cause a kind of avoidance of acting—which, in order to appear willful and not fearful, takes the form of the paralysis of analysis.

How does insecurity bear on the action faction? They seem to be impulsive, eager, primed for activity. Well, sometimes their readiness is just that and nothing more. But sometimes, perhaps more often, it is that this group thinks that if there is debate and discussion what they prefer will not occur. Their insecurity arises from feeling that they will not be able to convince others of the efficacy of their inclinations once those inclinations are subject to discussion, so it is better to just rush their views into practice. This is not only precipitous and arrogant, forestalling assessment, but also undemocratic—much less contrary to participation and self-management.

At any rate, whatever the roots of these dual problems may be, a solution is evident, albeit sometimes difficult. First, create movements in which there is sufficient mutual aid, respect, and, especially, development of speaking skills and political awareness in all participants, so that all have faith that a general discussion followed by a decision will be better than rushing to judgment. And second, have clear procedures for developing a program and discussing and choosing tactics which are organizationally followed each time, and which a) prevent endless exploration of the inessential, b) ensure sufficient assessment so that good ideas surface and all who are involved feel informed and confident that important issues have been aired, and, finally, c) whenever possible, also enact alternative plans of action, to preserve options and avoid a mistake being disastrous.

The Personal Is and Isn't Political

The phrase "the personal is political" first arose from the women's movement of the 1960s. In the 1950s to mid-1960s, there was sexism, racism, and poverty but little public recognition of these oppressions. Folks assumed each individual's plight was of their own making. To improve one's lot meant to overcome one's personal character inadequacies. The civil rights movement then demonstrated that many of the conditions that each black person faced were duplicated in the conditions most other black people faced. From blacks seeking food in restaurants to seats on buses to votes in elections, the public revelations of the era propelled new insights. The enemy was no longer one's own inadequacies. The enemy became systemic and was called "institutional racism" and, later, "white supremacy."

During the same period, spurred by civil rights momentum, a new resurgence of socialists—with Michael Harrington's book *The Other America* in the most visible position—showed that hunger and poverty were not personal prices that people paid for faulty preferences they harbored but were systemic outcomes operating against people's higher aspirations. Poverty wasn't a personal failure. It was systemic. The enemy became not self but capitalism.

The antiwar movement, in turn, revealed the causation and commonality in the patterns of U.S. foreign policy in Southeast Asia and throughout the world. Bombs weren't beneficent nor were they dropped due to the poor choices of the targeted victims. We weren't entangled overseas due to largesse. American foreign policy was greed and power writ large. The enemy became not U.S. errors or excess concern, much less the behavior of those blown to bits, but imperialism.

The 1960s women's movement came together, in part, when women in both the antiwar and civil rights movements noticed that their exclusion from leadership and their exploitation doing the most tedious work was not uniquely individual but was, instead, shared. Through consciousness-raising groups in which women told each other their life stories, women discovered that their situations in marriage, child-rearing, sex, work, culture, and even language were not unique but strikingly similar, and that the cause of their suffering was not themselves but something systemic and political. The enemy became not self but patriarchy.

In each instance, activism uncovered that "the personal is political." That is, the experiences, feelings, and possibilities of our personal lives were not just due to personal preferences but were overwhelmingly limited, molded, and defined by a broader social setting. Our problems felt personal, but their broad texture was systemic. They were imposed on us not caused by us. In this sense, a central contribution of the New Left was to say that we suffered a "totality of oppressions" that was systemic and mutually entwined and that all oppressions needed to be overcome by a revolution in existing institutions and the creation of liberating alternatives. In other words, "the personal is political" meant that our personal lives were, in considerable part, politically determined. Improving our personal experiences required collectively addressing political structures.

Time passes. A new generation picks up the phrase but reverses it to mean that our personal choices have political implications. Big deal, you might say. That's true too. The personal choice to support an activist project certainly has political implications. What's wrong with saying so? But redefining the phrase went further to imply that all the personal choices we make, even the ones that seem totally apolitical, have political implications and that those are especially important and even paramount. You choose to wear makeup or not, to watch TV or not, to eat this or that fish, to wear this or that pair of sneakers, to use a bank or not. That these are personal decisions but also political acts was the new apex of insight.

The idea that personal choices have political implications was, and is, true and certainly has some explanatory power and informative value. But the reversal of meaning went further. The most telling and instructive meaning of "the personal is political" became, in the 1990s and since, a feeling that the key thing for each individual to be concerned with in being political was to be personal in the "correct" way. Dress right, eat right, talk right, look right, read right, consume right, play right. That is how to politically be the best person that you can hope to be. "The personal is political" instead of meaning that personal outcomes are largely a product of systemic relations and of impositions on us by structures way beyond the reach of each individual acting alone instead came to mean that all political phenomena arise from the accumulated personal choices of individuals acting alone. What needed to be addressed to win better conditions were primarily people's personal choices.

This trend has been partially embodied in many sides of contemporary thought and activism, not least, for example, in elements of what is called "third-wave feminism," "identity politics," "food politics," "lifestyle politics," and so on.

Consider vegetarian activists insulting others who eat meat, anti-imperialists sneering at others who root for a football team deemed militaristic, anticapitalists putting down a small businessperson, feminists, socialists, and all manner of leftists criticizing others who enjoy elements of popular culture, mighty left intellectuals putting themselves above others who read "lowbrow" materials.

It is true that we need to try to live our lives in accord with our values. But it is also true that our values need careful assessment for their own biases and that our own ways of orienting our lives to our values have to be understood as not being the only ways to do it, or the best ways to do it, but most often just as our particular ways to do it. We need to abide and respect others who find other ways to live out good values. We can have patience and respect for those who are carving out ways of living in less (or more) propitious circumstances than we enjoy.

More, the impetus to wise, isolated, personal choices cannot replace the need for joining in collective acts and structures. "The personal is political" should mean society largely imposes our personal lives on us. We can change our personal lives only through collective action against unjust social relations.

And what does this have to do with movement stickiness? If you join a project—much less a movement to make a better world—and then a large part of your existence becomes being hassled and hassling others for their personal choices, moralistically judging and being judged, most often abstractly, without sympathy, without understanding, how long does it take to get fed up and move on? Not long. And what are your chances of attracting lots of people to join you? Not good.

And what is to be done about it? Common sense and mutual respect. You wear my shoes and I will wear yours before we claim we are debasing our beings by making constrained choices in complex settings. Let's bring back the real meaning of "the personal is political" and jettison the judgmental meaning.

Reform Can Be Strategic

One of the abiding issues of political, and particularly revolutionary, strategy is how to relate to reforms. To see if there are any near universal insights on the matter, first we need to get clear about some definitions.

A reform is a change in society that doesn't alter basic defining institutional relations. Getting higher wages is a reform. So is affirmative action. So is ending a war, changing tax rates, and so on.

Reformism, by contrast, is an approach to social change that takes for granted that basic defining relations are not going to change. Reformism seeks to win reforms, maybe lots of them, and reforms are the only end sought by reformism.

Rejecting Reform Means No Victory

To reject reforms as being insubstantial, insufficient, ignorant, etc. is to take a callous, uncaring, and even heartless stance for insubstantial and insufficient reasons. Yes, that is certainly a harsh judgment. And, yes, we know that rejecting reforms is an almost reflex position of many of the most committed and courageous activists currently engaged on the world stage. Nonetheless, we contend it is horribly wrong. Why?

To be against reforms is to say I am against demonstrating to end a particular war. It is to be against strikes to win better wages or conditions. It is to be against campaigns against pollution or global warming. It is to be against rallies for affirmative action or reparations. Very few who say they are against reforms are, in fact, against reforms. Virtually all of them would celebrate any victory of the sort just listed—even if no change of basic social relations occurred. But, by saying they are against reforms—by calling those who seek reforms ignorant or uncommitted—these same people exude a feeling of aloof callousness, as if they believe that reducing suffering is beneath their attention and unworthy of their effort. So to be against reforms—even if unintentionally and unknowingly—can be callous.

It is also insubstantial, meaning it is based on literally nothing of demonstrable weight. Instead, it typically arises from feeling that to be for a reform means one cannot be—now, or even ever—for more thorough and complete transformation. To favor reform, the feeling runs, negates any potential for favoring revolution. There is, however, zero logical or experiential evidence for such a claim. Of course some people who favor reforms don't favor revolution, just like some people who favor Facebook don't favor revolution. Does that mean to favor Facebook precludes favoring revolution? Some people who favor free access to clean water don't favor revolution. Does that mean to favor free access to clean water precludes favoring revolution?

Of course not. There is no connection between favoring Facebook or clean water and not favoring revolution. But what is the connection between favoring an end to a war, a higher wage for some workforce, or affirmative action or reparations and not favoring revolution? Of course some who favor clean water reject revolution. Some who favor Facebook reject revolution. Some who favor reform reject revolution. Favoring clean water is probably completely neutral vis-à-vis favoring revolution. Favoring things like an end to war, higher wages for workers, affirmative action, and pollution controls is arguably one component of favoring revolution—or very nearly so. In other words, the link between favoring reforms and not favoring revolution is insubstantial, as is the rejection of reforms on that basis.

People do not typically arrive at rejecting society's fundamental institutions in one giant leap. It often involves steps, or stages, during which one learns about society and about oneself, very often by way of movements seeking to win reforms—antiwar movements, women's movements, labor movements, no nukes movements, civil rights movements, and more. It is often not until one has experience with these movements and their limited goals that one decides the whole system is rotten to the core and needs to be replaced. If no one was seeking reforms—and no one ever had—then virtually no one would be revolutionary.

So to reject reforms is not only callous and insubstantial, it is also tantamount to rejecting revolution by rejecting aspects of the processes by which revolutionary movements are born, tempered, strengthened, and educated.

Advocating Reformism Also Means No Victory

The real reason activists reject reforms and use the word pejoratively is not because they reject reform, but because they rightly reject reformism. But they wrongly lump that very astute stance into a bundle with a self-defeating stance that rejects reforms themselves.

Reformism, by definition, rejects revolution. It says we are seeking an end to a war, and then will go home. We are seeking higher wages, and then will go home. We are seeking to shut down one coal plant or to force employers to hire minorities or to get wheelchair access in some public buildings and will then go home. Reformism says society's basic institutions are here to stay. They are a given, the basis of reality. We cannot touch them. Reformism says the only gains possible are those that take for granted those institutions. In fact, reformism typically says that to seek to alter those institutions is counterproductive. It drains energy by seeking to win specific reforms in a hopeless Sisyphean pursuit of the impossible.

Reformism comes in many shapes and forms, but we can perhaps best differentiate two main ones. Adherents of the first truly believe what they are saying—which is that basic institutions will last forever and that the only way to better the lot of society's worst off is to ameliorate their pains with reforms. And that is what many revolutionaries do not want to hear. People who think this can be just as caring, have just as fine values, and be just as courageous as the finest revolutionaries—and, indeed, can even be more caring and courageous.

To care about oppression doesn't imply believing basic institutions can be replaced. To have wonderful values doesn't imply believing basic institutions can be replaced. To be courageous doesn't imply believing basic institutions can be replaced. In fact, I can believe basic institutions cannot be replaced—even though I may wish more than anything that that wasn't true—and have fine values and be courageous, including working hard to win reforms and, again depending on my sincere beliefs, even literally opposing attempts at revolution. To be disdainful, even of reformists, is, again, insubstantial and ignorant, because the reformist one is disdainful of may be of the type just described—which most probably are. We should also note that the fact that these caring, motivated, and courageous folks are not revolutionaries is, ironically, a commentary not on them but on revolutionaries' failures to make a compelling case for the possibility of systemic transformation.

So is the activist pejorative inclination about reformists completely idiotic? No, because the second type of reformist may care and be courageous but not have fine values and ultimately be dishonest. This type of reformist rejects the possibility of revolution. Perhaps it is out of fear of revolution. It could be not liking that revolution would run contrary to this kind of reformists' own interests or it could be allegiance to a dominant constituency or class that bends their beliefs. But the point is, they don't wish that basic institutions could be altered. They don't adopt a reformist stance only because revolution sincerely appears utterly impossible to them, though they would be ecstatic to be proved wrong. Rather, they don't want to rock the boat or don't want new basic institutions but just want to ameliorate some of the worst pains—often only to ward off resistance and dissent and not out of true solidarity.

This latter type of reformism is what revolutionary activists rebel against but often in a ham-handed manner that indiscriminately includes unworthy targets—which is to say, sincere reformists. Still, it is certainly true that to become reformist for whatever reason means one is not seeking to transform basic institutions, so by definition, advocating reformism means rejecting revolution.

Nonreformist Reform Struggle Contributes to Victory

So, if it is revolutionary suicide to reject reforms but it is also revolutionary suicide to be reformist, what is the solution?

It is to reject reformism and embrace changing basic institutions. But it is also to fight for reforms in a way that seeks to change basic institutions. What does that mean?

For almost any reform, one can fight for it in a reformist manner that assumes preservation of the surrounding defining institutions. You demand the reform, raise consciousness about it—but about nothing more—and form organizations geared to winning it—but to winning nothing more. You work until you have generated sufficient power for the reform— at which point you go home.

Conversely, it is also possible to fight for almost any reform in a manner that is not reformist but radical or revolutionary. You not only demand the reform and raise consciousness about it, you also raise correlated issues that engender system-defying attitudes and understanding. You form organizations geared to winning the reform but also to persisting long after it is won. You work until you have generated sufficient power to win the reform, and then you fight for further gains in a trajectory leading to a whole new social structure.

Sometimes a reform itself—what is demanded—can be better or worse from the perspective of long-term gains and winning a new system. And, likewise, also for choices made and practices undertaken in the campaign to win the reform. For example, take fighting against a particular war. Do you, in the process, build opposition to the imperial causes of war and to the underlying economic and political and social institutions that propel war policies? Do you, in the process, build movement allegiance and organization that will persist when the opposed war ends? These are no small matters. On this difference hinges the difference between acting on caring, good values, and courage and having an impact that lasts or doing the same but having an impact that dissipates.

Seeds of the Future in the Present

There is a well-known anarchist slogan that says we need to plant the seeds of the future in the present. This is another strategic insight that is virtually universally applicable. What does it mean? It means build structures and projects and organizations in the present that incorporate as many key aspects as possible of the future you hope to win. But what does this mean more specifically? And why is this advisable?

What it means depends on what your long-term goals are—on your vision. Why it is advisable is basically because you want to attain those goals not goals you don't seek. The idea is that attaining our goals requires that we have sufficient informed, committed support. And it requires that we actually implement changes consistent with the goals—about which we learn more as we proceed—by building as we go.

To Learn

We incorporate structures into our projects, movements, and campaigns that embody aspects of our future aims in part to learn whether our ideas have merit. It is not a pure test, because we only have a part of our future embodied, because we are not yet future people, because the rest of the environment of the test is typically hostile to it. Nonetheless, if we are careful, patient, and take account of variables we can learn about the merits or the failings of our ideas.

Consider participatory economics. With that guiding our choices, we could implement elements of, or even a full version of, balanced job complexes in our work, in some project or a movement office, and beyond. Having done so, we understand that people have backgrounds that are contrary to it, that they have constant pressures all around that are contrary to it, including persistent markets, for example. But we can still learn about its merits. And the same holds for other structural features we may advocate attaining. So we plant seeds to learn the properties of the emergent plants and, if we discover problems, we can fix them.

To Grow and Empower

Part of our vision is participation and empowerment. This is, however, also essential for movements in struggle. If future structures are meant to convey those results to people in the future, why can't employing those structures, however partially, convey those results to us in the present? We have to try it to know if it will work, but it is surely a good bet. For example, we want a movement that is culturally welcoming for all communities, in which women are full participants, in which men are not made "macho," in which there is class-lessness, and so on. Part of why we try to incorporate future structures now is precisely because in the future we want the worthy results those structures are meant to convey, and we want those results, as best we can get them, now.

The idea is simple enough. If our vision has merit, even its partial implementation—planting its seeds—should convey some of its benefits, not just later but now. This will enrich the lives of people in our movements, give them more reason to stay, make them better able to attract others, reason well and without bias, and so on. So we plant tomorrow's seeds today, so that our movements can enjoy some of the fruits of the future now.

What fruits? Equity, solidarity, mutual aid, diversity, and self-management. Our movements, for example, can borrow from the approaches in our visions for handling responsibilities, for disbursing benefits, for making decisions.

To Inspire

When activists say they despise oppression and seek liberation, why should anyone believe us? When we say another world is possible, again, why should anyone believe us? Every politician on the planet says these things and we, the Left, say they lie. When we say these things, why shouldn't people deduce that we lie?

Well, actually, when someone says they are against oppression, when they say another world is possible, look at their practice and at what they advocate and call desirable. See if it is part of the current world, part of oppression. If so, do not believe their claim. The advocate of slave owning in the name of freedom is not worthy of belief. The advocate of wage slavery in the name of plenty is not worthy of belief. But if someone claims to be against oppression and argues that another world is possible, and the person advocates institutions consistent with that claim, and, even in the present, seeks to embody seeds of those institutions, then there is reason to listen carefully, look closely, and perhaps even believe.

A reason for incorporating the seeds of the future in the present is, in part, to inspire hope, trust, and desire.

To Get Where We Want to Go

Suppose we do not embody the seeds of the future in our endeavors. We get to the point of actually winning against opponents of change. Then what? We have no practice with new ways of organizing life. We have no experience with new ways of living. We know how to struggle but not how to live in new ways. We haven't embodied in our efforts new structures meant for a new society.

There is a great danger we will carry over the entrenched forms within our movements of struggle—which did not embody the seeds of a better future—into the new future we want to create. We will squander victory, turning it into failure.

Power Priorities

The issue in this section is how movements should deal with issues of power and its dispersal within the movement, as well as with power outside the movement. Are there any general insights that are universally valid, or nearly so, so that the advisories they imply are powerful and ought to be abided?

Power Corrupts

The famous formulation that power corrupts and absolute power corrupts absolutely is often repeated but rarely fully understood or effectively acted on. The claim is clear enough. But why does power corrupt?

There are three broad avenues of answer.

- The first is that power conveys the ability to enrich self and that is an enticement that few can resist. Thus, with power comes a shift of attention away from broad and worthy aims toward self-advancement. This interpretation says we need to vest power in particular people—so the solution is to erect barriers that prevent power's misuse for personal gain. This, when done well—which is hard to accomplish given that the powerful tend to obstruct the effort—can reduce corruption. But even when done well, it does not solve the more basic problems.

- Second, imagine that considerable power rests in a few hands. They have that power in everyone's view—including those holding power—not for personal aggrandizement and not to benefit some small constituency but for the greater good. Whether the argument is efficiency, coherence, or the brilliance and integrity of the relative few holding considerable power, the idea is that it is done to benefit the whole society. But this leads to those with power feeling that having the power is critically important. Challenges to it are antisociety. The mentality that emerges is not a flexible willingness and eagerness for participation and change but a bunker-like defensiveness warding off participation and change. The corruption is the elevation of self above society—even if it is done in the name of society and with full belief that society, not self, is the beneficiary.

- Third—and this one is perhaps least discussed and most germane in many instances—having disproportionate power leaves the holder with a problem. Looking in the mirror, how do they explain it? One explanation—the power isn't really for me, I am just holding it temporarily for all—may at first sustain the person's humility. But, in time, it becomes clear that this isn't enough of an explanation. Why am I holding it? The answer is not that I am lucky. Not that I grabbed it but that I deserve to hold it. I am smarter and more worthy. This is power corrupting by leading to delusions of personal grandeur. The inflated self-perceptions then fuel greater and greater excesses, and the bunker and aggrandizing issues arise.

And, of course, all of that is only about the trajectory from having some power in a few hands to more power in those few hands and how this leads to a distortion of motives and actions by the powerful. Even in the rare instance that the distortions don't arise, however, there is still a fundamental problem—the loss of power and participation and eventually wherewithal of those at the top. This has two harmful effects. First, any inadequacies of thinking and insight by those relative few with power goes less and less challenged. And second, the wisdom of the populace is excluded, which means most people are not having a say in the decisions that affect them. They are not just excluded but subordinated and ruled. The escalating centralization of power destroys not only self-management but democracy of any sort.

The corrective advisory, of course, is to try to avoid centralizing power in a few hands, particularly for any extended time. Dispersing power consistent with people's levels of involvement, commitment, and the extent they are affected by decisions is obviously ideal in any project, organization, or event. But when that is impossible due to outside pressures, lack of time, lack of preparedness, or whatever else, there should still be a high burden of proof on deviations from self-management and great care—when deviations must be implemented—that they are done in ways which protect individuals and movements from too long a time enduring corrupting influences. Likewise, the structural defense of dissidence, challenge, and debate, as well as provisions for recall and replacement of those overly powerful, need to be strong.

Weakness Debilitates

If power corrupts, and it does tend to do so, it is also true that weakness debilitates. There is only so long that a movement can function well when it is not affecting broader outcomes. People begin to doubt the efficacy of their efforts. This questioning tends to look within for a manageable opponent whenever those outside the movement seem too big to affect. Or whenever questioning leads to doubt, depression, and exodus from involvement. But the reality is that a movement, especially when starting out, doesn't have the strength to affect broader outcomes. So what can be done to prevent the ills of feeling weak?

The odd answer is: set aims that are attainable, albeit difficult, and use accomplishing those aims as the basis for evaluation. But also have as aims alterations that lead toward influencing society more broadly, however modestly at first. This includes, of course, recruitment and the enriching of the commitment of those already involved—both very real achievements on the road to further changes.

The short of it is this: if strategy involves consciousness-raising, construction, and contestation, then whatever stage one is at, whatever mix of those themes one is pursuing, judgments must focus there—not on distant aims that aren't yet in range.

Weakness should debilitate—but not misestimated weakness. Weakness is relative to where one ought to be at the moment, not where one seeks to be later. If the current agenda is to grow from tiny to small, generate some organizational structure, generate some fledgling projects—while the goal is a new society—then measuring one's achievements against winning a new society now is simply suicidal. The gap will be enormous, appearing even larger as one tries to measure and judge, and the debilitation will be profound. Measuring against the immediate agenda, however, should yield feelings of achievement and sometimes, when falling short, inform new choices.

There is one caveat. After all that was said above about what is and what isn't weakness and the need to measure against what is possible/sensible in the present, one must also always have in mind the ultimate element. Vision needs to inform the current agenda. So the psychologically hard part is to have in mind long-term aims—one's vision—yet not feel depleted by the distance to reach it.

Having such a mind-set in practice proves difficult. And the number of folks who either jettison vision completely— being brought down by its distance from achievement and wanting to eliminate that downer—or who retain vision but become debilitated by feelings of weakness is usually very high. Addressing this head-on to avoid the problem is a wise part of building a movement.

Finally, a movement that ignores power, even as it grows, and that never invests the agenda of the moment with efforts to exert power in changing immediate conditions is a movement that will eventually succumb to debilitation. Power corrupts, but the absence of power debilitates. Sometimes this debilitation is unwarranted due to being based on false expectations and not seeing what, in fact, at the stage one is at, constitutes worthy achievement. Other times, however, the debilitation is real. Despite ample time for development, despite considerable successes in growth and construction of project and organization, despite long and informed efforts, still, there is nary a sign that the movement can affect outcomes, improve lives, alter conditions to not only be less oppressive but also begin a better stage for further gain. This type of powerlessness should feel horrible, and we should not construct movements in a manner that leads to it.

Worthy Power Empowers

Suppose we look not at the whole movement but at individuals—who are, after all, the locus of the "power corrupts" insight. Can the individual have power but not be corrupted by it? And is influence the same as power?

First, what corrupts is having more power than warranted, and then (a) rationalizing it with an inflated view of self and a deflated view of others and (b) feeling one is not only responsible to enact good things but better able to do so than others, so that one must forcefully protect one's excessive power against criticism and dissent.

The answer to our first question seems clear enough. A person can have power up to the point of curtailing the comparable power of others. A person can influence events in proportion as they are affected by them, which permits others to do likewise. Worthy power, then, is that we each have decision-making options and responsibilities that are self-managing and respect that everyone should be welcomed to, prepared for, and expected to self-manage.

But what if you are fine with all that but lots of others abstain? They don't yet participate fully, or even at all. Or, even more so, suppose you have an organization that is just getting by—it has members but way less than it will have. This tends to leave your vote having more weight than it ought to or will in the future. The responsibility in that case is twofold. You can't magically force others to join immediately, or even jump in more fully. But you can work to make it so. You can see it as a priority, facilitate it, and understand it as the measure of your success in your own participation. And so long as it hasn't yet occurred, your other responsibility is to not simply exercise your vote in terms of your own desires. First, you might opt to hold decisions to a minimum, pending more people being involved. Second, if there are going to be decisions, your responsibility, to take an example, is to not take advantage of minority participation in decisions or low membership to cause things to go precisely where you might want. Instead, you can try to represent not only your own views but those of people who are missing but who should be and will, you hope, in time be involved.

These priorities, if held and acted on by a person who is participating and voting, will diminish the likelihood of their following the corruption path and will help empower others. Of course, there is a danger one will begin to think one can speak for others, but that too can be held in check. Worthy power empowers.

But what about influence? Here there is often some confusion. It is true that if Ted has more influence than others, then outcomes that Ted desires are more likely to be implemented than outcomes that others desire. But influence is not always power.

Power is that I get what I want simply because I want it— my will dominates not because others hear and agree but due to demand. Influence is that I get what I want because, after due deliberation, including hearing my views on it, others want it too. The former is forceful. The latter can be but may not be. What is the difference?

Well, the real issue is: Why am I more influential? If it is because I have some kind of structural advantage that others lack and cannot have and that advantage is constantly in play, then this is power. Suppose, for example, I have work that gives me greater skill, knowledge, contacts, and the like. Then when it is time to deliberate I have opinions and others do not have opinions. Decisions become choices about my views only. In this case, I have not just influence but power, because this is structurally asymmetrical, and not just in the moment but over long periods of time, from decision to decision.

Now take a different situation. Everyone is welcomed and facilitated in ways that ensure that they are able to participate, understand issues, and have opinions. But an issue comes up and because it is your area of involvement, you have more experience, etc. So you are more influential in the deliberations because others see your opinion and information as being quite relevant. This influence is not general power. And trying to eliminate this kind of influence differential is incredibly counterproductive.

What if someone is just good at thinking things through, and so in a free and open discussion their views predominate more often than others'? This is not power, it is influence. Yet it can be problematic if we get so used to it that we take for granted the person will be right and stop our own thinking, or if the person comes to feel they deserve obedience, for example. But it is not structural power, and attentiveness should be enough to offset negative potentials. We don't want to curtail good ideas, of course, but we want to be sure other ideas have opportunity to surface.

As a stark example, you go to the doctor and get a diagnosis. The doctor's knowledge and experience mean that his influence on your choice of medical regimen will be great—greater, perhaps, than even your own. But this influence is warranted, and if it does not aggrandize the doctor or get translated into material or other benefits and is not generalizable to other issues, it is desirable—of course, assuming that the actual decisions are self-managed, albeit highly influenced by the doctor's insights. On the other hand, if doctors use their excess of experience and knowledge in medicine to control general outcomes or to unduly aggrandize themselves or selected others, then there is a power issue.

Similarly, suppose in some workplace someone is really good at and communicates clearly about policy issues. At meetings everyone may want to hear from that person and that person's observations may often percolate through discussions into compatible policy choices. Again, this is influence not power, so long as it is not due to the person occupying roles that constantly convey greater knowledge and decision associated skills, so long as room for other views is not diminished, so long as there are no "voting" advantages, and so long as no material or structural benefits arise.

So the task is—as we have done with vision—to be sure that our strategies allow movements and organizations to benefit from highly informed participants who may, as a result, sometimes be more influential, yet to preserve self-managing, disallow personal aggrandizement, and ensure that all participants, while not equally informed about all things, nonetheless are generally adequately informed and confident enough to arrive at and express their own desires.

The Movement and Government

All the above leads to the big strategic issue bearing on power. How should a movement relate to existing governments? We are not here speaking of a movement that is literally creating a new polity with new virtues after having won and transformed society, but rather a movement considering the possibility of entering into and having to, in part, maintain an existing government, using its existing mechanisms, while trying to enlarge public benefits through those mechanisms—which were, of course, constructed for entirely different aims.

First, what are the central factors? Addressing only the most prominent, the first factor is the possibility that participating in existing governance—much less running it, whatever benefits it may deliver—can corrupt and make authoritarian those directly involved. Even just running for office can, of course, have these effects, since the process involves pumping up your own qualifications and perhaps running a party organization in which people follow your lead and serve your candidacy.

The second factor, as addressed above, is that not participating can marginalize and weaken.

The third factor is quite different. Existing governments have to, in part, maintain existing systems of political stability and viability. So, whether participating in or running an existing government, part of the task—which must be done at risk of failing to maintain relations that need to be maintained for people's well-being—is to administer existing structures unless or until transformed structures exist. This task, however, has virtually nothing to do with changing society, even if it meets needs. And it can take away from trying to change society by using up energies and people in maintenance and, even worse, by causing people to become what they do—maintainers not transformers, reformers not revolutionaries.

Thus, getting involved in government distracts from agendas of change to the extent it involves mainly maintenance instead of dissent and new construction, which it almost always does. To give just one example, in Brazil the Workers' Party was a very powerful grassroots entity working for change, dissenting, demonstrating, and building. Then, starting in a couple of cities and a particular Brazilian state, the party won government office—including mayor and governor and associated positions. Responsibility for the day-to-day affairs of governance—now in the old government structures—channeled most of the highly experienced movement actors into roles of maintenance not opposition, of delivery not change. The result was a loss of their energies, a loss of contact with radical emotion and desire, and a burgeoning commitment to system stability. By the time the Workers' Party founding member Luiz Inácio Lula da Silva won the presidency, there was a very stark indicator of what it might bring. His party—and movement—was, in that same election, voted out of power in the state it had been ruling for some time. In other words, even as they advanced in popularity nationally, locally, where they were administering the existing state, and where they had been strongest, they lost support. The reason was that they had lost their roots, ties, and agenda and could not deliver much using the old structures. This same scenario may have been unfolding in Bolivia over the past few years.

In Venezuela, in contrast, the third factor seems like perhaps it is being addressed/avoided, as the government continues to aid and promote the construction of new social relations, rather than entrenching those of the past. On the other hand, the issues of corruption (misuse of powers) and authoritarianism seem also to exist. There is the strange situation of steady gains in structures of participation, alongside steady growth of central power—with benefits due to the agenda being pursued alongside debits due to the dangers of entrenchment and elitism, and even sectarianism, dogmatism, and authoritarianism.

Typically, a movement can choose to relate to a government in many ways.

It can become part of it, or at least try to—typically by running for office. This has the serious debits mentioned above.

It can also advise a government by making suggestions to it—trying to communicate via reason. This has those same debits, although a bit less so, and another as well—delusion about the motives of existing elites. They do not care about our good sense, morals, etc. They have structural agendas.

Trying to force a government by making demands and seeking to compel the government to comply—even though it would not do so on its own—does not intrinsically have any of the above debits and is a natural path to exercising some power and influence—winning some changes, however modest—even at a point of a movement having relatively small size. Later, when movements are far more powerful, getting major changes via coercing existing government (rather than becoming part of it or advising it) intrinsically carries none of the dangers mentioned. But it also doesn't provide a direct kind of power that may be desired to enact changes.

There are no ironclad rules that will always apply. Different situations can make these options have different costs and dangers or different benefits and prospects. The best we can say, we think, is that to rule out or rule in approaches a priori is mistaken. To argue about participating or not, as if it is a mark of being for a better future or not, is mistaken. But there is a considerable burden of proof in taking up electoral participation—or participation in government itself. Developing movements that can compel existing governments to make desired changes is a somewhat safer path.

Here is a somewhat unusual example of a still different approach to government. Imagine the next presidential elections in the U.S. are over. Short of massive social transformations, the new president, who is minutely different from or still the old president, is waiting eagerly to commit domestic and international mayhem on behalf of his favored elite constituencies.

Suppose during the campaign movement candidates also ran—not to win but to educate. Suppose they did pretty well, say, garnering 5 percent of the vote, with many more who liked them best but who voted for a likely winner. Could that participation have been a worthwhile endeavor? The upside would have been, up to the day of the election, some education, perhaps in debates and public speeches, for larger than otherwise accessible audiences. The downside would have been the possible corruption of key participants, hierarchicalization of the movement around them, and channeling of energies and focus into the election not grassroots activism. If the left candidates basically stopped their activity on election day, and if the organizing in various states led to no lasting structures, odds are it wasn't worth it. But what if a different approach was considered and pursued?

Let's make it more real. What if after the 2012 presidential election in the U.S., Green presidential candidate Jill Stein, vice presidential candidate Cheri Honkala, the Green Party candidates for Congress, and party organizers, having run a campaign that inspired large audiences all across the U.S.—including having built apparatuses in many states—announced that they were establishing a shadow government, with Stein and Honkala at the head? They also announce a set of cabinet members (secretary of state, labor, etc.), a staff (press secretary, etc.), and a list of senators across the country—all worked out with the Green movement and whatever other movements may have been centrally involved in the prior campaigns. They announce a website that includes not only the biographies of the shadow officials and a statement by each regarding their aims and priorities, as well as forums for ongoing discussion, a sign-up mechanism to receive future communications, and an extensive, compelling display of ongoing shadow government policy priorities and positions contrasted to those of the actual government.

Then suppose that every week, starting with the inauguration in January, the shadow government website is augmented with at least three types of material:

- commentary on the major U.S. government undertakings for that week and on what the shadow government would have done differently on those matters—not constrained but operating precisely as it would if it were in power throughout the government—and the estimated difference in impact between the shadow choices and those of Washington;

- a presentation of what the shadow government would have undertaken/initiated differently from the actual government, explaining why the Washington government is unlikely to embark on similar actions and what the public gains would have been had the shadow government been able to pursue its very different aims;

- a summary contrasting the overall impact of the two governments for the week—plus a cumulative summary of major differences for the year to date.

Of course, the site could have sections relating to various spheres of social life—the economy, politics, cultural issues, family matters, foreign policy, and the ecology, for example. There could be sections for each person in the cabinet and for the president's staff and the senate. There could also be new appointments for the Food and Drug Administration and other regulatory agencies, as well as for financial institutions, courts, and so on.

There could be a section for a state of the week speech, given by Stein, with a press conference that would be broadcast on diverse independent radio stations, as well as being made available on the website.

Special events could also occur, such as a shadow inauguration, shadow state of the nation address, shadow press conferences broadcast over the site and to the press directly, shadow Senate votes, shadow Supreme Court appointments, shadow budget presentations and hearings, and even shadow White House cultural events, for example.

The shadow government site could include audio speeches and texts as well as ongoing dialogue between shadow government officials and the public in cumulative forum systems and live chat sessions. There could also be live speeches, live town hall meetings, gatherings of groups to discuss and make proposals, and so on.

The whole operation could educate the public on what the U.S. government actually does, on what its impact is, and especially on what an alternative progressive government would have done were it in office and free to pursue truly popular policies. The site would provide a record on which dissident candidates could run next time around. The site, press conferences and public campaigns, demonstrations, teach-ins, and other events would be a thorn in the side of elite government and, more important, an educational resource and organizing tool in the U.S.—and probably around the world—to create movements for pushing the actual government.

Now let's ramp it up. Imagine it was all fueled at every level by the kinds of views espoused in *Fanfare for the Future*. In that case, while it might start as noted above, it would quickly incorporate as a key aspect another set of aims—accountability, participation, self-management. The structures employed would bend toward local assemblies and means of voting and otherwise developing views that are participatory. Not only would the endeavor be about revealing the horrors of the incumbent officials within existing structures, it would also be about building new contrasting structures and thus planting the seeds of the future in the present.

Would all this replace getting out and organizing? Of course not. But the idea of a shadow government with shadow events, policies, statements, and results so people can judge if they want something far more radical than Washington offers, and then even with new structures and methods exemplifying more revolutionary aims, has a democratic, participatory, and engaging aura about it. The potential for developing in diverse directions is obvious, including public debates and teach-ins around the shadow government material and related activist challenges to the real government, to media, and to other institutions seeking the type of change people desire, and the construction of assemblies, and more.

What would be the obstacle to doing this? Well, the technology is easy enough. There is effort and creativity required, a lot of energy and ingenuity, but the project wouldn't have to cost too much in dollars and could even involve recompense for those giving lots of time. Since there is no dearth of good people to fill the cabinet posts, presidential staff, courts, joint chiefs, even the whole Senate, the only real difficulty is (a) the desire to do it and (b) getting along, coming to agreements, and being okay about going with X when some people prefer Y or even Z.

If we are going to win social change, eventually our movements will need to generate coherence, at least about short-term critique of events and immediate positive programs. Wouldn't this be an invigorating and productive way to do it?

There are lots of procedures that could be used. Even the worst option would probably be better than nothing: Stein or whoever appointing "from the top" all the officials and having the kind of overarching influence on choices that a real president does. Not ideal, with many risks of the sort discussed earlier. It would be better still, of course, for various parts of the undertaking to be overseen by appropriate grassroots organizations and projects interacting democratically and with relative autonomy in their own domains and then literally constructing new structures—in essence, creating not a shadow government, but a new kind of polity.

In any event, given the potentials as they now are, the first step would likely be for movements to decide they want to do it, for the movements to settle on candidates for high office and to choose a cabinet and other central appointments, and for the new shadow cabinet and as many other appointed officials as possible to together decide how to deal with each week's critical postings and policy and other determinations.

The above is merely one attempt at thinking through a possible way of relating to elections and government—in this case, trying to avoid debits and maximize benefits. Does it make sense? This is not an abstract question—it would or wouldn't, depending on actual conditions at the time. Can the dissident candidates garner 5 percent of the vote? Can a coherent shadow government be formed? Would its ideas galvanize support, educate, and mobilize? Would those voting for it immediately be positive about it, including donating some regular amount each month to help fund its operations? Would it be able to take the next step from good policies to new and vastly better political structures?

Deciding on any approach to power is contextual, though with certain insights about dangers and benefits highly likely to be relevant.

No Organization, No Victory

Social change is very rarely dependent on individuals acting largely, much less fully, alone. Rather, it depends on large groups, typically called movements. But for groups to have collective impact they have to operate with cohesion, at least in their major undertakings. This means when choices arise, movements have to arrive at shared decisions and enact those decisions collectively, likely with many different responsibilities for different members. They also have to have what we might call memory. Lessons learned need to be applied, which means they need to be preserved from one day, week, month, and year to the next. That way each new participant doesn't start from a state of ignorance but is able to quickly imbibe the insights prior participants have amassed. Without memory, there is no learning and no improving. Without cohesion, no power.

All of this is abetted, indeed made possible, by organization. Without organization, little can be achieved. With it, much can be achieved. But what attributes must desirable organization embody?

What to Attain

This depends on the purpose. What does the group desire to accomplish? Suppose it is a one-off endeavor where the group wishes to build something quite limited or block something or disrupt something—what have you—one time. The organization can obviously be quite minimal. There is not much cohesion and unity and not much memory needed, as the effort is not very complex and lasts a relatively short time.

But suppose the group instead wishes to engage in a sustained, long-term project, with much complexity and great need for effective action based on powerful insights. Now the situation is very different. Somehow the group must share an agenda and insights, for the present as a program and over the long haul as a vision. Memory is now critical. So too is the means to dispute differences and arrive at shared choices and views about what is sought and how to attain it.

Efforts to create a new society are quite obviously of the second type. So the group needs a means of making decisions, of working, of learning, and of preserving insights—and it needs these means to be well suited to its agenda, rather than having implications contrary to it. It needs shared tools of conception and implementation based on clarity about current situations and on sought-after vision.

This may all seem obvious, but the above advisory is rarely so explicitly stated and acted upon as here, despite being of fundamental importance.

Since our particular endeavor is to create a new participatory society, with a parecon, parpolity, participatory kinship, and participatory culture (as per *Fanfare for the Future, Volume 2: Occupy Vision*), this means we need an organization that will facilitate and meld into the institutional aims and conscious-ness aims we have for society.

So the resulting organizational advisory is for us to have a movement institution with roles that—by their implications for our behavior—promote diversity, solidarity, justice, equity, self-management, sustainability, and internationalism and that will sustain a program doing the same. And it is to have a movement institution with roles that—by their implications for behaviors—generate and sustain feminist, intercommunal-ist, antiauthoritarian—or, perhaps better put, self-managing and classlessness-seeking consciousness, both for its members and for those encountered outside.

This means having an organization that plants the seeds of the future in the present. One that, therefore, has a suffi-cient visionary commitment to know what constitutes seeds of the future and what doesn't, and an organization that—even as it has to deal with the historical legacy of the past, and has to overcome the obstructions that existing institutions and harmful consciousness impose on current choices—constantly pushes toward its sought-after shared future vision as best as circumstances permit.

This would be an organization that challenges external hierarchies by its operations and that excludes them in its own internal composition. An organization that has self-managing means of decision-making and that has mecha-nisms to preserve and benefit from a diversity of views and actions. An organization that internally develops the struc-tures it advocates for the society outside, which also means schooling its members in using all these congenially and effectively. An organization able to share sufficient insights and lessons from the past and to preserve sufficient differ-ences of opinion and paths for the entire operation to, in sum, move forward steadily, without getting mired in or blocked by obstructions.

Strategy Begets Tactics

Tactics are not forever. They are chosen at a moment, in a place, and typically for a short duration. Tactics include canvassing, leafleting, holding teach-ins, having classes, holding rallies, having marches, occupations, modes of making decisions, ways of describing self and others, and, yes, civil disobedience, rioting, even burning and fighting.

The importance of tactics has to do with whether they aid or subvert sought-after aims and whether or not they fit into the preferred strategy.

The point of our examinations has been to add that the sought-after aims should always include:

- enlarging not diminishing movement size;
- enriching not constraining movement intelligence;
- strengthening not weakening movement resources and structures;
- building mutual aid not paranoia or distrust;
- weakening not abetting state power;
- educating and inspiring not confusing and alienating a broader population;
- winning reforms in a nonreformist way not rejecting reforms or adopting reformism;
- planting seeds of the future in the present not replicating the ills of the present and carrying them into the future;
- dealing with power in ways that empower not corrupt;
- building lasting organization that itself adds to all these positive trajectories.

It is a lot to account for. You cannot usefully nuggetize winning a new world.

CHAPTER 14

Still More Strategic Issues

"You may encounter many defeats,
but you must not be defeated."
—*Maya Angelou*

Perhaps the most obvious strategic observation one might make is that if you don't try to win, odds strongly favor your losing. More generally, attitudes to winning and losing can be pivotal to movement revolutionary prospects in diverse ways. Enlarging on that observation is our focus in this chapter. Hopefully the discussion will not sound overly like a self-help manual. These matters are, in fact, very serious.

Mind-set

What is in—and what should be in—our minds as we try to win a better world? That is the question.

Winning Is Not Everything

The thing about winning is, it is pretty hard to say just what we mean. We strike for higher wages. We demonstrate to stop a meeting. We rally for a law. We disobey for a policy. We demand to end a war. We call it a victory if what we sought is accomplished.

The trouble is, to win the battle does not mean winning the war. To attain a step forward does not even guarantee that we are ready to win more steps forward. That a victory can lead to a debacle is one thing, and is actually widely understood, though sometimes largely ignored. But we have something different in mind.

Suppose we hold massive gatherings at some site to stop a meeting of the IMF or NATO or whatever. We successfully interrupt the meeting, or maybe even get it canceled. We typically call this a victory and, to an extent, it is.

Or suppose we are in an electoral contest. We go to some state in our country for a presidential primary or some analogous vote, and we tally more dissident votes than anyone thought possible. Or we seek some office and garner sufficient votes to win it. We call these accomplishments a victory, and to a degree they are.

So what does "winning isn't everything" mean? In the first example, we cancel the meeting. Nice. But a canceled meeting is only a small setback for the institution we're fighting. We might have won a small skirmish. There is a still a whole war ahead. So did our participants come away empowered to seek more and other gains in the future? Did our organizational capacity increase? Did the broader public get positively informed? Are larger numbers of people than before interested in our efforts and receptive to supporting and joining us? Think back to movement examples from the past and ask yourself: Did movement commentary focus more on the proximate aim (for example, stopping a meeting) or on the lasting dynamics (for example, developing more activist infrastructure and support than before the events)?

In the second example, we tally lots of votes or win an office. Nice. Winning includes that. But again, one more progressive representative in a corporate-dominated government is not really our end goal. So do those who worked on the campaigns come away empowered to seek more in the future? Do we leave a new organizational infrastructure in our wake that is able to galvanize new campaigns? Did the broader public, even beyond the immediate voters, get positively informed? Are larger numbers than before interested in our efforts?

If the answers to these types of question are negative, then the proximate victory for our campaign, demand, office seeking, or whatever is relatively hollow. When planning, later discussing, or finally evaluating our experiences, to focus mainly on some proximate aim and whether it was accomplished will likely be a delimiting, debilitating mistake. We are not reformists where each effort exists unto itself. We are seeking a new society. Each effort either contributes to that, or it has fallen short.

Losing Is Not Nothing

Take the same examples as above, or any others. We sit in but are removed without shutting down our target. We occupy but are removed without retaining hold on our turf. We run for office but get a paucity of votes. We demand X but fail to win X. And so on.

We lost our proximate aim in each case. Not nice but not necessarily nothing. Did our efforts yield more supporters than before we started? In the broader public, did we induce increased receptivity? Were our participants and supporters uplifted, made more conscious, and empowered—not at the moment but into the future? Do we have better organization and understanding after than we had before the events? Have we prepared ourselves to mount stronger and deeper efforts in the future?

If the answers to these questions are yes, then the proximate loss is actually not a failure. In that case, losing is not nothing. Rather, losing, when these answers are positive, is hardly even an apt descriptor. On the main points, which are those bearing on the long haul, we won.

You Lose, You Lose, You Lose, You Win

The phrase "you lose, you lose, you lose, you win" comes from the German revolutionary Rosa Luxemburg. What does it mean?

You lose. You fail to attain some immediate goal. Let's say it is worse still, you not only miss the proximate goal, you don't amass more support, you don't generate raised consciousness, you don't construct or strengthen your means to seek more. Still, though the loss can be devastating—as in stopping you cold and having no apparent positive benefits—it can, nonetheless, also be a source of insights that inform your development, and by those lessons help lead to better outcomes in the future. That is one meaning of Luxemburg's words.

The second meaning is that you only need to win once. Never let a defeat, even a comprehensive defeat, serve as anything other than a spur to do better as soon as possible.

Developing Virtues

One mind-set is to regularly look at self and see only perfection, finding whatever you can praise and defending it unto death. A nearly opposite mind-set is to regularly look at self and recognize and enjoy achievement, but mostly to look for flaws and vigorously correct them. Like all the other points made in this chapter, this seems trivial and obvious. We are not perfect. We get better only by finding faults and making corrections. But, in practice, it is not so easy to do.

Ego gets in the way. Defensiveness and insecurity get in the way. Jockeying for status gets in the way. So does a feeling that admitting weaknesses and flaws will somehow undermine potential, whereas keeping quiet about or even hiding those and reporting only positive attributes, even exaggerating them, will enhance potentials. Wrongheaded but prevalent.

Consider a large-scale instance. People who were active in the 1960s movements often talk about the 1960s, sometimes writing about them. When doing so, especially for public consumption, there is a tendency to get very agitated that any critique will hurt prospects to seek change in the future. A rose-tinted picture will inspire. Shoot the bringer of bad reports. This is nonsense. If reports are accurate, they convey real information. If reports reveal inadequacies, they convey useful information that can inform changes. If, in fact, there were no big flaws, or few, as many chroniclers like to believe, then that would be very bad news. We did not win a new world. If we did everything optimally, without problems of our own, how could anyone later do anything better?

Finding a real flaw is good not bad, whether we are looking at past actions, organizations, or ideologies. A growth-oriented approach doesn't trash what is worthy, but it doesn't shy away from truthful reporting of flaws either. This is the road to enhancing strengths and removing weaknesses.

In reporting and addressing problems, however, there is a pitfall that needs to be avoided. It is addressing everything but that which we can actually affect, whining about it, we might almost say, and to no avail, or, even worse, instead of addressing what we can fix.

To be more specific, think of activists as having a certain amount of time and energy available to focus on understanding some problems and trying to address them. Arguably, everything insightful helps, but some things have a greater likelihood of mattering than others.

Bemoaning, for example, that authorities—police and others—will oppose one's actions gets nowhere. It is whining. So is, for example, bemoaning that mainstream media will not honestly—or at all—report your endeavors. One can certainly analyze these factors to death, but it leads nowhere, save perhaps into depression. What matters, instead, is thinking through viable routes forward despite the media and the authorities acting on their agendas.

One of the most frequent and rightly worrisome conditions of activist efforts is composition. On the one hand, are there enough people involved to succeed? On the other hand, is the background of people involved diverse enough and balanced enough among different sectors of people for success to actually capture the desires of all those impacted?

Worrying about this often entails people trotting out the facts of the situation and bemoaning them ad infinitum. Maybe this occurs just at the level of society's ills—society is racist, sexist, classist—and, as a result, we don't have enough blacks, women, or workers. Sometimes it goes another step: due to society's oppressive features, people in different constituencies are under different time pressures, have different expectations, feel different burdens, have different levels of confidence, and so on, and so turn out to provide leadership in different proportions. So far, though, the observations, however insightful, are merely bemoaning root causes. Another step, however, which takes the whole discussion in a different direction is to ask: What are we doing that is hurting turnout from underrepresented sectors, whatever they may be, in the movement? Or even better: What might we do that would increase turnout from underrepresented sectors? This provides the hope of accomplishing gains not just bemoaning problems, of overcoming whatever types of imbalance our efforts may be suffering.

Do Not Snatch Defeat from the Jaws of Victory

We understand society's power to restrain and even crush dissent, and, when that fails, to co-opt its efforts. The logic is simple. If movements seek some goal—X—and elites want to block attaining X, then they will work hard to do so, surreptitiously, overtly, covertly, every which way that they can get away with without unintentionally strengthening our dissent. Suppose, however, that they fail. They have to give in. They must grant X. What do they do?

Consider labor movement victories for union rights, higher wages, better work hours, and so on. Or consider green victories for pollution laws, cleanup efforts, and so on. Or feminist victories for fairer wages, affirmative action, abortion rights, and so on. Or antiracist victories for affirmative action or civil rights legislation, for example. Or peace victories that curtail violence, or even win peace. Whatever it may be, elites are not dumb. They play to win. But when they lose, they try to make the best of it. This takes two forms.

First, they take credit for the humane change that movements won. They pass a law or enact a policy or whatever, and they say they are doing it despite and not because of the movement. It is their largesse, despite the movement's insanity, that has enacted change, they say. The reason they do this is simple. They understand that if they can usurp credit from the movement to themselves, they can turn the tide of the events—causing the movement itself to feel alienated, weak, and timid—and, at the same time, gain kudos for themselves from the broader public. Indeed, by claiming credit for progressive changes, politicians can even steal loyalty from movements. People begin to believe that they must keep those politicians in power in order to keep the gains that have been made and achieve further gains, instead of realizing that they can rely on movements.

Movements should expect this. Movements should not see politicians and other officials claiming credit for what the movements have forced them to do and become frustrated and alienated and ill-disposed to persist. The aim wasn't, in the first place, to elicit elite praise. The aim was to win the change—which was achieved—and to develop the capacity to win more changes. So movements should not steal defeat from the jaws of victory by letting elites alienate, disparage, and diminish them. Instead, movements should clarify the truth and prove it by pushing ahead even more strongly.

The second way elites try to make the best of a bad situation is to try to co-opt, corrupt, or later reverse the situation. They will oppose unions with incredible vigor and violence, but when unions clearly are inevitable start to engage with them, seeking to buy them off, distort their agendas, etc. You can see it at every level. Vigorously support the dictator—most recently, for example, Mubarak in Egypt—until he clearly is doomed, then prioritize infiltrating and engaging with the opposition you were trying to forestall, seeking to delimit its aims and, in time, to corrupt its priorities and means.

If movements win wage increases against strenuous opposition, elites only lick their wounds briefly. Let's now raise prices and prepare to get back the advantage by any means available. Elites play to win and never stop playing. The movement response has to be to take a comparably long view, plus to seek a steady accrual of movement members, allies, and means—or any gains movements achieve will be perverted or rolled back. Of course, if movements are to defend even prior modest gains, much less attain full liberation, the ultimate logic is that, in time, one must transform society whose old institutions are the source of the rollback pressures.

Claim No Easy Victories

Amílcar Cabral, the great Cape Verdean revolutionary, cautioned, "Tell no lies; claim no easy victories." This has diverse meanings. "The truth is always revolutionary," the Italian revolutionary, Gramsci, said, and that is one meaning. But Cabral's version was that we should not only be honest with others but also with ourselves. To pat ourselves on the back in the deluded belief that doing so will enhance our appeal, or because we will then feel better, is mistaken. Worse, claiming that we are making great progress—having victories—when we are not is a self-delusion that precludes assessing our own weaknesses and failings so as to try to correct them. It is a road, therefore, to our failings multiplying and diversifying and enlarging—even as we are celebrating, up to the point of full and total defeat.

It may seem that this is so utterly obvious that no one could possibly miss the point. But that would be mistaken. Consider the peace movement. Demonstrations around the world prior to the invasion of Iraq numbered in the many millions, let's say twelve million, as many reports at the time concluded. As time went on, there were other demonstrations. Each time, many would claim victory due to the hard-won turnout. But these turnouts were not "easy victories," but, in truth, harsh defeats, because the numbers involved were declining dramatically, when they should have been rising. In the past decade nothing should have been a higher strategic priority in the moment than to understand the decline in antiwar turnout, and in finding its causes to reverse them.

One could give numerous similar examples, but let's take just one more, from Venezuela. The Bolivarian movement there, with each new election, celebrated not just winning but a giant victory for the movement. Yet in many of these elections the margin of victory declined, rather than climbing, and certainly did not climb as it ought to have, given that the movement is in office. So the movement claimed "easy victory," while ignoring the real attrition and its causes and implications.

In such celebrations of victories that really are evidence of decline—or at least less than ought to be present—lessons are rarely assembled, rectification of reasons for decline are barely, if at all, proposed. The other side, meanwhile, notices the trajectory not the final tally, and goes back to work.

Patience Is Necessary, Audacity Is Essential

Apocalyptic organizing is a widespread and very understandable problem. Indeed, many act like it is a virtue and use the inclination to exaggerate it, rather than trying to overcome it.

What it means is that we organize as if the world will literally end if what we are doing is not perfectly successful. We organize as if full victory must come now or disaster unfolds forever. We organize as if the lives of people will be lost if we don't do whatever we have set out to do—or what someone else has set out for us to do—right now. It isn't that the dangers and costs are unreal. They are real. It is the mode of trying to motivate people—not by what can be achieved by the clarity and wisdom of the aims and the validity and prospects of the means, but simply by repeating, sometimes even exaggerating, the magnitude of the issues at stake.

More, we sometimes organize as if what we are urging is not only, without question, priority one, is not only the only moral thing to do, but also, as if our doing it will solve all problems, end injustice forever, and so on.

We have no long view. We have no patience. We are constantly urgent. We act like the world is heading for a cliff, and if the person we are trying to reach, or we ourselves, don't jump in and grab it, it will go over. We lose track of multiform variables and focus only on some proximate aim, which, in worst cases, is even rhetorically inflated to the point of being delusional.

This is the opposite of a sober and careful approach. It is the opposite of an informed sense of proportion. It is often even the opposite of honesty. Apocalyptic organizing may attract some reckless folks to act, but it does not build lasting and informed commitment and insight. Nor does it retain a sense of what success really is, and thus attention to the many variables that one must address to win lasting gains.

If every appeal of this sort over the past fifty years had been accurate the world would have literally expired many times over. Similarly, if every event or action that was organized on the grounds it would win gigantic change in and of itself—so that only a fool would refrain—had the attributes it claimed, then we would have won gigantic change over and over.

But the fact is, the world hasn't ended, and gigantic change on the heels of single projects has never occurred. What has occurred instead is people learning to discount movement rhetoric, including becoming skeptical of the integrity of movement organizers, and even movement people themselves, vested in their own rhetoric, becoming despondent when promises fail to materialize.

At the same time, what makes it hard to be patient and sober rather than apocalyptic about reality is that we also need to be audacious. It is a hard combination.

Audacity requires that we repeatedly challenge widely accepted norms. It means that we seek ends that seem distant. It means we stare at tremendous obstacles and ask, simply, which route will get us through, however long it may take. Audacity is the underdog who never for a moment gives the slightest thought to surrender, but who also never denies the real conditions at hand. What is hard is to be audacious but admit reality.

Envisioning Victory Is Useful

One aspect of audacity is not about behavior but about thought. It is a kind of method. Take for granted that there is to be eventual total victory and a new world will be won. In our case, take for granted that in the future we will attain a society with a participatory economy, participatory polity, feminist kinship, and intercommunalist culture, and with ecological steward-ship and internationalism. Okay, now comes the mental trick, the mind-set that can really help.

One way to think strategically is to think forward. Carefully assess current conditions. Assess the assets the movement has—consciousness, members, and organiza-tion. Assess desires that exist. And, in light of it all, formu-late demands or program or projects aimed to utilize assets, account for desires, and move forward.

Another way to think strategically is to work backward. Ask what is most likely to exist shortly before final victory. What structures will need to be in place? What mind-set attained? What membership committed? Then, go back another step, and another. One won't get the path perfectly envisioned, of course—even less so than thinking forward—but with this approach, one can begin to discern milestones that must be attained, and even the broad character of paths by which they might be attained. Take victory as a given and think backward. Take current conditions as a given—presenting them accu-rately—and think forward. Both are part of being strategic.

We Can Win; We Can Lose

The point here is simple but important, though perhaps redundant, given the things said already, so we will keep it very brief.

We undertake a campaign, a project, a struggle, a construction. We are audacious but flexible. We are steadfast, but we also have to realize what ought to be obvious; we might not succeed in the immediate effort. We function so that whether we succeed or not at our proximate aim, we learn, we leave gains, and we contribute to a long-term process, albeit perhaps less than we had hoped. But we cannot guarantee that everything we try will work or that every insight we have will prove accurate and operationally sound.

Because we can achieve, we try to achieve. Because we will win in the long-term, we try to be sure our efforts contribute to that long-term success. But we do not assume we are right. We do not assume our every thought is wisdom for the ages. We do not assume every disagreement with us demonstrates ignorance without limit. We are eager and we try. We are humble and we learn. This is not easy. We won't always succeed at this mind-set any more than we will always succeed at every other aim we have. But if we try, and if we support one another in trying, we will succeed in mind and practice—more often than not.

Fighting on the Side of the Angels Is Suicidal

There is a slogan that has existed for a long time on the Left, at least the American Left, and probably in variants elsewhere too: "Be on the side of the angels." It is horrible, not because it means we should do good, be ethical, etc., but because angels are dead. The slogan conveys an expectation of defeat. Be on the side of the angels communicates that I will go down fighting, but I will go down—I will lose.

The associated mind-set eliminates the need to be strategic. It eliminates the need to hone one's skills and talents. It eliminates the need to correct one's errors. Why should I bother with all of that if I am going to lose anyway? All one needs to do is to be sure one knows that one is good, others know one is good, and whatever will be will be.

This stance by a movement says to those assessing the movement that it is not about winning and does not expect to win. So, unless one is masochistic, why join?

Looking in the Mirror Is Preening

This is just more of the same. I want to be able to get up in the morning and look at myself in the mirror and smile. I want to respect myself. Nothing wrong with that, except, again, the implicit, and even explicit, message is that self-respect is just a matter of having the right values. If I have those, then I am ethical, I am moral, I can look at myself without seeing a monster.

But what about actually affecting the world? How about the fact that I should need to know not only that I have made ethical choices but also wise choices from the point of view of contributing to social justice, wise from the point of view of contributing to creating a new world?

If I don't believe such a world is winnable, obviously I cannot have that as a criterion for self-respect. If I do believe another world is winnable, I can. The slogan implies I do not. It correlates with people not believing they will win but just feeling a need to be virtuous in a losing cause. Again, this stance says to those assessing a movement that it is not about winning and does not expect to win. So, unless one is masochistic, why join?

Fighting the Good Fight Is Surrendering

Believing one will lose and exuding that belief, and, even more so, acting in ways consistent with it, comes in many forms—but it is always deadly.

Suppose you are going to play one-on-one basketball with Lebron James or you are going to have a running race with Usain Bolt or a sing-off with (a reincarnated, no less) Ella Fitzgerald. Clearly, you are going to lose any such contest. If you train hard, you are going to lose. If you study and strategize, you are going to lose. If you discover weaknesses you have, and work to fix them, you are going to lose. In fact, whatever you do, you are going to get obliterated. So what do you do?

Well, you worry about something you can affect. How will you look? What will be your posture? What will be your stance after losing? What will you wear? Will your smile maintain your friendships? And so on. You will address stuff you can affect which can, in turn, have implications. You will fight the good fight, looking good, trying to feel good, trying to help some others feel good, even as you lose. But as for training hard, studying hard and strategizing, correcting your weaknesses, you could do all that vigorously and endlessly and you would still lose pretty much identically, as if you did none of it—and so, why waste time on all that?

Fighting the good fight means looking good, feeling good, exerting fully, trying to put up a good show as you inevitably lose. It obviates any need for trying to win . . . because you simply cannot—and it is a prevalent stance of opponents of injustice, one that must be left in history's dustbin or it will guarantee that our projects wind up there.

CHAPTER 15

What Else Can You Show Me?

> "A moment's insight is sometimes
> worth a lifetime's experience."
> —*Oliver Wendell Holmes Jr.*

What demands might movements string together into a program, or the core of a program, bearing on all sides of life? And, more so, how does one even think about such a thing?

The goal of a program for some movement or organization is that working on its focused campaigns and winning them would augment movement outreach and participant desire, enrich movement members' consciousness, reach beyond the movement into other people's habits and beliefs, making them more receptive both to additional campaigns and to seeking a whole new social system, meet real and worthy needs within and outside the movement, display and enrich and even begin to implement future aims, and enhance movement means of winning steadily more gains.

Economy

Let's take a possible example. Someone proposes as a campaign—one among a few that would occupy people's focus—that the movement work to raise the income of doctors. To evaluate that as a central idea for a campaign one must ask: Will fighting for the aim and winning it have the desired effects? The answer is, no, it would not. It would aid a constituency that is already doing too well, economically—both in terms of its share of income and its share or power or influence. It would do little or nothing to aid those one should want to aid. It would establish and ratify values and structures at the heart of the current system not values and structures that lead toward a new system. It would be highly unlikely to lead to new movement relations and habits welcoming to most of the population, as compared to, say, welcoming to only doctors, and perhaps lawyers or engineers hoping to be the next beneficiaries. But if this proposal is not good, then what might be good?

Suppose we start by thinking about the situation of working people all over the world. One thing very typically true of economic life is that a great many people work long hours, yet many others don't have enough work to do and are underemployed or even unemployed. Of course, the share of social product people receive for their labor is also typically—at least for those in the working class—much lower than desirable.

Given our underlying analysis of class—and particularly of owner/coordinator/worker relations—and given our aspirations for new workplace features such as balanced job complexes, self-managed decision-making, and equitable remuneration, can we come up with a campaign that might appeal greatly to working people, deliver desirable and deserved benefits, arouse new consciousness leading to new desires, and empower actors more than before? That is how we need to think to arrive at something we can really get behind.

Okay, suppose the organization or movement pursues this line of thought and comes up with shortening the workday, perhaps in a plant or an industry or the whole country, or even internationally, as a possible campaign. This is immediately good for those who are working too many hours—but what about those who are underemployed or unemployed? Well, here too the proposal is good. If those who are now working too much work less, there will be work available for those now working too little.

But another problem arises. We are concerned not only about workload but also about income, which is each person's share of the social product. Suppose I was working seventy, sixty, fifty, or even forty hours a week. Suppose the demand is that everyone works, at most, thirty-five hours a week. It gives me more free time. It gives those who weren't working before a role in production. But what if I was just getting by at my previous income level? When I am cut back in the hours I work, my income drops, and I can't afford that. Suddenly I move from liking the program to fearing it.

What can we do? Our simple demand to cut hours won't work as is, but why does my income have to drop if my hours drop? Why can't my hourly wage increase, as a part of the change, so I wind up getting the same income as earlier, or even more, but now for less hours of work?

The total work done in a firm is what it was before. Now, however, the workers are each working thirty-five hours, but there are more of them. With the increased hourly wages, the overall wage bill for the total labor has climbed quite a lot. Where does that extra payment come from?

The first place is profits. Profits can drop as low as the movement is able to push them. The second place is the incomes of the 20 percent of the workforce that was previously earning five, ten, and even fifty times what the average employee was earning—the coordinator class. And how does that work? Do we really want to slash their hourly wages? Someday, yes, of course. We believe that remuneration should be for the duration, intensity, and onerousness of socially valued labor. With that norm, no one can earn five, ten, or fifty times what the average is. But for the moment our demand can be simpler than that, even though we can talk about our long-term values in our effort to win them. The coordinator-class members— engineers, doctors, lawyers, high-level managers and CEOs, etc. in the workplace, industry, or country—whichever is the focus of the campaign—are cut back to thirty-five hours, too.

But they keep their old hourly wages, with no increase per hour. So now they are working fewer hours and earning less overall than they were before, due to their shorter hours.

But there is still another problem. Getting a campaign right isn't rocket science, but it does take some serious thought and care. If the empowered workers of the coordinator class are now each working only thirty-five hours—and let's say before they were averaging fifty hours—who is doing the work that their lower hours are no longer able to accommodate? The answer has to be, those who were not doing it before. Sometimes other workers—members of the working class—can step right in, but other times they will need to learn the skills and gain the circumstances to do this type of labor as part of their overall workload. So there is a transition during which we have job training leading to more diversified job definitions. What occurs while the training is still happening? The coordinator-class members keep doing the empowered tasks but for the reduced income level of reduced hours, and their hours drop only as more people are able to take up the tasks they no longer do.

In one campaign, we have addressed issues of work duration, remuneration, and division of labor—and we can fight for it, putting forth our full analysis and aspirations, so that when we win, we have paved the way toward more gains to come.

Kinship

Consider one more example. A full program is going to address all the dimensions of life deemed central to winning social change and a new society. What, then, might be a component of that program related to matters of gender and sexism?

Following the same type of thinking as with the two previous examples, one might imagine a movement having a kinship campaign. The harder element will be that much that needs doing in this realm is not about demanding new "rules," but simply about our implementing them in daily life. There are, however, exceptions.

For example, the burden of individualized daycare is extreme, and one plank or aim could be the legal requirement for generalized, publicly funded daycare at all workplaces beyond some minimal size.

What about the period immediately preceding and following childbirth? Paid leave would certainly be a step forward. But there is a problem. If women get leave in their final months of pregnancy, and then, say, a year at the outset of each new child's life, an employer would be wise—albeit not very humane—to think twice about employing many women. If I employ a woman, there will be significant periods when she will likely be away, but I will still have to pay her, while also having to find a way to get her work done—perhaps by paying others overtime or hiring a temporary replacement or whatever. If I had employed a man, there would be no such problem.

Indeed, in Venezuela, some years ago, when a very advanced maternity leave law was passed, this is precisely what employers realized and acted on—reducing their inclination to hire women, and even trying to replace them. The government's solution wasn't to turn its back on women giving birth and becoming mothers but to extend the same rights to men becoming fathers. This is like the case above, where we propose a change in hours of labor, and then follow the implications to refine the aim and to create additional beneficial effects and eliminate unwanted negative effects.

Of course, additional demands regarding relations between men and women could address additional matters: full abortion rights accompanied by an appropriate focus on women's health in general, as compared to an excessive preoccupation with men to the exclusion of women. Free health care generally, for that matter. Equal pay for equal work. Alterations in child rights, full gay and lesbian liberation from restraints and violations—one can go on.

Another potential plank of a kinship sphere-related program, for example, could be to push for a change in the laws that convey partnership rights (hospital visits or end-of-life decisions, for example) and economic benefits (health insurance, tax benefits, co-ownership of property, or pension/social security benefits, for example) to some family arrangements and not to others. This is already happening throughout the world as the gay liberation movement wins gains in the legal redefinition of marriage. But the redefinition of marriage to include same-sex couples is a narrow gain. In reality, families are much more complex. The nuclear family—defined as two adults who are romantically involved and their offspring—is not a real reflection of the family that many people experience or would aspire to. One could imagine that group arrangements, multigenerational households, cohabitating friends, with or without kids, and many other combinations of consenting people who are committed to caring for each other and acting together as a household should not be underprivileged as compared to households that fit the "traditional" form of husband and wife with children.

Alterations in child rights could also be part of the program, starting with lowering the voting age and decoupling children's income from that of their parents, through high taxes on inheritance and government payments to children in poverty. Another area of work could be an overhaul of the education system to give children more say in self-managing their own education, providing uniform funding for public schools (rather than property tax-based funding), and free college education.

These programmatic aims could be part of a campaign that would open the door to gender equality, new living arrangements, and new opportunities for children to control their own lives.

Program Parameters

The above discussion of possible campaigns that we might combine into an achievable program is brief and in no way prescriptive. The campaigns could constitute a substantial part of a full movement or organization program, which would also presumably address matters of culture, politics, ecology, and international relations, at a minimum—all to allow work in these critical domains, to push forward consciousness, to win support and participation, to win gains that benefit people, to plant seeds of the future in the present, and more. On the other hand, in a particular place, at a particular time, a program might very well include none of the mentioned campaigns and be the better for it.

In any event, a program doesn't have to do everything imaginable or even everything desirable. A program is time-bound. Maybe only a year's program makes sense. It may well be confined to a city or region or country, or it could be international, and in any case wouldn't be mandatory for all actors but would have some focusing on one part and others focusing on another part. And, in any event, it would be flexible, adapting in light of lessons regarding what works well and what doesn't.

Campaigns and a program, modulating and morphing over time and from place to place, ideally contribute to a path forward, a path to where one wants to wind up.

CHAPTER 16

Paths Ahead

> "At eighteen our convictions are
> hills from which we look;
> At forty-five they are caves in which we hide."
> —F. Scott Fitzgerald

There is a sense in which the heart and soul of strategy is an image we can have in our minds of a broad path from the rejected present to the sought-after future. As with everything else about strategy, and contrary to what many think, there is no one right answer—not for all, not even for some. A path that works excellently in one country or time may not work at all in another country or at another time. A path that seems excellent at first could deteriorate later, to be replaced by another. Flexibility is paramount to avoid error and to capture opportunity.

Here we mention, very loosely, three broad types of path. Then we point out what seems to us the important insight for favoring any of the three scenarios, while nonetheless operating with other people who have different views—as long we are all committed to movements and organizations that truly embrace diversity.

An Electoral Path

Elections are public tallies of preferences to yield decisions, most typically the choice of some person or persons to occupy official positions conveying authority, up to electing presidents with incredible power.

An electoral path to a new society with new economic, kinship, cultural, political, ecological, and international structures doesn't just mean a path that includes electoral participation. Rather, it means a path that takes electoral activity and election results as paramount, whatever else may be occurring or being pursued.

It is a path where the priority focus is trying to garner more votes than in the past, and eventually enough votes to win offices or plebiscites. Following this path, the accrual of such victories and the support that they evidence are the main interim aims and evidentiary signposts of movement achievement and prospects.

This doesn't mean that nothing but electoral work occurs. There may also be, for example, insurrectionary demonstrations and the creation of alternative institutions. What it instead means is that whatever else does occur, it is undertaken in light of positively benefitting electoral activities. Winning votes, and particularly winning offices, and then using them on behalf of change is seen as demonstrating movement support and establishing conditions of further movement victories.

Holding office—and the prerogatives that accompany it—is central to this path. Elections and derivative actions by those who are elected are the main indicators of gains and losses and the main basis for enabling more gains and losses. In short, the electoral path, while it would aim in the case of seeking a participatory society to utterly revamp political, economic, cultural, and kinship structures, would also, even as a binding condition, retain respect for voting and the choices of voters.

Examples of projects that might compose an electoral path are forming a faction within an existing party or forming a whole movement party and running in elections to increase vote tallies and, in time, to win offices. Upon winning offices, still within the electoral path's logic, there is also the use of the prerogatives of the positions won to legally enact changes on behalf of suffering and supportive constituencies, including eventually constitutionally altering structural relations in society and welcoming mass activism and initiative.

Consider, as an example of all this, the Bolivarian revolutionary process in Venezuela. No path is pure and pristine, but this example is perhaps the closest one can find to an actual real world electoral revolutionary process.

An odd set of historical realities led to a populist military man, Hugo Chávez, taking office as president—then turning left as a result of polarization and pressure from the opposition. Winning the presidency after decades of other types of struggle in Venezuela, including the alternative institutional and the insurrectionary, up to and including clandestine violence, was both critical and pivotal to the new approach. The office, once held, provided cover for, and even enabled instigation of, all manner of official, legal, and to some extent extralegal activism trying to further transform society.

Elections remained central, including emphasizing enlarging support, using official channels to abet change, and functioning within laws, even while seeking to legally change laws singly and in sum via constitutional rewrites. Instigating popular participation, including demonstrations and even insurrection (against an aborted coup), and especially the construction of new political structures for grassroots decision-making and the delivery of social benefits (health care, education, etc.) also became paramount.

Without going into excessive detail of this current and highly advanced and informative case, we should note that it does reveal the incredible complexities of having a revolutionary process in a society by winning the key electoral office—and thus controlling the executive branch of government—even while old owners remain, old governors and mayors remain, old police remain, old media remains, and these old elements all aggressively obstruct progress. One can see in Venezuela the historically specific unfolding of an electoral path approach to seeking revolutionary social change.

Venezuela shows the motivation and benefits of the approach when it has great success—such as having the officials who are elected advancing change, while avoiding civil war and violence more generally. But it also shows the debits of the approach, again, even when it has great success—such as a centralizing dynamic that runs the risk, against popular and even leadership desires, of trumping participatory aims, plus the persistence of great power in the hands of small sectors of prior elites, who then use their massive assets to obstruct progress by every means they can muster.

Of course, most electoral approaches have historically had much less success than the Venezuelan case, as in major campaigns that have diverted attention from most other possible pursuits but then lost and dissolved or major campaigns that won only to have the victory lead to outcomes very different than hoped for. Examples of the former would include, in the U.S., the Citizens Party, Rainbow Coalition, and Green Party efforts. And an example—indeed, perhaps the prime example—of electoral victory bringing about much less than hoped would be the victory by the Workers' Party candidate Lula in Brazil, with over 60 percent support, yielding not a government inciting and leading an ongoing revolutionary transformation but a government administering the current system, albeit far more progressively than its predecessor.

At the moment, around the world, the effort by diverse self-defined socialist parties to win growing electoral tallies is, to the extent this is strategically well-defined at all, an example of an electoral approach.

An Insurrectionary Path

An insurrection is a public uprising that, when it is revolutionary, seeks to seize control of society's key institutions or to move forward on a path toward eventually doing so, and then to employ them, and, even more so, to employ continued mass actions, to transform society's structures.

An insurrectionary path to a new society with economic, kinship, cultural, political, ecological, and international structures like those outlined in this book doesn't just mean a path that includes an insurrection. Rather, it means a path that takes insurrectionary mass activism and the gains won and held by such activism as primary, whatever else may be occurring and pursued, such as some elections and some building of alternative institutions.

It is a path where the priority focus of those seeking a new society is to wield popular pressure to force elites to enact demanded changes and to eventually begin to seize control over society's institutions and enact defining changes in them—in part by the accrual of such victories and the benefits and better conditions they bring, as well as by the growing support that they evidence and manifest. In the insurrectionary approach, popular demonstrations and displays of power and support are the main interim aims and evidentiary signposts of movement achievement and prospects.

This doesn't mean that nothing but insurrectionary work occurs. It instead means that whatever else does occur—such as, for example, running in an election or trying to win some plebiscite or building some new institutions in the interstices of the old—is undertaken in light of positively benefitting and manifesting the implications of insurrectionary activities. Amassing popular power, and particularly using it to retain control over growing aspects of social life, is seen as demonstrating support for and establishing the conditions of further victories. Demonstrations and the derivative changes they compel are both the main indicators of gains and losses and the main basis for enabling more gains and losses. In short, the insurrectionary path has no particular respect for old laws and rules, or even for elections, save insofar as they augment insurrection.

Insurrection certainly doesn't require violence and may even foreswear it, but it could also include or even prioritize it. Without going excessively into the details, perhaps the most recent highly advanced and informative—and by its own terms highly successful—case was Cuba, which revealed the incredible complexities of having a revolutionary process of construction in a society that is based in large part on trampling old norms and rules, often by force. In Cuba, one can see an insurrectionary path to seeking revolutionary social change.

Cuba shows the motivation and benefits of the approach in areas where it has had great success—such as having the heights of society scaled and controlled by a movement apparatus and stripping the opposition of its massive means of obstruction, its offices, and its property and other institutional powers. And it also shows the debits of the approach, again, even when it has great success—such as a very strongly centralizing, and even coercive, dynamic that in violating all prior notions of law runs the risk of becoming so instrumentalist that it reduces the public to recipients and bystanders of actions that are, however, undertaken by new—albeit very popular and generally progressive—elites. It may also polarize opponents into violent tactics abetted not by their domestic holdings—which they have lost—but by aid from international allies.

Of course, most insurrectionary approaches have historically had less success than the Cuban example, as in major uprisings that diverted attention from all other possible pursuits, but were then beaten and dissolved, often with massive repression, death, and incarceration—Che Guevara's attempt in Bolivia, for example—or as in major campaigns that win power only to have the victory lead to outcomes even more different than those most participants had hoped for than was the case in Cuba. Additional examples of the former would be, for example, various insurrectionary approaches over the decades in the U.S., not least the abortive and distractingly destructive Weatherman path of the 1960s, and, as perhaps the prime example internationally, the victory of the Bolsheviks in the Soviet Union, with the revolutionary party repressing and finally obliterating all vehicles of popular participation and instituting highly repressive and reactionary rule.

A Constructivist Path

By construction we refer to creating what are sometimes called alternative institutions in the present to accomplish some important social functions in ways seeking to implement values and structures desired for all of society in the future. The slogan that might best apply is "creating the seeds of the future in the present." Acts of construction, if they mean to be revolutionary, seek to develop and federate together ever larger and more important structures, providing a model of future aims and incorporating ever more people into their definition and process.

A constructivist path to a new society doesn't just mean a path that includes creating new institutions. Rather, it means a path that takes the creation of new institutions and the gains and examples constructed and operated in that manner as primary, whatever else may be occurring and pursued, such as elections, insurrection, etc.

It is a path where the priority focus of those seeking the new society is to construct instances of new institutions, partly for the immediate benefit of those who will enjoy their dynamics and fruits, and partly for the "showcase effect" that their existence can have on others—inspiring more participation in such efforts—and, finally, for the lessons that can be learned about future relations and structures preparatory to their being implemented more widely. The ultimate aim, however, is for the constructions of the movement to become so widespread and so viable that they compete for allegiance and eventually become the infrastructure of a new society. The construction of alternative institutions and the demonstration of their viability and merit to those involved, and to society more broadly, are the main interim aims and evidentiary signposts of movement achievement and prospects.

This doesn't mean that only creating alternative institutions occurs. It instead means that whatever else does occur—such as, for example, running in some election or trying to win some plebiscite or engaging in some mass activism or other insurrectionary type activity—is undertaken to manifest the implications of constructivist activities. Amassing new institutions, and particularly using them to attain control over growing aspects of social life, is seen as demonstrating support and establishing conditions for further victories. The constructing and the gains that accompany it and are made possible by it are central. Benefits and changes the construction generates and inspires are the main indicators of gains and losses and the main basis enabling more gains and losses. In short, the constructivist path has no particular respect for old laws and rules, even elections, save insofar as they augment construction, and for the most part sees them as entirely peripheral.

Perhaps the most recent highly advanced and informative case was, at least to some degree, the Spanish anarchist revolution, which revealed the incredible complexities of having a revolutionary process in a society that trampled all old norms and rules without actually operating the old state. The creation of liberated zones in China might stand as another example, however much each would reject the other as a model. In the Spanish case, at least, one can see a largely constructivist path to seeking revolutionary social change.

Spanish anarchism shows the motivation and benefits of the approach in its great success—having the functions of society steadily and increasingly controlled by a movement apparatus that in turn inspired activism of all sorts. And it also shows some possible debits of the approach, again, even when it has great success—a very polarizing dynamic that in eventually violating all prior notions of law runs the risk, even against its desires, of polarizing opponents into violent tactics abetted not only by their domestic holdings but by aid from international allies, without having attained a national organization to counter the assaults most efficiently. The Chinese case, again oversimplifying greatly, arguably reveals instead how under pressure the constructivist approach can, like others, become centralizing.

Of course, most constructivist approaches have historically had less success. Major alternative institutions have in some cases diverted attention from other critically important pursuits, later often atrophying and even collapsing under external pressure or due to internal failings. Separatist stability often compromises internal intentions and, in any event, largely forswears the broad political stage. An example of the former would be various constructivist approaches over the decades in the U.S., such as the distractingly self-oriented food and other co-op efforts of the sixties and since, and, as perhaps the prime example of the latter, the successes, ironically, again in Spain, of the Mondragon movement, which had almost no effect on the broad character of Spanish society or even its contemporary mass political struggles.

Three Phases of Revolutionary Struggle

If you read through the above summaries of three approaches, something striking begins to emerge. Specifically, they are not, in fact, totally at odds. While each prioritizes its way of thinking and evaluating— elections, insurrectionary activity, or creating alternative institutions—instances of each have, in fact, also included aspects of the two others. The real difference is only what is put in a central position for the other parts to augment and aid. But what happens if we admit that this choice is not a matter of principle or inviolable necessity, but instead is based on what works and what doesn't at different times and in different places.

Once that kind of insight is admitted, all three are, in fact, mixed paths, with different combinations distinguishing them. But, in truth, one could easily imagine each moving from one prioritization to another as circumstances alter. The Chinese revolution, albeit never seeking a participatory society as we have envisioned it, certainly did have phases that were primarily constructivist, as well as others that were primarily insurrectionary. The Bolivarian revolution has had primarily electoral phases but, arguably, also primarily constructivist phases.

Consciousness-Raising

As we have repeatedly noted, all efforts to transform society, winning significant gains against elite opposition or, even more so, attaining new social institutions, such as those advocated in this book, require wide and informed participation. This means associated organizations and movements must be advocated in ways that attract support while creating informed involvement.

This indicates one aspect of any revolutionary effort. There must be great attention given to (more so at the outset but continuing for the duration) recruiting additional participants, as well as ensuring that many or even most become not mere supporters or even "foot soldiers" but highly informed participants able to assess events, aims, and choices themselves, adding their own inputs to the mix.

We call this phase or moment of revolutionary activity consciousness-raising. It involves outreach and the continuing development of confidence and awareness once people are on board. We must find ways to communicate with people who are not in our movement, conveying its purpose, logic, morality, and prospects in ways that cause them to become interested, supportive, and involved. Once folks become involved, we must also have sufficient engagement, so that all members' awareness of movement ideas and aims grows steadily, as does their ability to relate those ideas and aims to others and, even more so, to assess them, to assess strategy, and to participate in conceiving and reconceiving movement agendas. They move from opponents to supporters who are actively involved, informed, and capable participants.

At the outset of organizing, consciousness-raising is paramount. Nothing else can proceed far without advocates and participants. As time passes and movements become ever larger, outreach to new recruits must continue alongside the steady development of the commitment and skills and knowledge of those who are recruited, but other activities begin to become even more central.

Contestation

Winning social change involves pressuring elites to make changes. What constitutes pressuring? We want X. Elites don't want to institute X. You can think of X as winning a neighborhood stoplight, ending a war, changing educational policies, cleaning a local dump-site, instituting reparations for the racist policies of the past, enacting free medical care for all, changing election rules and procedures, or anything else you wish.

We want X because it will benefit people who need change. Because winning X will put us in position to win more—especially if we seek X in a manner that raises new awareness and desires and develops new means of outreach and organization. Elites don't want X, not because they are sadists, but because they feel X will diminish their rewards and, even worse, perhaps be part of a process leading to more losses for them.

So how do we get them to enact X? We act in ways that raise social costs for them that are so great that they decide giving in on X to get us to relent in our efforts is better than not giving in on X and having us continue our efforts. What can achieve that?

If you consider their perspective, it becomes obvious. To give in to your demand and deliver X reduces their benefits. Worse, delivering X may augur still more demands and losses they must endure. Why would they do this? It won't be because they are convinced by moral arguments. What can work is elites coming to believe that by withholding X they are provoking a reaction which is more dangerous to them than relenting on X. They have to believe that it is in their interests to give in because not giving in has even worse prospects. In essence, we make them an offer they cannot refuse. Give in or we persist.

Of course, we intend to persist in any event, but they believe that we won't be able to persevere once they not only give in on X but claim to have done so out of their own ethical goodness despite our moronic actions. They try to turn their defeat into a victory by spinning it like crazy.

So by contestation, referring to the second phase of all variants of revolutionary strategy and program, we mean engaging in acts that convey to elites the threat we represent and why, therefore, they must succumb to our agendas. It can involve all manner of activity, depending on context, on issues sought, and on the characteristics of movements involved.

Construction

A new society is not designed by elites who give in to our demand for a new world. There is no such thing for two reasons. First, they are utterly incapable, mentally and morally, of such an undertaking, given their life histories and experiences and the attitudes, habits, and values these have conveyed. Second, they (with rare exceptions) will not come around to such a stance. There is no threat great enough to get them to give in and build a new society in which they no longer rule.

The construction phase of revolutionary process involves conceiving new institutional relations and, even more so, beginning to enact them in the present. This is planting the seeds of the future now. It is creating what we seek in embryo and, as time passes, to a greater degree on a larger scale. This is done partly for those involved to benefit from the virtues of the new way of operating, partly as a showcase to help convince others of the efficacy of movement aims, and partly to learn about the practical realities of visionary aims, so as to continually improve and otherwise refine them. It is everything from having our movements embody the values and ways of operating we favor for a future society to literally constructing institutions of the future standing alongside those of today.

Three Phases as One Process

In thinking about a revolutionary process spanning years or decades as a mix of consciousness-raising, contestation, and construction, we don't want to become confused about the relation of each phase to the other two phases.

First, they overlap, in that we consistently do them all, and it is only the emphasis of our activity that tends to shift—first most of our attention and effort is on consciousness-raising, followed by contestation, and then construction, even though we are always doing all three in varying degrees.

Second, even an activity primarily aimed at one of the priorities will be relevant to the other two. For example, when raising social costs, we are communicating to those who see our activity—which, at the extremes, either recruits or repels them. Our approaches at the extremes either cause those involved to become steadily more committed and informed or to become estranged and alienated. We are also either constructively paving the way toward new institutions by the methods we incorporate in our effort, or we are repeating and even ratifying the ills of the past. Similarly, when constructing, we are either abetting and perhaps engaging in raising social costs for elites and in outreach and membership development, or we're not. And when reaching out and developing member participants, we are either abetting and perhaps engaging in raising social costs and enhancing the creation of alternatives, or we're not.

If we think of consciousness-raising, contestation, and construction as three entwined and overlapping moments of all revolutionary process, enacted differently in different times and places, we have an approach that can actually incorporate, respect, and yield all three of the paths discussed in the last chapter, including any mix of the three, as appropriate.

Indeed, it can even incorporate people favoring different options.

It isn't that differences between people about the efficacy of electoral, insurrectionary, or constructivist approaches simply disappear. It is that when there is shared vision and shared understanding of the logic of struggle, the differences are not a matter of principle, morality, or aim but of how we read a situation. A movement that favors diversity and is self-managing can opt for the approach with the best mix of emphases, even as those with each different slant can pursue activities consistent with their beliefs. Even a movement that has a large majority of members who are, for example, highly doubtful of the efficacy of electoral work—in some country at some time—should be able to see that having some folks energetically engaged in it in a manner in accord with the rest of the movement's priorities is better than having them barred from it and doing other things less energetically and against their inclinations. It is a hedge against the majority being wrong in its estimates. It is a means of learning. It keeps all movement members respectfully and passionately involved, and so on.

All too often we have a self-serving definition of diversity. That which we like is accepted, that which we don't isn't, and somehow we label the result diverse. In a movement consistent with this book's formulations, diversity certainly doesn't extend all the way to including folks who reject the underlying tools of analysis, vision, or general strategic insights and commitments. But differing about the balance of how they are implemented, about tactics, and even paths forward should not be a matter of hostility, much less separation. Instead, once there is a shared perspective, such differences should be seen as perfectly reasonable matters of open exploration, with as much effort to keep alive dissident preferences as possible, even while vigorously pursuing more widely supported options.

CHAPTER 17

The Logic of Revolution

"A habit of basing convictions upon evidence, and of giving to them only that degree of certainty which the evidence warrants, would, if it became general, cure most of the ills from which the world is suffering."
—*Bertrand Russell*

We have emphasized throughout this book that strategy and tactics are contextual. While good in one context, a tactic, or even a strategy, can be suicidal in another—or vice versa. This imposes on revolutionary thought some tight boundaries and advisories.

We must conceive our strategies—our paths from one condition to another, and ultimately from where we start all the way to implementing our vision—and the tactics we use within our strategies with a grounding in what exists and in the limits of our assets, as well as in regard to their fit with where we wish to wind up and what that requires.

After we weigh the aspects of any strategy or tactic against our assets, we must ask the question: Can we do what is implied? We tally the implications of proceeding for attaining immediate goals and especially for enriching our prospects of attaining future goals. How will it enhance our numbers, our commitment, and our means and desires? We address consciousness-raising, contestation for gains, and construction of new means and infrastructure, all with these same guides to thought.

We should modestly be prepared for what we know will turn out to be numerous errors. When I think path A, method B, and tactic C are ideal, you instead may think path W, method X, and tactic Y are ideal. The difference, while it may be great and highly important, is rarely beyond discussion. The gap should not preclude mutual respect, assuming we share a broad vision and theory. Most often, indeed, the resolution of such differences is not attainable by endless debate, much less by application of some principle, but depends on reactions and relations among countless variables, not least human perceptions, and so can only be the result of experience.

We try to evaluate wisely. We try to account for what matters and not get caught up in trivia. But we know we may err, so we also know it is very wise, whenever possible, to keep alternatives alive and to experiment with those alternatives even when some other path is currently our main focus. In this way we protect against the possibility that the minority was right and the preferred path was less desirable than anticipated.

There is no winning without trying, and the reason for being a revolutionary is to win. While we should hold our strategies and tactics cautiously and with respect for those who favor alternatives, we should nonetheless conceive them ambitiously.

Our strategies, tactics, and programs are always part of an overall process, and whatever their proximate aim may be, the ultimate aim is that we want the world and nothing less. We measure our choices and efforts not in terms of proximate aims only, or even mostly, but in terms of the overarching process of winning a new world.

Minimalist Maximalism

Minimalist maximalism is a mind-set that bears on theory, vision, and strategy. Regarding theory, minimalist maximalism realizes that society is way too complex to theorize the way one theorizes a radio, a football game, or a nuclear reaction. Indeed, even calling what we use to think about society and history or about vision and strategy a theory is a bit of hubris, at least if one takes the word *theory* seriously. That is why we call our intellectual offering a toolbox of concepts and urge that it be used to guide thoughts and choices not to dictate them.

Minimalist maximalism guards against dogmatism and sectarianism and favors flexibility and dissent. It seeks constant growth—not reflex defense of past claims and views but their careful and thoughtful improvement.

Minimalist maximalism is modest about what we know, always testing, always proposing variations and alternatives— but it is immodest about what we try to achieve.

The toolbox of concepts rejects a priori pronouncements about focus and importance. It rejects extrapolating our desires into choices that go beyond what our experience and insights can sustain. It rejects attaching our beliefs to our identities and assessing people by their contingent views and their assessments of contingent variables—rather than by their actions and values.

History is chock full of intellectual systems meant to advance social truths and guide liberating social practice, which, however, have in the past solidified into dogmas causing dead people's minds to inhabit the hopes and dreams of the living. Hopefully participatory theory, vision, and strategy can avoid such a disastrous outcome, instead always orienting toward its own continuous development and growth. Only time will tell.

Index

"Passim" (literally "scattered") indicates intermittent discussion of a topic over a cluster of pages.

About the authors

Michael Albert is an organizer, publisher, teacher, and author of over twenty books and hundreds of articles. He cofounded South End Press, Z *Magazine*, the Z Media Institute, ZNet, and various other projects, and works full time for Z Communications. He is the author, with Robin Hahnel, of the economic vision named participatory economics. In 2012 he helped create the International Organization for a Participatory Society (IOPS).

Radicalized in the mid-1960s, Albert has been uncompromisingly revolutionary and active ever since. He has taught in universities, prisons, and at the Z summer school, Z Media Institute. He has given lectures in dozens of countries and debated in almost as many. His numerous other books include *Parecon: Life after Capitalism* and *Remembering Tomorrow: From SDS to Life after Capitalism, a Memoir*.

Noam Chomsky is a linguist, philosopher, cognitive scientist, historian, social critic, and the author of many bestselling political works, including *Hegemony or Survival* and *Failed States*. A professor emeritus of linguistics and philosophy at MIT, he is widely credited with having revolutionized modern linguistics. He lives in Cambridge, Massachusetts.

ABOUT PM PRESS

PM Press was founded at the end of 2007
by a small collection of folks with decades of
publishing, media, and organizing experience.
PM Press co-conspirators have published and
distributed hundreds of books, pamphlets,
CDs, and DVDs. Members of PM have
founded enduring book fairs, spearheaded victorious tenant organizing
campaigns, and worked closely with bookstores, academic conferences,
and even rock bands to deliver political and challenging ideas to all walks
of life. We're old enough to know what we're doing and young enough to
know what's at stake.

We seek to create radical and stimulating fiction and non-fiction books,
pamphlets, T-shirts, visual and audio materials to entertain, educate,
and inspire you. We aim to distribute these through every available
channel with every available technology—whether that means you are
seeing anarchist classics at our bookfair stalls, reading our latest vegan
cookbook at the café, downloading geeky fiction e-books, or digging new
music and timely videos from our website.

PM Press is always on the lookout for talented and skilled volunteers,
artists, activists, and writers to work with. If you have a great idea for a
project or can contribute in some way, please get in touch.

PM Press
PO Box 23912
Oakland, CA 94623
www.pmpress.org

FRIENDS OF PM PRESS

These are indisputably momentous times—the financial system is melting down globally and the Empire is stumbling. Now more than ever there is a vital need for radical ideas.

In the years since its founding—and on a mere shoestring—PM Press has risen to the formidable challenge of publishing and distributing knowledge and entertainment for the struggles ahead. With over 300 releases to date, we have published an impressive and stimulating array of literature, art, music, politics, and culture. Using every available medium, we've succeeded in connecting those hungry for ideas and information to those putting them into practice.

Friends of PM allows you to directly help impact, amplify, and revitalize the discourse and actions of radical writers, filmmakers, and artists. It provides us with a stable foundation from which we can build upon our early successes and provides a much-needed subsidy for the materials that can't necessarily pay their own way. You can help make that happen—and receive every new title automatically delivered to your door once a month—by joining as a Friend of PM Press. And, we'll throw in a free T-shirt when you sign up.

Here are your options:

- **$30 a month** Get all books and pamphlets plus 50% discount on all webstore purchases

- **$40 a month** Get all PM Press releases (including CDs and DVDs) plus 50% discount on all webstore purchases

- **$100 a month** Superstar—Everything plus PM merchandise, free downloads, and 50% discount on all webstore purchases

For those who can't afford $30 or more a month, we have **Sustainer Rates** at $15, $10 and $5. Sustainers get a free PM Press T-shirt and a 50% discount on all purchases from our website.

Your Visa or Mastercard will be billed once a month, until you tell us to stop. Or until our efforts succeed in bringing the revolution around. Or the financial meltdown of Capital makes plastic redundant. Whichever comes first.

In, Against, and Beyond Capitalism: The San Francisco Lectures

John Holloway
with a Preface by Andrej Grubačić

ISBN: 978-1-62963-109-7
$14.95   112 pages

In, Against, and Beyond Capitalism is based
on three recent lectures delivered by John
Holloway at the California Institute of Integral Studies in San Francisco.
The lectures focus on what anticapitalist revolution can mean today—
after the historic failure of the idea that the conquest of state power
was the key to radical change—and offer a brilliant and engaging
introduction to the central themes of Holloway's work.

The lectures take as their central challenge the idea that "We Are the
Crisis of Capital and Proud of It." This runs counter to many leftist
assumptions that the capitalists are to blame for the crisis, or that crisis
is simply the expression of the bankruptcy of the system. The only way
to see crisis as the possible threshold to a better world is to understand
the failure of capitalism as the face of the push of our creative force. This
poses a theoretical challenge. The first lecture focuses on the meaning
of "We," the second on the understanding of capital as a system of
social cohesion that systematically frustrates our creative force, and the
third on the proposal that we are the crisis of this system of cohesion.

*"His Marxism is premised on another form of logic, one that affirms
movement, instability, and struggle. This is a movement of thought that
affirms the richness of life, particularity (non-identity) and 'walking in the
opposite direction'; walking, that is, away from exploitation, domination,
and classification. Without contradictory thinking in, against, and beyond
the capitalist society, capital once again becomes a reified object, a thing,
and not a social relation that signifies transformation of a useful and
creative activity (doing) into (abstract) labor. Only open dialectics, a right
kind of thinking for the wrong kind of world, non-unitary thinking without
guarantees, is able to assist us in our contradictory struggle for a world free
of contradiction."*
—Andrej Grubačić, from his Preface

"Holloway's work is infectiously optimistic."
—Steven Poole, the *Guardian* (UK)

Anthropocene or Capitalocene? Nature, History, and the Crisis of Capitalism

Edited by Jason W. Moore

ISBN: 978-1-62963-148-6
$21.95   304 pages

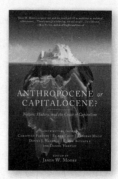

The Earth has reached a tipping point.
Runaway climate change, the sixth great extinction of planetary life, the
acidification of the oceans—all point toward an era of unprecedented
turbulence in humanity's relationship within the web of life. But
just what is that relationship, and how do we make sense of this
extraordinary transition?

Anthropocene or Capitalocene? offers answers to these questions from
a dynamic group of leading critical scholars. They challenge the theory
and history offered by the most significant environmental concept of our
times: the Anthropocene. But are we living in the Anthropocene, literally
the "Age of Man"? Is a different response more compelling, and better
suited to the strange—and often terrifying—times in which we live?
The contributors to this book diagnose the problems of Anthropocene
thinking and propose an alternative: the global crises of the twenty-first
century are rooted in the Capitalocene; not the Age of Man but the Age
of Capital.

Anthropocene or Capitalocene? offers a series of provocative essays
on nature and power, humanity, and capitalism. Including both well-
established voices and younger scholars, the book challenges the
conventional practice of dividing historical change and contemporary
reality into "Nature" and "Society," demonstrating the possibilities
offered by a more nuanced and connective view of human environment-
making, joined at every step with and within the biosphere. In distinct
registers, the authors frame their discussions within a politics of
hope that signal the possibilities for transcending capitalism, broadly
understood as a "world-ecology" that joins nature, capital, and power as
a historically evolving whole.

Contributors include Jason W. Moore, Eileen Crist, Donna J. Haraway,
Andreas Malm, Elmar Altvater, Daniel Hartley, and Christian Parenti.

Birth Work as Care Work: Stories from Activist Birth Communities

Alana Apfel, with a foreword by Loretta J. Ross, preface by Victoria Law, and introduction by Silvia Federici

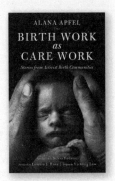

ISBN: 978-1-62963-151-6
$14.95   128 pages

Birth Work as Care Work presents a vibrant collection of stories and insights from the front lines of birth activist communities. The personal has once more become political, and birth workers, supporters, and doulas now find themselves at the fore of collective struggles for freedom and dignity.

The author, herself a scholar and birth justice organiser, provides a unique platform to explore the political dynamics of birth work; drawing connections between birth, reproductive labor, and the struggles of caregiving communities today. Articulating a politics of care work in and through the reproductive process, the book brings diverse voices into conversation to explore multiple possibilities and avenues for change.

At a moment when agency over our childbirth experiences is increasingly centralized in the hands of professional elites, *Birth Work as Care Work* presents creative new ways to reimagine the trajectory of our reproductive processes. Most importantly, the contributors present new ways of thinking about the entire life cycle, providing a unique and creative entry point into the essence of all human struggle—the struggle over the reproduction of life itself.

"*I love this book, all of it. The polished essays and the interviews with birth workers dare to take on the deepest questions of human existence.*"
—Carol Downer, cofounder of the Feminist Women's Heath Centers of California and author of *A Woman's Book of Choices*

"*This volume provides theoretically rich, practical tools for birth and other care workers to collectively and effectively fight capitalism and the many intersecting processes of oppression that accompany it.* Birth Work as Care Work *forcefully and joyfully reminds us that the personal is political, a lesson we need now more than ever.*"
—Adrienne Pine, author of *Working Hard, Drinking Hard: On Violence and Survival in Honduras*

We Are the Crisis of Capital: A John Holloway Reader

John Holloway

ISBN: 978-1-62963-225-4
$22.95   320 pages

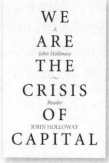

We Are the Crisis of Capital collects articles and excerpts written by radical academic, theorist, and activist John Holloway over a period of forty years.

Different times, different places, and the same anguish persists throughout our societies. This collection asks, "Is there a way out?" How do we break capital, a form of social organisation that dehumanises us and threatens to annihilate us completely? How do we create a world based on the mutual recognition of human dignity?

Holloway's work answers loudly, "By screaming NO!" By thinking from our own anger and from our own creativity. By trying to recover the "We" who are buried under the categories of capitalist thought. By opening the categories and discovering the antagonism they conceal, by discovering that behind the concepts of money, state, capital, crisis, and so on, there moves our resistance and rebellion.

An approach sometimes referred to as Open Marxism, it is an attempt to rethink Marxism as daily struggle. The articles move forward, influenced by the German state derivation debates of the seventies, by the CSE debates in Britain, and the group around the Edinburgh journal *Common Sense*, and then moving on to Mexico and the wonderful stimulus of the Zapatista uprising, and now the continuing whirl of discussion with colleagues and students in the Posgrado de Sociología of the Benemérita Universidad Autónoma de Puebla.

"Holloway's work is infectiously optimistic."
—Steven Poole, the *Guardian* (UK)

"Holloway's thesis is indeed important and worthy of notice."
—Richard J.F. Day, *Canadian Journal of Cultural Studies*

Theory and Practice: Conversations with Noam Chomsky and Howard Zinn (DVD)

Noam Chomsky, Howard Zinn, Sasha Lilley

ISBN: 978-1-60486-305-5
$19.95   105 minutes

Two of the most venerable figures on the American Left—Howard Zinn and Noam Chomsky—converse with Sasha Lilley about their lives and political philosophies, looking back at eight decades of struggle and theoretical debate. Howard Zinn, interviewed shortly before his death, reflects on the genesis of his politics, from the Civil Rights and anti-Vietnam war movements to opposing empire today, as well as history, art and activism. Noam Chomsky discusses the evolution of his libertarian socialist ideals since childhood, his vision for a future postcapitalist society, and his views on the state, science, the Enlightenment, and the future of the planet.

Noam Chomsky is one of the world's leading intellectuals, the father of modern linguistics, and an outspoken media and foreign policy critic. He is Institute Professor emeritus of linguistics at MIT and the author of numerous books and DVDs including *Hegemony and Survival: America's Quest for Global Dominance*, *Chomsky on Anarchism*, *The Essential Chomsky*, and *Crisis and Hope: Theirs and Ours* published by PM Press

Howard Zinn was one of the country's most beloved and respected historians, the author of numerous books and plays including *Marx in Soho*, *You Can't Be Neutral on a Moving Train*, and the best-selling *A People's History of the United States*, and a passionate activist for radical change.

Sasha Lilley (interviewer) is a writer and radio broadcaster. She is the co-founder and host of the critically acclaimed program of radical ideas *Against the Grain*. As program director of KPFA Radio, the flagship station of the Pacifica Network, she headed up such award-winning national broadcasts as *Winter Soldier: Iraq and Afghanistan*. Lilley is the series editor of PM Press's political economy imprint, Spectre.

"Chomsky is a global phenomenon… perhaps the most widely read voice on foreign policy on the planet."
—The New York Times Book Review

Capital and Its Discontents: Conversations with Radical Thinkers in a Time of Tumult

Sasha Lilley

ISBN: 978-1-60486-334-5
$20.00   320 pages

Capitalism is stumbling, empire is faltering, and the planet is thawing. Yet many people are still grasping to understand these multiple crises and to find a way forward to a just future. Into the breach come the essential insights of *Capital and Its Discontents*, which cut through the gristle to get to the heart of the matter about the nature of capitalism and imperialism, capitalism's vulnerabilities at this conjuncture—and what can we do to hasten its demise. Through a series of incisive conversations with some of the most eminent thinkers and political economists on the Left—including David Harvey, Ellen Meiksins Wood, Mike Davis, Leo Panitch, Tariq Ali, and Noam Chomsky—*Capital and Its Discontents* illuminates the dynamic contradictions undergirding capitalism and the potential for its dethroning. At a moment when capitalism as a system is more reviled than ever, here is an indispensable toolbox of ideas for action by some of the most brilliant thinkers of our times.

"These conversations illuminate the current world situation in ways that are very useful for those hoping to orient themselves and find a way forward to effective individual and collective action. Highly recommended."
—Kim Stanley Robinson, *New York Times* bestselling author of the *Mars Trilogy* and *The Years of Rice and Salt*

"In this fine set of interviews, an A-list of radical political economists demonstrate why their skills are indispensable to understanding today's multiple economic and ecological crises."
—Raj Patel, author of *Stuffed and Starved* and *The Value of Nothing*

"This is an extremely important book. It is the most detailed, comprehensive, and best study yet published on the most recent capitalist crisis and its discontents. Sasha Lilley sets each interview in its context, writing with style, scholarship, and wit about ideas and philosophies."
—Andrej Grubačić, radical sociologist and social critic, co-author of *Wobblies and Zapatistas*

Catastrophism: The Apocalyptic Politics of Collapse and Rebirth

Sasha Lilley, David McNally, Eddie Yuen, and James Davis with a foreword by Doug Henwood

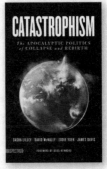

ISBN: 978-1-60486-589-9
$16.00   192 pages

We live in catastrophic times. The world is reeling from the deepest economic crisis since the Great Depression, with the threat of further meltdowns ever-looming. Global warming and myriad dire ecological disasters worsen—with little if any action to halt them—their effects rippling across the planet in the shape of almost biblical floods, fires, droughts, and hurricanes. Governments warn that no alternative exists than to take the bitter medicine they prescribe—or risk devastating financial or social collapse. The right, whether religious or secular, views the present as catastrophic and wants to turn the clock back. The left fears for the worst, but hopes some good will emerge from the rubble. Visions of the apocalypse and predictions of impending doom abound. Across the political spectrum, a culture of fear reigns.

Catastrophism explores the politics of apocalypse—on the left and right, in the environmental movement, and from capital and the state—and examines why the lens of catastrophe can distort our understanding of the dynamics at the heart of these numerous disasters—and fatally impede our ability to transform the world. Lilley, McNally, Yuen, and Davis probe the reasons why catastrophic thinking is so prevalent, and challenge the belief that it is only out of the ashes that a better society may be born. The authors argue that those who care about social justice and the environment should eschew the Pandora's box of fear—even as it relates to indisputably apocalyptic climate change. Far from calling people to arms, they suggest, catastrophic fear often results in passivity and paralysis—and, at worst, reactionary politics.

"This groundbreaking book examines a deep current—on both the left and right—of apocalyptical thought and action. The authors explore the origins, uses, and consequences of the idea that collapse might usher in a better world. Catastrophism *is a crucial guide to understanding our tumultuous times, while steering us away from the pitfalls of the past."*
—Barbara Epstein, author of *Political Protest and Cultural Revolution: Nonviolent Direct Action in the 1970s and 1980s*

Wobblies and Zapatistas: Conversations on Anarchism, Marxism and Radical History

Staughton Lynd and Andrej Grubačić

ISBN: 978-1-60486-041-2
$20.00   300 pages

Wobblies and Zapatistas offers the reader an encounter between two generations and two traditions. Andrej Grubačić is an anarchist from the Balkans. Staughton Lynd is a lifelong pacifist, influenced by Marxism. They meet in dialogue in an effort to bring together the anarchist and Marxist traditions, to discuss the writing of history by those who make it, and to remind us of the idea that "my country is the world." Encompassing a Left libertarian perspective and an emphatically activist standpoint, these conversations are meant to be read in the clubs and affinity groups of the new Movement.

The authors accompany us on a journey through modern revolutions, direct actions, anti-globalist counter summits, Freedom Schools, Zapatista cooperatives, Haymarket and Petrograd, Hanoi and Belgrade, "intentional" communities, wildcat strikes, early Protestant communities, Native American democratic practices, the Workers' Solidarity Club of Youngstown, occupied factories, self-organized councils and soviets, the lives of forgotten revolutionaries, Quaker meetings, antiwar movements, and prison rebellions. Neglected and forgotten moments of interracial self-activity are brought to light. The book invites the attention of readers who believe that a better world, on the other side of capitalism and state bureaucracy, may indeed be possible.

"There's no doubt that we've lost much of our history. It's also very clear that those in power in this country like it that way. Here's a book that shows us why. It demonstrates not only that another world is possible, but that it already exists, has existed, and shows an endless potential to burst through the artificial walls and divisions that currently imprison us. An exquisite contribution to the literature of human freedom, and coming not a moment too soon."
—David Graeber, author of *Fragments of an Anarchist Anthropology* and *Direct Action: An Ethnography*

William Morris: Romantic to Revolutionary

E.P. Thompson
with a foreword by Peter Linebaugh

ISBN: 978-1-60486-243-0
$32.95   880 pages

William Morris—the great 19th century
craftsman, architect, designer, poet and
writer—remains a monumental figure whose
influence resonates powerfully today. As an intellectual (and author
of the seminal utopian *News From Nowhere*), his concern with artistic
and human values led him to cross what he called the 'river of fire' and
become a committed socialist—committed not to some theoretical
formula but to the day by day struggle of working women and men
in Britain and to the evolution of his ideas about art, about work and
about how life should be lived. Many of his ideas accorded none too
well with the reforming tendencies dominant in the Labour movement,
nor with those of 'orthodox' Marxism, which has looked elsewhere for
inspiration. Both sides have been inclined to venerate Morris rather than
to pay attention to what he said. Originally written less than a decade
before his groundbreaking *The Making of the English Working Class*,
E.P. Thompson brought to this biography his now trademark historical
mastery, passion, wit, and essential sympathy. It remains unsurpassed
as the definitive work on this remarkable figure, by the major British
historian of the 20th century.

"*Two impressive figures, William Morris as subject and E. P. Thompson
as author, are conjoined in this immense biographical-historical-critical
study, and both of them have gained in stature since the first edition of the
book was published… The book that was ignored in 1955 has meanwhile
become something of an underground classic—almost impossible to locate
in second-hand bookstores, pored over in libraries, required reading for
anyone interested in Morris and, increasingly, for anyone interested in one
of the most important of contemporary British historians… Thompson has
the distinguishing characteristic of a great historian: he has transformed
the nature of the past, it will never look the same again; and whoever works
in the area of his concerns in the future must come to terms with what
Thompson has written. So too with his study of William Morris.*"
—Peter Stansky, *The New York Times Book Review*

Organize! Building from the Local for Global Justice

Edited by Aziz Choudry, Jill Hanley & Eric Shragge

ISBN: 978-1-60486-433-5
$24.95   352 pages

What are the ways forward for organizing for progressive social change in an era of unprecedented economic, social and ecological crises? How do political activists build power and critical analysis in their daily work for change?

Grounded in struggles in Canada, the USA, Aotearoa/New Zealand, as well as transnational activist networks, *Organize!: Building from the Local for Global Justice* links local organizing with global struggles to make a better world. In over twenty chapters written by a diverse range of organizers, activists, academics, lawyers, artists and researchers, this book weaves a rich and varied tapestry of dynamic strategies for struggle. From community-based labor organizing strategies among immigrant workers to mobilizing psychiatric survivors, from arts and activism for Palestine to organizing in support of Indigenous Peoples, the authors reflect critically on the tensions, problems, limits and gains inherent in a diverse range of organizing contexts and practices. The book also places these processes in historical perspective, encouraging us to use history to shed light on contemporary injustices and how they can be overcome. Written in accessible language, *Organize!* will appeal to college and university students, activists, organizers and the wider public.

Contributors include: Aziz Choudry, Jill Hanley, Eric Shragge, Devlin Kuyek, Kezia Speirs, Evelyn Calugay, Anne Petermann, Alex Law, Jared Will, Radha D'Souza, Edward Ou Jin Lee, Norman Nawrocki, Rafeef Ziadah, Maria Bargh, Dave Bleakney, Abdi Hagi Yusef, Mostafa Henaway, Emilie Breton, Sandra Jeppesen, Anna Kruzynski, Rachel Sarrasin, Dolores Chew, David Reville, Kathryn Church, Brian Aboud, Joey Calugay, Gada Mahrouse, Harsha Walia, Mary Foster, Martha Stiegman, Robert Fisher, Yuseph Katiya, and Christopher Reid.